EISENHOWER
Was My Boss

Tossed by the fortunes of war into close association with World War II's top leaders, Miss Summersby tells the inside story of military command from a woman's point of view. Hers is a portrait of General Eisenhower as few could see him, continuously, at moments of tension, making great decisions, during long hours of routine work, and while he relaxed at bridge or horseback riding.

To Captain Kay Summersby — W.A.C.
A. valued assistant of these war[...] with
best wishes
Dwight D Eisenhower

EISENHOWER
Was My Boss

by

Kay Summersby

Captain, WAC,
Army of the U.S.

Edited by Michael Kearns

PRENTICE-HALL, INC.
NEW YORK

PRINTED IN THE UNITED STATES OF AMERICA
AMERICAN BOOK—STRATFORD PRESS, INC., NEW YORK

To
Kul
and
one other

ILLUSTRATIONS

EISENHOWER
Was My Boss

CHAPTER I

ATRIP-TICKET and a two-block ride changed my entire life. The place was wartime London; the time, May of 1942. And I saw nothing special or miraculous about the ticket. It merely noted that I, as a civilian Army driver, was to pick up a passenger at Paddington Station. He was listed as a "Major General Eisenhower."

I had never heard of the general. And, quite frankly, I was doubly disappointed in the assignment.

Half of the disappointment was natural. Five of us drivers had waited around American Army headquarters three days, to pick up a packet of Very Important Persons due in from the United States via Scotland. The first two mornings we staggered down to the motor pool at 5:30 A.M. And we stayed there until dark both times, only to be finally advised that the weather still held all London-bound planes at Prestwick Airport.

This morning, it looked as though the Brass had abandoned their original plan. They were coming on down to London by train. Just when, no one knew. We had been jailed in the motor pool since 5:30, waiting—in moods as gray as the early-morning fog outside.

The other half of my disappointment came from snobbery. An army driver's prestige is based solely on the rank of the uniform in the back seat. So I had hoped to get General George Marshall or General "Hap" Arnold. Both were in this group, we knew. Both were known to all of us by name and reputation; either would be a bright feather in a driver's cap.

But Sheila and Betty had them. Sheila was one of those nonchalant, likeable girls to whom everything seemed to come easily, without thought or effort. Betty was a proud redhead who used plenty of thought and effort to make absolutely certain everything came her way. And, intimating that I had nobody, Betty lost no time in whispering *she* was picking up a *three*-star general. She said it in such a way I could almost feel wrinkles in my face, braces on my teeth.

I turned apprehensively to Sheila. "Surely, *you've* heard of General Eisenhower?" As an American (married to an English officer from Sandhurst), she was my only hope.

"Eisenhower?" Sheila thought a moment. "Eisenhower? Never heard of him."

By the time we arrived at Paddington Station, everyone's spirits were as low as mine. London was so misty that morning we couldn't see the lead car, that of the late John G. Winant, then United States Ambassador to Britain. We lined up our five cars behind his limousine, then sat around griping. Instead of showing up at 5:30, the train was three hours late. We smoked and fumed and shivered in the cold.

."Here they come!" The shout pulled us all out of our cars . . . and out of our gloom. All we could see was the tall figure of Ambassador Winant and, beside him, Major General Chaney, the only Yank general in London. (Colonels were real "rank" in those sparse days.) Someone identified General Marshall; we all recognized him from newspaper photos. We also managed to pick out General Arnold and Mr. Harry Hopkins.

"One of those fellows must be your General Eisenhower," Sheila said, pointing shamelessly. All I could see was a mass of uniforms and much handshaking. There seemed to be *three* major generals in the group.

The six V-I-P's walked away from their special track, moving toward the line of automobiles. We ran to our staff cars, opened the doors, and tried to stand at soldierly attention.

They all climbed into Ambassador Winant's car.

It rumbled off in important haste, leaving a procession of five empty staff cars attended by five lonely and very angry drivers. That was my first "meeting" with General Eisenhower.

I followed the others back to headquarters, hardly impressed by the name of Eisenhower. At our motor pool office the beefing was as bad as earlier. In fact, it was worse: we had orders to wait around for further instructions. That was at nine o'clock. By 1 P.M., I was starved. No one else would risk it, so I went out alone to have tea and a sandwich.

Coming back to Grosvenor Square, I noticed with alarm that things were happening. The other cars were pulling out. Mine was the last in line; the one just ahead already was halfway down the street. Two officers were walking toward my khaki-colored Packard. They were nondescript, although one was taller than the other. Both wore two stars on each shoulder. The smaller general, I noticed, had nice broad shoulders.

I rushed up, completely confused. Finally I looked from one to the other and puffed, "I'm General Eisenhower's driver. Are you looking for me?"

The shorter general nodded, his full face breaking into a grin destined to spread across half the world's newspapers. "I'm General Eisenhower. This is General Clark. We would like to go to Claridge's, please." I drove them there without incident. As they got out, General Eisenhower remarked, "Thank you. Tomorrow at nine, please."

I had driven them exactly two blocks, after waiting three days for that trip.

Then, I had no feeling one way or the other about General Eisenhower or General Clark. If there was any reaction, it wasn't exactly cordial. After all, I had crawled out of bed at 5:30 three mornings in a row—to drive these Yanks exactly two city blocks.

Yet that quickie trip was to start me on travels through England, Ireland, Scotland, North Africa, Egypt, Sicily, Italy, France, Belgium, the Netherlands, Palestine, Iceland, Denmark, Hungary, America, Luxembourg, Germany, Austria, even Russia. The square where that almost anonymous general stood as I walked up that afternoon was to change from the quiet heart of Mayfair to the crowded nerve-center of an invasion army. And that same Grosvenor Square was to become known, unofficially, as Eisenhower Platz.

But in that May of 1942 there was no hint that the smiling general would become our Supreme Commander, that his quiet companion would lead a bizarre submarine mission to the enemy soil of North Africa. To me they were only temporary passengers, in London for a ten-day visit.

As the days flew by, I began to like both my generals.

Their working hours were staggering, after the gay and easy life of other Americans I hauled around London. They had come over to work and they had little time. From the nature of high offices we visited I sensed that something very top-level was going on.

Yet both took time to treat me as a human being, not as a uniformed machine. I liked that. It was a complete turnabout from the chill dignity of British staff officers, not as tiring as the dirty wisecracks, wandering hands, and childish chatter of many American and Canadian officers.

When we journeyed over to Dover Castle, headquarters of "Bomb Alley," both generals talked easily throughout the long, pleasant trip. There was no stiff reserve between them or with me. We were three People, not two generals and a driver.

Because of General Clark's natural reticence, General Eisenhower did most of the talking. And he had an unassuming curiosity that I can only describe as charming. If he didn't know something, he asked questions. There was no pretense at the God-like knowledge many generals seem to believe their rank demands. He asked questions about everything from Canterbury Cathedral to bomb damage; he asked them as a friendly, curious man—not as a general patronizing his driver. Later, I was to see that blessed gift directed at chiefs of state and chiefs of staff with phenomenal but natural success. It is one of General Eisenhower's greatest assets.

The next few days were long and very official. We hit every important war building in London, plus a few elsewhere in the British Isles. Both my passengers grew weary and taciturn. Instead of bouncing in and out of the car, as before, they climbed out slowly and returned to that rear seat with heavy sighs. Time seemed to evaporate; there was a distinct air that hours were much too scarce. There was no relaxation in their crowded schedule.

One noontime they collapsed on the seat and General Eisenhower said, "Kay, I think the war can get along without us for a while. Let's take the afternoon off. And as a starter, where's a good place to have lunch?"

I blushed like a ten-year-old schoolgirl. It was the first time he had bowed to the universal custom of calling me "Kay."

I suggested the Connaught. When we got there I let them out at the door, then drove around the block to park. Finishing that chore, I looked up to find both of them standing there. "You'll join us, of course?" asked General Clark. I nodded dumbly as we strolled past the astonished doorman. (I say "astonished" doorman because most London attendants are old British soldiers; they'll never quite recover from the easy discipline of American military men.)

Lunch over, we went on a little trip up country, around Oxford. General Eisenhower displayed an amazing grasp of English history, as he did consistently throughout his visit.

It was a warm afternoon. I was dying for a drink. On impulse, I pulled up in Beaconsfield and said, "You *must* see an English pub before you leave!"

They were out of the car and inside before I realized just how bold I had been to two major generals. At the bar, they couldn't make up their minds what to have. "You tell us, Kay," General Clark said.

I considered. "You wouldn't like whiskey without ice, I know. It's too hot—gin and tonic, that's the thing! A real summer drink and a real English drink." They seemed to enjoy it almost as much as I did.

I gave Sheila a ring as soon as I got home. She didn't believe a word of my story about the lunch, let alone the drinks. Still, I knew she would pass it along to the other girls.

The day our V-I-P's were scheduled to leave for Prestwick and the United States, British weather closed in again. Their trip was postponed until the following morning. By now I was brazen, almost drunk on the friendliness of these two American generals. So I called up General Eisenhower. But when he answered, I apologized in a rush of embarrassment: haltingly, I suggested that he and General Clark might like to do some sightseeing now that they had an afternoon of leisure because of the canceled departure.

To my relief he was intrigued by the idea and overlooked my brashness. "Just the thing," he said. "Wonderful idea. This is the first day we haven't had any conferences and we're completely free. In half an hour, please."

Our tour ranged from the Tower of London to Westminster Abbey and the Houses of Parliament. My passengers showed such interest in bomb damage at the House of Commons that I took them on down to the East End and a section I knew as well as my own mind: Lambeth.

"Kay," General Eisenhower remarked as we cruised around the skeletoned and blasted tenements of Lambeth, "you seem to know a lot about this section."

"I should," I replied solemnly.

With little encouragement, I found myself telling the story of my life to these two Yank generals.

Nothing in childhood had prepared me for wartime London. My father was a retired army officer and I, as Kathleen McCarthy-Morrogh, led what is commonly known as The Sheltered Life. Our home, *Inish Beg*, was a somewhat run-down estate on a small but lovely emerald island in a river in County Cork. Our favorite pastime (I had a brother and three sisters) was to sail down that river four miles, to the Atlantic. There was a succession of governesses, hunts, spatting parents, riding in the fields and along the long avenue fringed with old trees . . . the usual pattern of that obsolete world. The only tragedy which could becloud life in those days was a sudden Irish thundershower—because it might spoil my lovely tennis party.

But London drew me away from Ireland. There was some traveling on the Continent with Mother, who stayed in London most of the time and rarely went back to *Inish Beg*. Eventually I was on my own, utterly unprepared to do much more than sit a horse properly and pour tea correctly. Someone suggested photography; I drifted into that. There was a period of "extra" work at the film studios just outside London. Inevitably, there was marriage, a dismal failure.

By 1939 I was a mannequin at "Worth's of Paris," near Grosvenor Square. As war clouds grew blacker I felt more and more ridiculous modeling exquisite clothes, pretending that everything was the same. In late August I gave notice of my intention to leave. And on September 4—the day after hearing Prime Minister Neville Chamberlain broadcast the declaration of war—I walked out of that life forever.

The nearest service was the Motor Transport Corps. I joined up immediately.

I soon learned, however, the MTC was looked upon as a sort of social sorority. A newspaper writer had noted that the qualifications for admission seemed to be (1) ability to drive a motorcar and (2) ability to drape oneself in chic fashion at the Ritz or Dorchester bars. One joined the MTC because it was The Thing One Must Do, Y'know . . . *if* one had the money. With disappointment, I discovered there was no pay. (When we finally received a pittance, the girls at headquarters looked down upon us for accepting it.) The smart uniform—a skirted version of that worn by British officers, complete with Sam Browne—consumed almost fifty pounds of my thin savings. I was assigned to Post No. 1, which area took in the docks and Lambeth. Our uniforms there drew only pure hate from the class-conscious Cockney. There was no war in Lambeth or anywhere else that autumn or that winter. We endured the disgust of our neighbors, the snide remarks of our friends, and "played war" in our headquarters, an old schoolhouse.

The *Luftwaffe* arrived in August of 1940 in full, terrifying, horrifying strength.

Our little social set became the busiest rescue squad in all of London. Lambeth and the dock areas rocked under the Nazis' bombs. We had twenty-four hours on duty, twenty-four off, rarely got even a wink of sleep on the broken cots.

Now, it's difficult to try to re-create that life. I was an ambulance driver. The only concession granted me as a woman was unofficial permission to stuff cosmetics in my gas-mask bag. It was sheer Hell, living and driving and working in a bomb-made Hell. Blood and death became as commonplace as a cigarette.

I remember houses razed to the ground, yet alive with cries of the wounded and buried . . . Careening through gutted streets with only bomb-light and huge fires to light the way . . . A Bobby who threw himself atop me as shelter from a blast . . . Our old Cockney enemies, now friends, pulling us in off the buckled sidewalks, for a welcome shot of gin or whiskey . . . A motion picture house with the lights still on but the front stalls filled with bodies, all headless . . . Bodies, bodies, bodies, each with a tragic tag on one foot, if there was a foot . . . Driving ambulances loaded with bodies . . . Sick with the stench of burnt flesh . . . Being turned away by morgue after morgue: "Sorry, we're full."

". . . and that's why I know Lambeth so well," I concluded.

The two generals were grim. "Poor Kay," General Clark said. "Poor people, poor London," General Eisenhower added. After their ten-day visit they realized what the new war was all about—it was impossible for people from the unbombed United States to visualize exactly what the Blitz meant.

General Eisenhower hurled dozens of questions at me about women ambulance drivers: how we got along with our male colleagues, how we managed in the rough spots. Then he asked about women who acted as air-raid officials. He went into the subject of our auxiliary forces in the army, navy, and air force. His large forehead crinkled in long lines of concentration as he bombarded me with questions about British women's role in the war. Later, that intense interest was to grow into a near-obsession that women could safely and efficiently replace fighting men—a conviction which he helped translate into actual practice long before Normandy and still supported vigorously after the war.

His curiosity about people, and the individual, eventually overwhelmed his broader interest in women at war. "Tell me," he said, "how did you ever wind up with the Americans?"

I explained that the big Blitz, the steady Blitz, was over by the summer of 1941. About that time, I ran into an American Colonel at a cocktail party. He mentioned that his little group of seventeen officer "observers" (then in civilian clothes, as America wasn't in the war) needed drivers who knew London. I told him about our work and how life at Post No. 1 had turned dull. Several days later, a few MTC girls were transferred to U. S. Army headquarters. Sheila and I were among them.

"And I've been with the Yanks ever since," I ended.

General Eisenhower suddenly winked at General Clark and seemed to shake off his serious mood. "Do you enjoy driving us around London?"

I answered that it must be obvious.

"Well, one of your girls wouldn't!" He laughed. "Remember that first afternoon when we got here? I walked up to the girl at the head of the line of cars and asked if she were our driver. She looked me straight in the eye and said, 'Oh, no! I'm driving a *three*-star general!' "

I howled, wondering if any other general could laugh at such a story on himself, if any other would mention it to someone not a major general also. "That's Betty, General. Red hair, snooty—"

"That's enough," he said. "That's the one."

At the time I was only amused that Betty had snubbed her way out of a wonderful ten days. I didn't know then that she also had missed a chance at serving three years with the Supreme Commander.

The next day I drove my two generals out to Northholt. The weather was lifting. They were heading for Scotland and then the United States. We all got out and shook hands. "Be sure and let me know if you ever come back to London," I said. "It would be a pleasure to drive you both again." It *had* been better than most jobs; still, I was just saying the usual goodbyes, wartime goodbyes.

General Clark mumbled something about my "efficient driving." General Eisenhower went back into the car. When he stepped out there was a precious, priceless box of sweets in his hand. "Here you are, Kay. We want you to accept this little box of candy as some sort of appreciation. And if we're ever back this way, we want you to drive us."

Right then I wasn't a bit impressed that *he*—General Dwight Eisenhower—had given me a box of candy. All I wanted to do was get away and dig into that lovely box of unrationed sweets.

But I did stay at the airport long enough to see my two generals off. As their plane left the ground, I waved and thought: They're both nice—but I'll never see either of them again.

Then I started on that candy.

CHAPTER II

245

Within a fortnight I was driving a new general, Carl (Tooey) Spaatz.

The now-famous and retired Tooey Spaatz was, in early 1942, a grimly silent major general. As chief of the new Eighth Air Force, he had a gigantic job. And he spent every waking moment pondering over problems involved in the daring principle of daylight bombing. A rather unspectacular, balding man who would hardly stand out in a crowd, he called to mind that pensive statue: The Thinker. He concentrated so intensively that I often thought he was asleep. Naturally, he had no time for the ordinary little details of everyday life. He was, in fact, coldly impatient with them.

That's how I came to drive for General Spaatz.

His temper had finally boiled over because his sergeant was late again in arriving at a conference. The Yank chauffeur was naturally bewildered—like many other Americans—by the maze of tangled little streets which history had forced upon London. When the General heard of my MTC experience, he requested that I be loaned out to his headquarters immediately.

The job was a complete change of pace. I soon learned General Spaatz had no time for the relaxing chats and side-trips which had highlighted the Eisenhower-Clark visit. My assignment was to keep my mouth shut and get him from one place to another as quickly as possible.

"How long will it take you to get to the Air Ministry?" he would ask. If I estimated fifteen minutes, he replied, "You can make it in ten!" Then he would come out from that particular meeting, already five minutes late, expecting to make the trip in *less* than ten minutes.

Thanks to the absence of civilian traffic, we usually did. But I began to feel more a fighter pilot than a staff-car driver. Our automotive airport was "Pinetree," the U.S. air headquarters set incongruously in lovely countryside once reserved for wealthy female pupils of the school at Wycombe Abbey; that was succeeded by "Widewing" at Bushey Park.

Gradually, I also became experienced in a part I was to play for General Eisenhower: that of "unofficial aide."

It was rather embarrassing the first time. I had just let General Spaatz out at Claridge's after a long, tiring day. He leaned in the car window and said, "You'd better come on up, Kay. I may need you later." I parked and joined him at the elevator.

Walking into his suite was very much like walking into a Hollywood version of a cocktail party. In fact, it was a Hollywood version, because the General's aide, Major Sy Bartlett, was and is a writer in the movie capital. Using the exclusive hotel and the high-Brass atmosphere as props, he had begun to stage a straight run of parties attended by other Hollywood-Broadway figures and the show people of London's West End. The smoke, the noise, and the rank were overpowering.

The General nodded briefly to everyone and strode into another room. I trailed along. He closed the door, sighed heavily, and sagged into a chair. I stood there uneasily, then sat down stiffly.

We sat like that—without a word—for the better part of two hours. He sat and thought; I sat and fidgeted. Finally, he looked up. "Thanks, Kay. Guess I won't be needing you any more tonight."

The scene became a common occurrence. I think it was partly because the General wanted me to stand by for any sudden trips, partly because he liked to have company during those mighty thinking bouts. I learned to smother any feminine instincts at conversation. Instead, I took along newspapers, magazines, and books to while away the hours as he dug into voluminous reports or drowned himself in meditation. They were curious periods, those. Yet I grew to understand the deep concentration of General Spaatz, to respect the enormity and loneliness of his task, and, finally, to feel perfectly at ease in the silent hours at Claridge's.

The General's one off-duty delight was poker, all-out poker. Staff members spoke of his ability (and his astronomical stakes) with awe. Upon infrequent occasions he joined festivities in the other room at Claridge's, sometimes pulling out his guitar and strumming away at West Point songs. I thus became a sort of combination driver-hostess, mixing and serving drinks (the General liked a tiny jigger of whiskey buried in a long glass of water), detouring bores, acting as suite doorman, and always holding myself ready to rush down for the car at any late-hour telephone call from the airfields.

Mostly, however, the job involved a steady cycle of trips around London offices and out to Eighth Air Force headquarters.

Several times General Spaatz directed me to tour bombed-out sites around London. It was no morbid, sight-seeing curiosity. He had been in battered London during the original *Luftwaffe* assault, sitting on roofs during the heavy raids and making notes on Nazi tactics. Now, he studied the debris itself with all the intensity of an engineer. He was studying bomb damage first-hand; there was no better laboratory, outside Hitler's Europe. In the Lambeth district I pointed out our old MTC headquarters and he soon got me talking about those experiences. It knocked a few chips from the wall of reserve between us . . . I even told him about Dick.

I didn't tell him all the details but I did confess that Dick was my own, my very special American, that he had been ever since the days when I was an ambulance driver and he was a United States Army "observer" at the Embassy.

My two-star passenger leaned forward. For once the furrows were gone from his forehead, the cold-steel missing from his eyes. "Kay," he said, "I don't talk much. But I've hung onto you as a driver because you have a conscience something like mine. You never complain if I keep you late or if I ask you to do some odd job any other driver would bitch about." He smiled. "I never realized what these evening chores mean. From now on, any time your captain isn't away on a trip—just let me know. We'll arrange time-off, somehow. War stops for some things."

He turned again to the bomb damage, his brow ridged, his shoulders hunched, his eyes squinted in that old intensity of concentration.

That's the way things were until one fine summer evening when I pulled up at Claridge's, almost four weeks later. General Spaatz jumped into the back seat and muttered, "Important mission. Hendon Airport—and don't spare the horses!"

There's something special about an airplane coming in to land, no matter how many you've traveled on or how many you've met. Judging from the array of awaiting Brass and the way General Spaatz dashed out on Hendon's runway, there was something extra-special about this plane. I ran over to see the V-I-P's unload.

Two wide shoulders appeared in the door, each bearing two stars. Above them, a broad grin—General Eisenhower.

He greeted the dignitaries and returned the barrage of salutes. Then he came over to chat with General Spaatz. I stood at attention, assuming he wouldn't remember his ten-day driver.

But the future Supreme Commander extended a friendly hand and an equally friendly greeting. "Kay, how are you? I've been wondering where you were ever since I returned to London. Thought you wanted to drive for me?" He glanced at General Spaatz. "Tooey, you've been hiding her in the air force."

I muttered shyly that I had been busy at air-force headquarters, out of touch with Grade-A gossip at Grosvenor Square. But I did remember to congratulate him upon his appointment as commander of European Theater of Operations, which fact I had learned in the newspapers.

"Would you like to come back and drive for me again?" he asked bluntly.

I didn't know what to say. Air-force life was free and easy; I also liked the happy-go-lucky staff. General Eisenhower was a pleasant passenger but I had come to like the dedicated Tooey Spaatz. Besides, the latter now allowed me free time when Dick was in town.

General Spaatz spared me the embarrassment of a reply. "Now don't you take Kay away from me," he growled. "She's the only driver I've found who really knows London."

Dropping the subject, General Eisenhower turned back to me. "Well, when are you coming to London?" He smiled again. "I've got some fruit for you. Sort of crushed, but still fruit."

Fruit! After almost three rationed years in wartime London, with fresh fruit as rare as nylons, I was over-anxious in replying. "I'm driving General Spaatz in tomorrow, Sir. Tomorrow *morning.*" He laughed, "Well, be sure to come in and see me."

Next day I hurried up to the first floor (second floor, American style) of the modern Grosvenor Square block of flats which had become Theater headquarters. The General's offices were surprisingly small and unpretentious. Through his windows I could see the park square itself, with the usual barrage balloons anchored in the center.

"I'm Kay Summersby," I announced hopefully to a tall captain. "I believe the General expects me?"

He introduced himself as Captain Ernest (Tex) Lee. "Yes," he said, "the General expects you. To tell the truth he has expected you ever since he got back to London. I even left a note for you in what someone at the motor pool said was your staff car." (I remembered that note, signed by a Captain Lee and asking me to stop by his office. I regarded the paper as a joke at the time; I hadn't known that Captain Lee was an aide.)

General Eisenhower, although in the midst of new staff conferences, took time to chat and to hand me a veritable treasure: oranges, lemons, and grapefruit. I handled them as eggs covered in gold leaf. They were part of a load he had brought back for top British commanders; I was humbly appreciative for a share.

The General apologized because some of the fruit was bruised, then asked directly, "Would you like to come back again, for good?"

"Of course," I murmured, still not certain.

"I'll see what can be done about it," he concluded in dismissal.

Back at air-force headquarters that afternoon I described the situation to General Spaatz. "Maybe you've seen it," he said. "London put out an order about a week ago calling back to 20 Grosvenor all you temporary-duty drivers. But I'm trying to keep you here. We'll see."

Even his stars didn't change that order. I was transferred back to London. Before leaving, I spent several days training General Spaatz' driver, who by that time was quite accustomed to driving on the left side of the road and beginning to know his way around. I taught him the fastest routes to the city and the quickest way to travel around the hundreds of Allied offices.

Returning to London, even I could see the sharp change in American Army discipline. The motor pool had once been rather a social center; we went to work around 10 in the morning, took an hour and a half for lunch, knocked off about tea-time in the afternoon. Now it was run on strictly military lines. Headquarters had been reorganized. Instead of the easy-going group of "observers," whose schedules included long liquid lunches and early cocktail hours, 20 Grosvenor Square was peopled by army men who comprised the hard core of America's new European Theater of Operations. And they were on a *seven*-day week. General Eisenhower had come over to do a job; he was wasting no time.

Within a few weeks numerous men-who-had-been-in-London-too-long were on their way back to the States, unable to adjust to the new order. Their rank was high. General Eisenhower often remarked, when irritated by some too-social officer: "I'd like to send him back on a slow boat, without destroyer escort!"

The General was far from a martinet on spit-and-polish. But he emphasized that good discipline made good soldiers and often saved lives in combat. So, among other things, he bucked up the Military Police. They were outfitted in white helmet-liners, white belts, white gloves, and white leggings. London, hardened to the sloppy and carefree Yanks of earlier days, laughed at the new M.P.'s and called them "Snowballs."

The Theater Commander made increasingly frequent references to the disregard of salutes. He liked to drive about London with covers over the star-studded license plates, to avoid ostentation. But now the tags were uncovered for a series of "test runs." Along one stretch of Audley Street jammed with Americans of every conceivable rank, we once collected but one salute. That was from a British officer.

During those early days, I actually had little driving. Most of the General's time was consumed by staff conferences, planning, paper work. In the evening he usually called upon Old Gilbey (Lord Gilbey, to the aides), a British veteran of World War I who chauffeured at the American Embassy. Old Gilbey was lovable and sweet but a little slow. I got most of the few daytime trips; he made the night runs.

Boredom set in, after the constant activity with General Spaatz and the fun with his staff officers. But things began to pick up as the General started getting outside more and more and, sometimes, visiting installations in the field.

With the comparatively slow business, I got to know the rest of the General's "official family," as he called us.

The charmer of the group was that genial navy officer, Harry C. Butcher, former vice-president of Columbia Broadcasting System and then a lieutenant-commander. A tall, smiling, and very social chap, Butch was front-office boy, full-time aide, personal friend, eager publicist, and chief diarist. (That diary was later recognizable the world over as the best-selling *My Three Years With Eisenhower*.) Butch's only failing was an over-zealous enthusiasm for public relations. The General occasionally stormed when his naval aide gave out some highly personal sidelight to the press. But it was Butch who lived with the General, traveled with him, and served him most ably as Friend.

The Butcher zeal for publicity work was equaled only by the army aide-de-camp's energy in executive work. Tex was the be-spectacled, booming-voiced, towering captain who rode herd on the General's paper work. He was the administrative titan, the red-tape artist, the office chieftain, the official worrier.

Another character in the innermost cast was Sergeant Mickey McKeogh, the black-haired, blue-eyed little Irishman who had been a bellhop in New York. Mickey was everything to his General, his walking memo pad and his left hand, an impeccable and loyal orderly who did anything from shining shoes or brass to shopping. Above all, he shared his unfailing, bubbling Irish humor. And he wrote a personal report regularly each week to Mrs. Mamie Eisenhower, the General's wife.

I gradually oozed into this circle because all my off hours were spent waiting around the General's office until he was ready to take a trip anywhere from the War Office to supply headquarters in Cheltenham. Also, I started to recognize, then know, all the senior subordinates who poured into that little office with their problems. I gingerly attempted some paper work and helped out on 'phone calls. Without knowing it, I was joining the Unofficial Official Family: Butch, Tex, Mickey, and Kay.

(The Boss objected strenuously if anyone else sent us out on a tiny mission. He reminded one and all that we constituted his personal staff. Any order by Butch or Tex was to be assumed as coming from the Commanding General. Similarly, we were to take orders from no one but him. "And that goes for you too, Kay," he said pointedly, knowing I had fought boredom by going on dozens of personal errands for other members of the headquarters staff. Actually, our Boss was only making certain no section chief misused or treated us as personal flunkeys.)

A sudden increase in motor trips about this time started a series of runs to a bomb-proof building on the edge of St. James Park just off famous Downing Street. Usually, I sat in the car while my passenger conferred inside; I read and chatted with the high-ranking Allied men who pulled up at that entrance.

One morning General Eisenhower emerged from that dull-looking building with a companion. As they strolled over to the car, I jumped out and assumed my own peculiar brand of attention: it was Mr. Winston Churchill, the Prime Minister.

It may be difficult for Americans to understand the wide-spread, absolute worship for Winston Churchill in those weary days. It was close to what many Americans must have felt for President Roosevelt—a feeling I shared immediately at my first meeting with that great man. Churchill represented a tired but defiant wartime Britain, all molded into a very human figure we could love and follow. He was a more real and intimate symbol than the strains of *"God Save the King"* or the bongs of Big Ben. He was England; more important, he was London for all of us who had stayed there throughout the Blitz.

I was frankly thrilled and excited just seeing him for the first time. The now-familiar jutting chin, the round shoulders, the fat cigar—all these were just as press photos had pictured them. But I was astounded at the cherubic face superimposed on the bulldog head, a face nevertheless capable of portraying grumpiness incarnate. His eyes were a vivid blue, at times those of a gurgling infant, at other times those of a cold wartime leader, at still other times those of a laughing, socially accomplished diplomat and politician. I was impressed by his clear, pink, baby-like skin. As a woman, I was more attracted to that characteristic than to any other single item of his appearance. He wore the usual shapeless "siren suit," of course, and his flapping, initialed slippers.

General Eisenhower accomplished an introduction as though all three of us should be very good friends.

Churchill glared. "I hope you'll take good care of our General," he growled. Then that impish look in his eyes: "Mind you now, don't you lose him in London!"

The General laughed. "Don't you worry. Kay knows London as well as any Cockney taxi driver."

Watching the celebrated pair, it was plain they shared a mutual respect and sincere natural friendliness despite many arguments on a military plane. I soon took General Eisenhower down to Downing Street for dinner once or twice a week; to those Cabinet meetings in the Park annex, more frequently. Upon the latter occasions the Prime Minister always walked out to the car with General Eisenhower. And at Churchill's insistence the General spent many a week end at the freezing, drafty country estate known as Chequers.

Perhaps Churchill's fondness for the American commander was best revealed at the dinner parties. Although Eisenhower normally was the lowest-ranking general present and in spite of the rigid protocol which rules Government and military circles in England, the P.M. invariably placed General Eisenhower in the highest chair of honor, to his immediate right. The General told me of the custom in an evident mood of appreciation.

Later I got to know the P.M. quite well. And he always acted on impulse socially, without thought of false dignity—the same characteristic which so many persons found attractive in General Eisenhower. For example, when the General met the train which brought to London Mrs. Eleanor Roosevelt (whom Butch immediately tagged in official correspondence under the code name of "Rover"), the King and Queen chatted easily with him. And he called over his faithful chief of staff, Walter Bedell ("Beetle") Smith, for an almost boyish introduction. Likewise, Mrs. Roosevelt talked to me about dogs as though we were next door neighbors. Mr. Churchill, similarly, once plowed across a broad airfield, scattering Brass and V-I-P's like a bull stomping through a chickenyard, just to say "hello" to me. All three—General Eisenhower, Mrs. Roosevelt, and Mr. Churchill—have that same common touch in human relations.

General George Patton impressed me almost as much as Mr. Churchill.

Introduced by General Ike as one of his oldest and closest friends, Patton at once displayed that Old World gallantry which all his biographers seem to have missed. When he shook hands and bowed, everything was there but a Continental kiss of the hand. There was no hint of the expected American backslap or the wolfish eye. All he needed was a cavalier's cape and a sword. I also found him the most glamorous, dramatic general I'd ever met. His chest was covered with more ribbons than that of any officer down at the Imperial General Staff; it fairly blazed with ego, experience, and pride of profession. And the chest underneath his brilliant tunic was every inch that of a soldier. Blindingly polished cavalry boots and tailored jodhpurs completed the picture.

When Patton mentioned interest in bomb damage around London, General Eisenhower remarked, "Give him the sixty-four-dollar tour, Kay—Lambeth."

The future Third Army chief was just as appalled by the Lambeth desolation as Generals Eisenhower, Clark, and Spaatz had been. Although his G-I's probably wouldn't have believed it, he sat on the front seat with me. And his ramrod back never once unbent, never touched the seat. "Those sonsabitches," he would mutter, "those sonsabitches." Then, he'd turn to me. "I'm sorry, Miss Summersby. Excuse me, please."

I had to point out that I had been with the American Army long enough to realize that Yanks used curses in such a natural way that no one could take offense.

I even told my passenger of the time I had yelled "Godamn!" in the office at Grosvenor Square. "General Eisenhower buzzed me right away," I told Patton, "and asked where I had acquired such shocking language. He smiled weakly when I admitted I had learned that particular word from Dwight D. Eisenhower."

General Patton laughed at the story, then turned back to his study of the bomb damage. In a few minutes he was at it again: "Those bastards, those sonsabitches!" Always, the immediate apology. I've heard Patton swear like a docker many times but

I never felt actually embarrassed; he was a man's man, a real soldier, and yet he unfailingly treated women with an eighteenth century flourish. Also, he was second only to General Eisenhower in his intellectual interests and his knowledge of history.

The Patton ego was, to me at least, more a superb self-confidence (which he always justified) rather than empty bragging. I'll admit that I heard him *ask* for medals; but he had earned them a hundred times over; he knew, further, they strengthened his men's respect and added visibly to his chosen lifetime career. Patton referred to "clusters" as *self-starters*. He once admitted, in that high-pitched, creaking voice which seemed so foreign to the rest of his makeup: "There's only one medal here I don't want a self-starter for—my Purple Heart!"

General Patton was curious about the behavior of women in Britain's war effort. But it was only a flurry of interest compared to the storm of questions General Eisenhower poured on Colonel Oveta Culp Hobby when she visited London.

"If you don't send me WAC's over here," he exclaimed, "I'm just going to hire a regular army of civilians. I've seen what women can do in wartime; I've seen how they can free men for their primary duty—fighting."

Colonel Hobby, the charming WAC director who retained all her newspaper executive ability from civilian days in Texas, attempted to explain that her girls still were training. Furthermore, she wasn't certain how America would react to the new idea of women going overseas.

"I've *seen* what women can do," the General insisted. "And I'm going to have them in this Theater, whether they're British or American or French or what." As a beginning, he asked for a wholesale shipment of some five thousand WAC's.

Colonel Hobby explained quietly that her feminine troops weren't ready for foreign duty as yet. "Anyhow," she added, "you're asking for well over a third of all the WAC's we have." She made a discreet reference to the existence of a war in the Pacific.

Finally, the Colonel agreed to send over large numbers of WAC's as soon as they were trained, equipped, and available. She kept her word. The first group was hand-picked, for all-around ability. They made a tremendous hit among the homesick G-I's and buckled down to administrative work with dazzling efficiency. I heard many a staff officer remark that British office workers were wonderful, but couldn't measure up to the secretarial ability and morale-uplift of American girls.

And I'm happy to add that, despite the fantastic collection of backgrounds, those women behaved so conscientiously that I never heard a word of scandal about any WAC in England. *That* was a real achievement in a gay wartime capital like London, where occasional raids fed the here-today-gone-tomorrow philosophy, where anything a girl might do was off the hometown scoreboard.

As an advance cadre, Colonel Hobby sent to England five WAC officers. We all lived together before and after I got my commission, lived together in many countries, through every conceivable condition, for some three and one-half years. We came to know each other as sisters, with that intensity war provides. The five were Ruth Briggs, a Rhode Islander who ended the war by going to Moscow with Beetle Smith turned Ambassador; Martha Rogers, a Dixie belle from Mississippi, and Louise Anderson, of Denver, both now living as civilized Californians; Mattie Pinette, of Maine, and Alene Dresmal, of St. Paul, both of whom migrated to Washington, D. C., after the war. There couldn't have been a more diverse group; maybe that's why we got along so famously.

The only time Colonel Hobby was close to danger in London came when she stopped at an open elevator door and stiffly refused to go in until General Eisenhower entered. She didn't know it, but the General's flaming neck and face had nothing to do with a blush. He was angry.

"Just because you put a woman into uniform, it doesn't change her sex," he once scolded me when I, too, waited for him to step

through a door. He always, with his inborn chivalry, stepped aside
to let female companions enter the door first—a small thing, perhaps, yet to a woman an important and revealing trait.

But to many women General Ike was an unsocial ogre. Soon
after his arrival in England, British and American hostesses sent
a Niagara of invitations cascading over his desk. They clogged
the telephone wires with both coy and demanding invitations to
parties, week ends, receptions, dances, dinners, luncheons, even
breakfasts.

The harassed General at first tried to comply, in keeping with
his near-fanatic insistence upon practical Anglo-American relations, both social and military. But several bad experiences
changed all that. One time he lost an entire afternoon's work because he agreed to lunch very simply with Norway's royalty; although intrigued and charmed by King Haakon, he fumed over
the protocol which forbids commoners to leave until the King
has departed. (Still, I heard the General mention on one occasion
that he thought staff section chiefs should remain at their offices
until the "Old Man" left.) Another time, he returned from a
large social gathering with hands so sore from the endless reception line that he swore never to go out again.

Staff advisers worked out a policy to which he adhered from
then on: no social events unless directly connected with military
duties. Even Lady Astor failed to tempt him with rare social
bait—George Bernard Shaw.

This same lack of social pretense led him to evacuate his first
London residence, luxurious Claridge's. It was too rich for his
military blood. He moved into a suite at the Dorchester, the
Americanized hotel which fronted on Park Lane and permitted a
restful view of Hyde Park. The flat had one parlor. Until he
asked Butch to move in and take the other bedroom, General
Eisenhower was a lonely man.

With his limited social activity, I felt quite honored when he
asked my mother and me up to dinner in his flat. It was a wonderful, wholly natural evening. He asked after my brother and

sisters as a real friend of the family, displaying particular interest in my brother Seumas, then in the Royal Engineers and overseas with Wingate. Obviously a family man, the General was greatly touched by my story of the morning when, after a horrible night of Blitz ambulance work in Lambeth, I had gone over to Warwick Court to surprise Mother for breakfast and found the building a hideous heap of smoldering rubble. Luckily, she had been saved. The General shook his head and remarked, fervently, what a blessing it was that his wife—and the wives and families of all Americans overseas—were safe in the unbombed United States.

The entire evening was so mutually pleasant that he invited Mother back several times; they shared a bright interest in history, as well as other subjects. She was most impressed by my Boss. "You'll laugh," she said, "but he's every bit as great a leader as Lincoln—you'll see. He'll grow taller and taller in history as the years go by."

With the 1942 calendar growing thinner, General Eisenhower found no peace even in his hotel suite. The parlor and even the bedroom became mere annexes of his Grosvenor Square office. His appointment pad might start at 8:30 A.M. and continue through till after six in the evening, with candy or peanuts for lunch; going "home" to the flat meant only that he moved over there for additional and often more important meetings. The wrinkles deepened in his face; he showed increasing signs of impatience and nervousness. He probably had less sleep than any non-playboy member of his growing Theater of Operations. Beetle, Butch, Tex, Mickey, and I all began to worry about him.

Finally, he gave in and asked that someone try to find a little retreat on London's outskirts. After much thrashing about the suburbs by staff personnel as well as British and American billeting officers, Butch found just the place late that August.

Telegraph Cottage had been appropriately but mysteriously named decades ago by its elderly lady owner. It was as picturesque as an English Christmas card—so tiny and quaint that visiting Brass, accustomed to huge houses and giant estates as prerogatives of their wartime nobility, were appalled at the ridiculously small hideout their Theater Commander had chosen.

The house offered everything General Eisenhower needed. There was no telephone; when Signal Corpsmen did put in a line it was direct to the General's office at Grosvenor Square, unlisted and unknown outside of our little clique. The slate-roofed little cottage was off the beaten track, nestled in a ten-acre wooded tract near Richmond Park, with a private road. The grounds were utterly pastoral, beautifully peaceful: a high wooden fence protected the privacy of a landscaped lawn in the rear; a small rose garden, an overgrown pathway through the wood.

Inside, the house was miniature but cozy and comfortable. French casement windows looked out upon rustic scenes; the living room had long ceiling-to-floor windows opening onto the lawn itself. There was a cheerful parlor complete with fireplace, a dining room with small oak table. Doll-house stairs led to the little bedrooms and one bathroom. The comparatively ridiculous rent was something like $32 a week, including the services of a gardener. Mickey took over as major-domo, assisted by two likeable Negro soldiers, Chef Hunt, of Virginia, and Waiter Moaney, of Maryland.

Happily, the grounds fringed a golf course. The General had no time for a complete round but he was to spend many easeful hours playing the several holes nearby. He became expert on the thirteenth in particular. The diversion marked the only occasion when he would discard his necktie as a symbol of complete relaxation. I occasionally joined him in puttering attempts at onehole golf; Butch was a more frequent companion. Sometimes they engaged in .22 pistol practice near the cottage.

Only twenty-five minutes from London, Telegraph Cottage was a literal but sympathetic retreat for our tired General.

He went there on every possible occasion to spend the night and, when not summoned to Chequers, the week ends. If anything saved him from a mental crack-up in those tense days it was Telegraph Cottage and the new life it provided. While a strong disciple of official military discipline, the General agreed with the British that a man's home is his castle. And he fortified it against his greatest enemy—shop talk. When new visitors appeared at the cottage he offered the same welcome employed at the Dorchester flat: "As soon as you step in this door, you're my *guests*. Say what you like, do what you like. Relax and enjoy yourselves." Here, he broadened that custom to include the prohibition of official chatter.

One of the first evenings, when I drove him out and then waited to see if there were any night trips, he sank into a chair and grumbled, "Kay, I never seem to have any fun and I get so bored. Must be boring for you people around me, too. What can we do? What do you like?"

"Well," I said, "bridge is fun. It'll take you far away from the war." Then I remembered past experience. "That is, it's fun if there are no post-mortems. They're deadly. I used to love bridge but had to give it up, what with all the rows and post-mortems. One time my husband and I didn't speak for three days, all because of a post-mortem!"

"Okay, that's it. A good idea, bridge." He grinned. "And no post-mortems."

That began a heavy round of bridge. I often played partners with the General; our accounts—at threepence per 100 points— eventually turned into an accountant's nightmare, a financial hodgepodge of dollars, pounds, francs, and marks. The General was as expert at cards as at military strategy and, as at the office, barely hid his impatience with incompetents. General Clark, a close friend for more than two decades and now the deputy chief planner, was a constant companion. So were Butch and Beetle. Another was T. J. Davis, the General's best good-time friend, a jovial and genial Falstaff from South Carolina and yet the extremely competent Adjutant General of Theater headquarters; he had known his present commander intimately since old days in the Philippines. Still another bridge shark was the good-looking, dark-eyed dispensary nurse, Ethel Westermann, who had come to England early as a civilian nurse.

General Ike, as all of us began to call him in the sanctuary of Telegraph Cottage (unless outside guests were present), had really found a sort of home.

He lounged around the living room in G-I slacks, old shirt, a half-suede, half-leather jacket, and a shabby pair of straw slippers which dated back to duty in Manila. Determined to shun official worries momentarily, he snubbed newspapers, books, and general magazines. His only reading fare—indulged to excess—consisted of the inevitable paper-backed cowboy magazines. Mickey managed to scrounge up a seemingly limitless supply of the Westerns.

"I think they're frightful," I told General Ike. His answer was a stopper: "After these long days at the office, worrying about operations which will involve the lives of hundreds of thousands, I don't want to worry when I get out here. That's the idea of this place. And that's the idea of my Westerns—when I read them I don't have to *think.*" No one complained about his one vice after that; in fact, there was an attempt to show Wild West movies in the living room, but it proved impractical.

When I pulled up at the cottage about 7:30 in the morning, the General usually was well into his second or third cup of boiling-hot coffee. I sometimes joined him and any guests for a brief A.M. meal, especially grateful for the occasional egg sent over by some self-sacrificing British admirer.

No one could call Dwight Eisenhower a big eater. He ate whatever was put before him, with relish but never with wild pleasure. His rare temper flared only when the coffee was cold (usually through his own fault). He did, however, maintain a continual campaign for the one dish he really loved—baked beans. No one was quite able to cook it just right. One night, Butch, Hunt, and I each brought in a plate of beans cooked to our respective recipes; the Boss turned up his nose at all of them. He also liked rare steak, lemon-curd and all kinds of pies, leafy artichokes, fried onions; there were no complaints about the pet hates of all Americans in Britain, Brussels sprouts and Spam. Parsnips were exiled from his table.

Steady visits to the War Office resulted in an overdue liking for the British habit of stopping for tea every afternoon; in that, he was far behind the Yanks who screamed louder than Englishmen if cups of tea failed to appear in their offices every afternoon about four o'clock.

Evenings at Telegraph Cottage always started with that "sundown high-ball" served by Mickey to the tune of tinkling ice and gigantic let-down sighs by all present. With General Ike, liquor was only a social custom, necessary but pleasantly enjoyable after one becomes hardened to it; he treated it lightly but with respect. There's no likelihood that anyone will ever see General Eisenhower drunk, or even tight. He handles liquor as respectfully and carefully as an old soldier handles a gun, a loaded gun.

Except for those Westerns, his only vice was cigarettes; he had the habit, to an intensity which approached the chain-fashion stage. Two packs a day were quite normal. In the office I often got away with handing him a few with the warning, "This is your ration for the afternoon." He was surprisingly good-tempered about it. But he blew up one day when I mentioned to a press correspondent that the General smoked a certain brand of cigarette. He was deathly afraid some such chance remark might result in an unintended endorsement.

(This lusty independence was even carried to the point that he instructed Tex Lee, who handled his accounts, to make certain a large part of his personal pay was applied to expenses; he wanted no criticism that he had taken advantage of his position.)

The official General Eisenhower probably worked harder and longer than anyone under his command. Any of his staff will bear out the statement that his working day, his *average* working day, stretched anywhere from ten to twelve hours. After instituting the seven-day week, he once shipped home a key Colonel for being unavailable when a crisis arose; the Colonel was off on a country house party. The C.G. was among the first to appear at 20

Grosvenor Square early Sunday mornings; upon at least one occasion of which I heard, he hit the roof because most of his section
chiefs had failed to show up by 10 A.M. Charwomen reporting for
cleaning duties in the early hours became hardened to the shock
of seeing the General already hard at work.

Atop all else, every decision the C.G. made during his long
day was one of staggering importance and implications. Staff
members took care of the minor problems and passed along to him
only those which required superhuman responsibility and, often,
sheer courage.

Fortunately, all these demands upon his mind and body had
little noticeable effect upon General Eisenhower's health. True,
he was inclined to suffer from high blood pressure. And neuritis
was likely to visit his shoulder. (The all-powerful C.G. was so
afraid of an Army medic's possible orders that he slipped down
to London Clinic for injection treatments. At the same time, he
had to *order* his suffering chief of staff, Beetle, to Army hospital
for ulcer treatment—but didn't have the heart to say a single
word when Beetle later disobeyed Ike's explicit orders and
walked out of the Oxford hospital without doctor's approval.)

Those times we made trips out to supply headquarters, airfields, or troop concentrations, the General always remarked that
his feeling of freedom in getting away from headquarters was
second only to that of escaping to Telegraph Cottage. "I wish
I had seen England in peacetime," he remarked frequently as we
cruised by concrete-and-wire roadblocks, nameless railway sta-
tions, piles of bomb debris, and other reminders of the nation's
desperate early days in the war.

Coming back to London from Cheltenham one lovely day
early in October, we both began talking about the trim little farms
of the Cotswolds. General Ike was choked with nostalgia for the
Middle West.

"I really miss animals in London," I remarked offhand, thinking back to carefree days of rural childhood in Ireland.

My passenger pulled up to the edge of the seat. "Would you

like to have a dog, Kay? You've been awfully nice to me, working all sorts of hours and running all kinds of errands—I'd like to do some little thing."

I was as excited as a little girl. "Would I!"

We talked about dogs the remainder of the trip, agreeing that a Scottie would be the best pet. In the rush of duty over the next few days, however, I forgot all about the idea.

But the staff soon reminded me. There had been a mixup in the meantime. General Eisenhower apparently mentioned he was looking for a dog, a Scottie. The aides and staff chiefs jumped to the natural conclusion it was for him; by the time he realized his mistake, it was too late. They were out combing the city and the countryside for a Scottie appropriate for the top general of a war. The dog would be presented to General Ike on his birthday, less than a week away. I fell in step with the scheme.

Beetle and I eventually came across a pair of Scotties in kennels just a few blocks away, near Selfridge's huge department store. I loved the puppy, but Beetle favored the other one, a much older dog. He pointed out it wouldn't be necessary to house-break his choice. "I know what it means," he added. "I've had dogs all my life" As a compromise it was agreed that we should take both to the Boss and let him decide. Beetle said the General had put so much pressure on Tex to find a dog that they had had to admit they were planning to give him one as a birthday present. So, he emphasized, there was no harm in letting the General make a choice.

Back at Grosvenor Square we barged into the Commanding General's office with our struggling burdens, laughing and kidding like children. "Which one's it to be, Ike?" Beetle asked as we put out two Scotties on the floor

Beetle's older dog sat down with a whimper, shy and dull. My puppy, only six weeks old and fat as a baby, wobbled uncertainly. "Come here, fella!" General Ike yelled hopefully to both.

My puppy staggered and skidded across the floor, toward what was obviously a master's voice.

The General laughed happily. "Beetle, that's the one for me!"

Excited and barely able to stand, the favored puppy proceeded to celebrate the occasion with a defiant little puddle smack in the center of the Commanding General's office.

On October 14 the General's birthday was celebrated with a little gathering at the cottage. Beetle, T.J., Butch, and his few other intimates roared as the sixty-dollar puppy was presented with appropriate ceremony. Someone at Eighth Air Force had sent over a midget-sized parachute and harness for the friendly little black dog destined to become second only to the renowned Falla in wartime fame. There was a cake with three candles and three stars to commemorate the honor guest's new rank, which, incidentally, had come about so quietly in the summer that his two aides first learned of it in the newspapers.

Beetle and General Ike tried out several possible names for the bewildered Scottie. "I've got it!" the General shouted. "*Telek!*" We all looked mystified. "After Telegraph Cottage," he explained. Then he glanced over at me. "This place is secret, Kay. So the reason for Telek's name will have to be Top Secret till after the war!"

I managed a weak smile.

Amidst all that festivity, I couldn't tell them I was suffering from woman's oldest wartime pain:

Dick was leaving Scotland that very night—for North Africa.

CHAPTER III

INEVITABLY, I had heard of the impending North African invasion. Talk in the back seat of my staff car was more Top Secret than anything on paper. In general, I knew about as much about "Torch" Operation as most senior commanders in the early autumn of 1942.

One month before the birthday party I had taken General Eisenhower out to Telegraph Cottage in a hurry. For once he seemed preoccupied. He obviously didn't want to talk; I had long made it a habit not to ask questions, ever. As we sped through Kensington he mumbled something about "big doings for a colonel." The rest of the ride was in heavy silence. But Generals —three-star Generals—don't usually get excited over colonels. I knew something *big* was up.

"I don't know how long we'll be here," the General said as he got out at the cottage. "Mickey will look after you."

There was an air of hush-hush inside. Hunt, Moaney, and Mickey walked on tip-toe. I retired to the kitchen and learned that the General was outside talking in literal whispers to a tall, unmilitary lieutenant-colonel. As darkness fell, they came inside and sat beside the crackling fireplace. Kitchen gossip soon established that the cottage housed a queer assortment: Beetle, General Clark, Brigadier Eric Mockler-Ferryman, and Mr. William H. B. Mack. Beetle himself, it seemed, had gone to Hendon to pick up the colonel, to whom they referred as McGowan. Butch had gone to Norfolk House, closely guarded HQ of Allied forces planning the invasion, for the others. Colonel Julius Holmes, the

British-looking United States Embassy officer with the Guards mustache, also was present.

They had dinner in the tiny dining room, to the accompaniment of drinks, whispers, cigars, and clouds of smoke as thick as any London pea-souper fog. Butch left in a car around 7:30, returning with Ambassador Winant, Mr. Harriman, and H. Freeman Mathews.

Sitting nervously in the kitchen, I found my imagination running riot. Was this the final invasion council? Were the Nazis planning some new horror? Who was this stoop-shouldered, civilian-looking lieutenant-colonel who commanded such attention from his top-level companions?

Around 9 P.M. I was dismissed without explanation. I went home to Kensington Close completely bewildered. Lying awake in bed that cold September night, I thought of the friends who always remarked, "Kay, you must have a terribly dull job. You never talk about it." And I thought of Dick.

In the next few days details of that secret meeting at Telegraph Cottage gradually seeped up to the front seat of my car.

"Lieutenant-Colonel McGowan" was none other than Mr. Robert Murphy, the American underground chief in French Morocco. The conference had been concerned largely with one frightening question mark: would the French fight when we landed in North Africa? Equally important, it had been concerned with French leaders' demand that the Allies send a top commander to the scene down there to discuss practical details. This, then, was the meeting when it had been decided to send General Clark on his submarine mission to the North African coast, for a clandestine parley which might have been dreamed up by Hitchcock, or Oppenheim.

Shortly afterward, General Eisenhower asked the question I had been framing in my mind for weeks, to ask *him*. "Kay," he said, unusually serious, "would you like to go along?"

I was almost shouting as I explained that Dick undoubtedly would be heading the direction of the forthcoming invasion. I would do *anything* to be somewhere near him. Ike knew about Dick. No further emphasis was required. "It'll be in about a month or so," he said, warning of the need for extreme security.

Excited by this new development, I took a personal interest from then on in plans I heard discussed. When we went up to western Scotland for assault exercises in the bleak country around Kentallen, north of Inveraray, I watched the maneuvers with keen feeling. And I drove so long in the murky blackout that, for the first time in my official driving career, someone (Butch) had to take the wheel. At one point I suddenly remembered that the honor guest back at Telegraph Cottage the night before we left for Scotland had been General Clark, now en route to that secret rendezvous.

The tempo around London headquarters increased to a crescendo. One wire-service correspondent was given to understand the invasion would take place in Norway. Another trumpeted that it was planned for Dakar. Some of the staff purchased arctic clothing; others, tropic garb. A few of these items were left around for reporters to see and use as "inside" speculation. There was a bad day when Butch reported the loss of a page from some Top Secret documents which covered the entire Torch Operation. And another when one of the press associations sent a straight story to the States suggesting that arrangements be made to provide coverage at Casablanca, not Dakar, as Casa was the point of invasion.

Just thinking of Dick, I was thrown into a dither by such slip-ups. I could imagine the added strain on General Eisenhower, who bore the responsibility for the lives of thousands of men like Dick.

As October drew to a close, my three-star passenger decided to drive himself out to Telegraph Cottage one evening. He wanted to be alone, I'm sure, although he said it was merely to see if he could find the way. (He made it, but I've since wondered what some conscientious M.P. would have done in stopping that big Packard and finding a three-star general driving alone.)

The next day after that solo journey, all our tension eased. General Clark appeared at Telegraph Cottage for dinner. He told his now well-known story well, with all the polish of the born story-teller. Each of his usually blasé listeners—including his relieved friend Eisenhower—was openly thrilled and happy that everything went off so well. Surely, it was one of the most fabulous dramas of a fantastic war. I got a tremendous kick out of his sidelight story, that he returned a hero without pants.

Ike took General Clark with him to say goodbye to the King. Telek and I drove them down to Buckingham Palace and waited in the historic courtyard; Telek was quite unimpressed by his surroundings and insisted upon committing a blatant indignity upon the Royal property. When our passengers returned, General Eisenhower revealed that he had worried needlessly over one major point of protocol: how to back away from His Majesty, without falling flat on his face. "He came right to the door with us," Ike laughed.

In addition to all his staggering official worries, General Eisenhower had a very personal fret about leaving for Gibraltar. It had been directed that a story be put out he was returning to Washington for an official visit—to explain his sudden absence from London. General Ike knew Mrs. Eisenhower would have a huge welcome prepared. He couldn't bring himself to disappoint and worry his own family so. Yet he felt the Supreme Commander shouldn't have the right to break security silence any more than the lowest-ranking G-I.

All of us felt his personal pain at deciding to stick to the story that he was going to Washington, without using his official position to tell his own family it was all a "cover plan."

After a final week end at Chequers he had a small farewell dinner—a dinner, not a party—at the cottage. General Clark, Butch, Beetle, and T.J., his most intimate friends, were the only guests that Saturday night, the last day of October. Mickey packed the few belongings the General was taking along to Gibraltar. The festivities hardly could be described as gay.

Sunday was quiet, then a Monday dull for me but filled with last-minute staff conferences for the General. The weather was bad, typically early-November; the darkness was charcoal-black as I drove him down to Addison Road Station. There were few, people around; the yard was used mostly as a goods station.

"Well, Kay," the General said as he got out, "tomorrow's the day." There was a quick flutter of goodbyes in the blackout, shouts of "Good luck!" and "Godspeed!" and the train puffed away into the night.

Tuesday morning was sheer torture; I hate to be left out of anything. Still wondering when my own party would leave, I loafed in the near-empty office. The atmosphere was that of a theater after the show's over.

The 'phone rang. I recognized Beetle's voice. "Go down," he said cryptically, "and pick up the same party you saw off last night!"

General Eisenhower and his entire group were waiting at the station. The wisecracks about "a dry run" failed to hide deep disappointment. They had arrived safely in Bournemouth only to find their B-17's grounded by nasty weather. Flight to Gibraltar was out of the question; authorities refused to let the rank-packed train stay in Bournemouth as a juicy target for Nazi air raiders. So they all came back to London.

All the party were ordered to stay out of sight, particularly out of their offices. Inasmuch as the newspapers had proclaimed he was on the way to Washington, the General himself had to hide. The Dorchester or Grosvenor Square were strictly "off limits" this time.

We took the General back to the old reliable security hideaway, Telegraph Cottage.

Every man there was as nervous as an expectant father and, as one irreverent companion put it, I was as nervous as a pregnant nun. Steaming black coffee disappeared by the pint. Even the usually imperturbable General was frankly nervous, lighting one cigarette from another. Dinner was quiet and glum. After dark the group traveled to the heart of London's commercial film district, Wardour Street, to quiet nerves with a private showing in one of the trade-show offices.

The film was *Road to Morocco.*

Tension eased somewhat by the hilarious humor, we returned to Addison Road Station. This time, goodbyes were anti-climax. I smothered a thousand questions while shaking hands with the General. "You'll be off before long, Kay," he said. "And look after Telek!"

The Boss being away, I had no duties the next day. And the succeeding days were little better.

Beetle, with whom the General had advised me to keep in touch, said I and the other civilians probably would go by sea instead of air. There had been some trouble with the official air party, it seemed. Weather had continued bad at Bournemouth and the pilot declined to take off. But time was running out. General Eisenhower, for the first time in his life, had disregarded the pilot's estimate; he *ordered* the take-off. As a safety measure, however, he put General Clark, the one man most familiar with all invasion details, in a separate plane. Beetle said Mr. Churchill called London headquarters several times an hour until advised his commander was safe at Gibraltar.

I talked unhappy office-talk with the General's new junior aide, Lieutenant Craig Campbell. But I couldn't talk to anyone about the one subject uppermost in my mind: Dick was in that invasion fleet on the high seas.

I spent the night of November 7 virtually inside my radio. Not long after 1 A.M., which I knew to be H-Hour, the good news came through. The invasion was on. I heard some remarks by President Roosevelt and others by a "spokesman" giving instructions to people in the invasion areas. And I heard a proclamation by General Ike, in beautiful French. Since he spoke no French, I knew the carefully modulated voice with the polished accent belonged to our suave Colonel Julius Holmes. I slept very little that night, listening to the dramatic broadcasts and the continual martial strains of the *Marseillaise*.

Foolishly, I packed everything of value, including my best luggage and a few precious bits of jewelry. North Africa meant war, but it also meant Dick—and marriage. I packed accordingly. Mother maintained the best tradition of British privacy and awareness of war security. I could tell her only that I was leaving London. Although undoubtedly certain I was headed for North Africa and a long war, she asked no questions and was a great comfort.

Time evaporated quickly. There was a mad round of shots for everything from typhoid to lockjaw, the arrival of WAC's and civilians who were joining the party. Luckily, one of my driver friends was going along: Elspeth Duncan, a friendly Scot who later became the wife of a British general in Berlin.

We civilians had to have passports, which involved so much red tape that the staff finally shoved them up to highest levels in order to get around civil servants who insisted upon long, time-consuming procedure, war or no war. Mine was dated November 12 and gave my occupation as "driver." There were visas for Portugal and Spain, just in case. The exit permit read: "Valid for departure before Feb. 12, 1943, and for one journey only. Holder is traveling to North Africa." (Trust the Government to squeeze all excitement from an official document.)

That last day they issued us gas masks and helmets at Norfolk House. The war seemed much closer.

The first leg of our journey was a long, hungry, night time trip from Euston Station to Scotland. Arriving at Greenock village on the Clyde, the same port first seen by hundreds of thousands of Americans who came to England, we were welcomed by more mountains of red tape. The military enjoyed hot coffee and doughnuts while we civilians shuffled to one side for paper clearance.

The weather couldn't have been more miserable. Even the

English usually find Scotland's climate wet. And this was a superbly typical day: great sheets of cold, gusty rain soaked us to the skin while painting the whole scene in depressing grayness.

After endless delays, we loaded into small boats. Embarkation was slow; we circled around the harbor for the better part of an hour, shivering in the open tender, using anything from baggage to newspapers to hide from that cold downpour.

Finally, we scrambled onto the ill-fated *Strathallen*, off to war . . . and disaster.

CHAPTER IV

Troopship life evolved into a world without privacy, a world of restless boredom and endless rumor.

Fortunately, my two "cabin" companions were old friends: Ethel Westermann, the dispensary nurse who had been out to Telegraph Cottage for innumerable bridge sessions, and Jean Dixon, a friendly Washington girl whose British husband had been killed in the Royal Air Force. We took turns sleeping on a dirty mattress wedged into the floor beside a double-decker bunk.

With three separate sittings for each meal, we spent much of the days inching along the deck in snake-like lines. Even loafing space was rationed. We queued, slept, and strolled; strolled, slept, and queued. Between-times, we joined the gossip-manglers.

Finally, to escape the endless chatter, we set up a marathon bridge game. Our fourth was Margaret (Peg) Bourke-White, the *Life* photographer, whose slim slacks, natty uniform, and neat blue-gray hair drew a symphony of wolf-calls with every appearance on deck. To us she was a Godsend, a vivacious fourth in our bridge battle against the old shipboard enemy, boredom.

Every night, without fail, we packed the "torpedo bag" prescribed by regulations. This was our regular-issue "musette" shoulder bag, which was to be stuffed with warm clothing and other necessities. But, being women, we ignored such male logic and, instead of necessities, piled luxuries into our emergency kits. Mine bulged with nylons, a few bits of jewelry, silk undies —things I thought invaluable in the event of submarine action.

Meanwhile, our convoy began to take shape. Ships joined

up unobtrusively as we ploughed through the rolling Atlantic, stretching as far as eye could see through rain and fog. The commander ordered three lifeboat drills daily, two in the morning, one in the afternoon.

Several days out, a wild gale struck with terrifying ferocity. Rough seas kept most passengers in their bunks. Queues for meals shrunk, then disappeared. The dining room was empty, almost ghost-like. Whenever the ship lurched, waiters dashed full trays to the deck. Lifeboat drill was canceled.

The storm thrashed us about for days, reducing life to its barest minimum, gloomy and dreary. Then, in the dark hours after midnight, it scurried away to the west. We hurried topside.

"Look!" one of the British nurses cried, "*lights!*" It was Tangier, a sparkling necklace of a city—the first land sighted since Scotland, the first lighted city some of us had seen since 1939.

Morning brought hope and a cheerful sky, plus the rich blue waters of the Mediterranean. Pale-faced, sad-eyed officers and nurses appeared on deck for the first time in days, soaking up the sunshine. The *Strathallen* shivered that night as she dropped a frothing succession of depth charges, but no one seemed concerned over reports of German subs in the vicinity. Boat drills were resumed; only one daily.

Amidst all this reassuring normality, the loudspeakers blared forth a long-awaited announcement: we would land the next day.

Every cabin held a "last night" party. After unpacking the emergency torpedo bags and carefully tucking all those items into our luggage, we went to join some friends in a party as bright and gay as any peacetime celebration aboard a cruise liner.

It was 1:30 in the morning before we tip-toed back, anxious to pin up our hair and grab some sleep. I sank onto the bunk and kicked off my shoes. Pictures of Algiers bubbled up, pictures where all the women looked like Hedy Lamarr and the men spoke like Charles Boyer. I pulled off my necktie and lazily unbuttoned my collar—

A tremendous explosion threw us forward.

All lights went out. The ship shuddered, then rocked back and forth.

No one moved or said a word. Several minutes later, Ethel muttered, "This is it, kids."

The ship settled at a list. We banged our shins against luggage and the double-decker before Jean found a flashlight. I grabbed my shoes. Cursing at our empty torpedo bags, we each grabbed a coat and headed for the lifeboat station.

Dim moonlight showed the rest of the convoy moving on by. Scores of dark figures ran around the deck, getting groups organized, while crew members readied the boats. All of us shouted, trying to locate friends. Half the nurses and WAC's had pajama tops or nightshirts over slacks. Everyone was half-dressed; some were barefoot. A determined minority dragged barracks bags or other belongings. Most of us were empty-handed.

There was no confusion, no panic. Every face was sleepy, presenting a half-sheepish, half-astonished expression.

After we stepped into our lifeboat, the sailors lowered us gently until we hit the tossing waters. Any fears I had about being sucked under with the *Strathallen* were calmed by the coxswain, who handled us, the boat, and his dark-skinned, jabbering Lascar crew with superb skill. We pulled away quickly. The stricken ship became a dark hulk in the distance.

Adrift in the Mediterranean and the fast rescue work over, our boat seemed lonelier than ever. We could see the convoy steaming by. Tiny lights of other lifeboats and rafts bobbed on the water. We could hear occasional shouts.

The sea was filled with soldiers swimming around aimlessly, yelling for help. I jerked blankets from the Lascars, who muttered angrily while their coxswain swore at them in disgust. We pulled in a good twenty or thirty men before our boat became overcrowded. Other lifeboats then edged into the area to pick up the few remaining survivors.

Among those we rescued was a chap with a broken leg; he wouldn't have made it much longer. Another collapsed at our feet and gasped, "Whole boat turned over when they lowered us down the side. Lot of nurses and officers drowned . . ."

A British destroyer came close by. A megaphone voice announced survivors would be picked up in the morning. Our neighborhood still was alive with U-boats, the voice explained; it would take hours to clear the area.

The rest of the long, long night was spent trying to keep warm—and trying to keep from getting sick.

The Mediterranean's normal swell was churned into angry waves by hundreds of depth charges. Each bomb sent a volcanic explosion up in the air, then huge rings of waves, one after another. Our little lifeboat rocked and plunged.

I was one of six, at most, who failed to become ill—and it was a constant battle, minute after minute, hour after hour, *not* to get sick. The boat was packed full; fellow passengers, wet and cold and downhearted, were sick in each other's laps. Ethel and I cracked jokes to keep from turning ill. We cuddled to keep warm, talked to overcome the noises of the sick. It was a rough, cold, nauseating, interminable night.

Just before dawn the sea calmed as the barrage of depth charges lessened. And the sun came up, pouring warmth and light and color over the scene.

It was impossible to remain glum in the new day. Our ill gained new strength. Clothes steamed, then dried. The men began talking about food. We women were most concerned with our appearance. The lipstick and comb in my pocket were great morale-boosters. Only Peg White showed no interest; she was busy with her cameras, recording an admittedly dramatic tableau.

The morning's climax came when our old friend, the British

destroyer, hove into sight. In an incredibly short time she was picking up the survivors in each lifeboat. When our turn came, I helped Peg up the rope-ladder with her cameras. The deck felt wonderfully solid and very, very welcome. Far below, empty lifeboats floated by, grim wreaths in memory of those who had died during the night.

Hot tea and meager emergency rations helped kill time aboard the destroyer. We spent most of the hours reuniting with old friends, talking over the torpedoing.

Late in the afternoon our destroyer pulled into Oran, tied up alongside a pier, and dropped the gangplank. The usual women-and-children-first tradition was reversed; we women waited for the men to disembark. They organized into original outfits and marched off, a ragged military parade of half-dressed soldiers and officers.

Searching for Dick at Oran headquarters, I was regarded with open suspicion. The guard, however, admitted there was a Lieutenant-Colonel Arnold in the section; in that very building, in fact. "I'll get him for you," he said cryptically.

He asked Dick to come down to the lobby, then hung up without mentioning my name on the phone.

I asked to telephone Algiers. That request brought out another guard, a lieutenant in charge, a major, and, finally, a full colonel. Each of them studied my torn skirt, shredded nylons, open-necked shirt and my straggly hair, covered by a peasant-like handkerchief. They whispered among themselves.

"Look here," I said in exasperation, "I've just been rescued from a torpedoed ship. I want to call General Eisenhower and tell him his staff is safe. And I want to get orders what to do next. *Do you mind?*"

The one magic word—Eisenhower—got me the telephone. I was weak with relief when the operator got me through to the General's office and Tex Lee came on the line. "Tex," I said with complete lack of imagination, "we're here."

Tex said the office knew we had been torpedoed, but didn't know if we had been picked up. "Just a minute," he added, "the General will want to talk to you."

General Eisenhower asked after each of the office gang, put on General Clark for a moment, then concluded the conversation by ordering us to Algiers the next day.

I hung up thoughtfully and turned to ask the guards where Ethel, Jean, and I could spend the night.

My vision blurred. The guards faded from sight.

All I could see was a tall, dark lieutenant-colonel who thought I was in London. Thoroughly bewildered, he couldn't utter a word.

"Dick!" I cried, running toward him, breaking down in a most unmilitary fashion.

CHAPTER V

WITHIN twenty-four hours, the war ripped us apart again. Dick waved forlornly, shin-deep in mud, as Ethel, Jean, and I climbed into General Eisenhower's B-17, dispatched to make certain that we proceed to Allied Force Headquarters without further delay. When the plane pulled itself from Oran's swampy airfield I could scarcely keep from bawling as Dick gradually diminished to a mere pinpoint near the airstrip far below. His last words still rang in my ears: "I'm trying to get up to the front, darling."

In Algiers, I found AFHQ located at the old St. George Hotel. I also found the army had displayed its usual impatience in rushing me back to work, away from Dick. There was no work. The Boss was up front on a quick trip. His office, a trio of rooms each about the size of a linen closet, offered me no desk space. The staff cars still hadn't arrived. Tex, sincerely happy to see us and to hear all about the torpedoing, nevertheless hinted that I might be in the way around the office until the General returned. "Why don't you all go up and look at your new quarters?" he suggested. "I'll get you a car. Tell the driver you want the *Clinique Glycine.*"

Climbing to the top of a hill overlooking Algiers, we found the *Clinique.* The army's rare sense of humor was billeting us in a maternity hospital.

We piled inside, inspected the dormitory rooms, gobbled a foul dinner concocted by the French cook from our strange G-I rations, and washed the one shirt each of us possessed.

Then we piled into warm cots for a long overdue good night's sleep.

Next morning, Tex supplied ration coupons. Elspeth Duncan and I set out on a day-long search of the city for clothes to replace those now at the bottom of the Mediterranean, along with the poor *Strathallen.*

Algiers, an intriguing mixture of French and Arab, of city and desert, was a colorful and foreign change from the wartime drabness of London. Instead of the fictional white, flowing robes, the Arabs were wrapped in clothes distinctly similar to unwashed bedsheets. The more fashionable cut holes in G-I barracks bags and used them as baggy pants. All were indescribably filthy, partially responsible for the sickening range of odors which shifted with each step along the cobbled streets. The dirt seemed contaminating even at fifty yards. These men were horribly cruel; when horses stumbled under heavy loads, their gaunt masters wielded whips with a savagery which seemed to indicate a form of revenge on all the world for reducing humans to such a way of life. I often saw Yanks and Tommies angrily grab whips from Arabs.

Arab women? Their traditional veils were little more than small handkerchiefs which hid none of the heavy makeup so thick it reminded me of girls on movie sets back in London. Dirt was no stranger to them, either. And they suffered the same treatment as the animals from the men.

Arab children were close cousins of slum kids in every city of the world, tough, prematurely adult, and bitter, accomplished beggars. In the past month since the liberation they had learned to swoop down on stray American and British soldiers. The chant started with coy requests: "Candy? . . . Gum? . . . Soap? . . . Cigarettes?" Then it shifted to sly bargaining: "Shoeshine, Joe? . . . Woman? Nice sister? . . . Wine? . . . Feelthy pictures? . . ." They badgered until bribed, then slid away only to be replaced by another gang of wheedling yet demanding little ruffians. One urchin had been in contact with a Brooklyn teacher; he shouted at every G-I, "Who win Series, Mac? Dodgers?" Another had been taught to approach officers and smirk, "What's date of your rank, Bud?" The most accomplished boy was one who had learned to scream President Roosevelt's most unfortunate and most widely warped remark. In serious sing-song, he yelled: "I *hate* wahr, mah frans, I *hate* wahr . . ."

Elspeth and I found the shops modern and pleasant, the sales-girls chic and friendly. Only one thing was wrong: the shelves were empty. Even a hairpin was a real treasure. Hours of weary search turned up only a few pairs of panties and bras, very French. American supply people fixed us up with ties and overseas caps; the British quartermaster came through with gloves, shirt, and a badly needed raincoat for each of us. (British nurses from the *Strathallen* didn't fare as well; those long-suffering girls went around Algiers for months in shapeless battledress and *hobnail boots*, because their supply officers simply couldn't be bothered to provide proper equipment. In sharp contrast, American nurses soon received feminine equipment direct from States supplies to replace their lost items.)

The following day—Christmas Eve—Admiral Darlan was assassinated.

Guards appeared throughout the city, nestling tommy-guns under their arms. Some were stationed at the *Clinique*. The civilian population slithered around in ominous quiet, whispering instead of shouting; headquarters personnel openly worried about the possibility of an organized uprising or, more frightening, a chain of assassinations. The most astute wondered just how this new calamity would affect General Eisenhower, who was already under home-front fire for appointing Darlan, for permitting a Vichy-like atmosphere, for favoring such characters as Nogues, Peyrouton, and scores of other major administrative officials. Tex managed to reach the General up at the front; he started back to tense Algiers on Christmas evening. And he found the Yuletide spirit a definite casualty throughout Allied ranks.

But Beetle Smith came to our rescue with a sudden invitation to his Christmas turkey dinner.

The combination of his villa and his cordiality was a happy relief from the nervous pessimism in the city below. Although even an outhouse in Algiers is described as a villa, Beetle's residence truly deserved the luxurious name. It was smart, attractive throughout, bright, cheerful, and beautifully landscaped, with garden and terrace. Among the many unique furnishings was an intriguing drawing room carpet woven in the topographical form of an African desert, buff in color, with graduated ridges to represent sand dunes of varying heights.

The villa's charm was exceeded only by that of our Santa Claus host. Most of the headquarters staff, especially the junior officers, regarded General Smith as a complete Prussian. He could be, too—tough, humorless, driving, with all the sentiment of an S.S. general. As Beetle himself often put it, "Someone around the top has to be an absolute S.O.B. and Ike's not in a position to do it all the time. So that's my job." Actually, General Eisenhower frequently emphasized he would be, quite literally, lost without the services of his able Chief of Staff, who was a master of paper work, who protected his Boss from minor problems and decisions, who had the ideal of cold military logic. That's **why** the General had been forced to play every high card in his powerful deck to get Beetle away from General Marshall, who likewise regarded the dimple-chinned officer as one of the Army's finest executives.

But Beetle also can lower his official guard, revealing a warm, friendly, and very likeable gentleman. Too few persons have seen that second-layer personality of Beetle Smith, the personality **we** gloried in that Christmas Day at his Algiers villa.

Christmas became a memory. The weather continued cold and rainy, much like that of London in late December. General Eisenhower went off to the front once more and, as the motor pool still wasn't set up, I fought off boredom by trying to make myself useful in the Adjutant General's office, basking in the genial atmosphere set by my old friend from Telegraph Cottage days, "T. J." Davis.

The five WAC officers arrived from Oran and they, together with another civilian woman and me, were moved into a separate little villa not far away from the *Clinique,* which became a billet for nurses only. We were quite pleased to have a billet to ourselves and eventually arranged to operate our own tiny mess. The water system, of course, broke down with dismaying regularity. And any good script writer could have made an hilarious comedy scene out of the picture of all seven of us crowding into the one bathroom at the same hour every morning.

The high point of my first week in Algiers came on the last day of December, when General Eisenhower invited Elspeth and me up to his villa for dinner. I was glad to see the Boss, who appeared tired and suffering from a cold which landed him in bed shortly afterward with a touch of flu. But the real treat came when a barking, jumping, skidding, fat bundle of black fur assaulted me at the doorway: *Telek!*

He made me almost ill with my first real attack of homesickness; I hadn't known till then just how much I had missed that yelping little Scottie. We played noisily for the better part of an hour. When Hunt and Moaney came out of the kitchen to say "hello," they complained that Telek wasn't house-broken. I snorted. "You're just too nice to him. You've spoiled him rotten— I had that dog well-trained before you great big tough soldiers got your hands on him!" (By the time General Marshall arrived in the middle of January, Telek was so undisciplined and disrespectful to rank that he piddled twice on Ike's bed, while two of the world's greatest disciplinarians stood by helplessly.)

As usual, General Eisenhower had chosen a house more appropriate for a captain than for the Allied commander. I found it ugly, filled with uncomfortable French furniture and a general appearance of dreariness. The view from the terrace, however, was lovely. We all rushed out there when German planes came over on a raid, the first I saw in Africa. Sergeant Clay Williams, who acted as a major-domo of sorts, clapped on his helmet; the more veteran Telek scurried under a couch, trembling and crying softly. The raid was terrible to the rest of us, too, but armed with our London baptism we were able to see the awful beauty of the ack-ack fireworks which illuminated the harbor and the city in the bowl down by the Mediterranean. The initial sense of beauty disappeared when hunks of shrapnel began falling on the terrace; we went inside.

That night marked the first talk about a spectacularly secret conference to be held at Casablanca.

At the mention of names the caliber of Roosevelt, Churchill, De Gaulle, Hopkins, Giraud, Tedder, Pound, and Mountbatten, I tingled with anticipatory excitement. The General certainly would be a star delegate and I most certainly would drive him. It seemed a sure thing. It soon was evident, however, that the only female guests would be those capable of super-stenographic work. I wasn't invited to the biggest party in Africa.

Still more disturbing news—that Dick had been transferred up to II Corps and possible front-line action—was partially off-set by a blessed gift from the limitless store of Eisenhower thoughtfulness. When he heard Dick was coming to Algiers on brief Corps duty, the General called me in. "Kay," he said, "I understand Dick's coming to town?" I nodded. "Well," he continued, "you two can't talk or have much privacy up there at the billet with other women hanging around." He smiled. "When Dick arrives, tell him I want him to stay at my villa, as my personal guest, as long as he's here."

"Thanks" is such a tiny, clumsy word for a man who can take time from directing an historic army to realize that his driver and her boy friend would appreciate solitude. Both Dick and I tried to emphasize our appreciation, but the General only countered by tossing a special dinner for us one night; Butch, Ethel, and a few other friends added to the festive spirit, despite another air raid which reminded me, soberly, Dick was going back to the real war.

Shortly after the Casablanca conference and its iron demand for unconditional surrender by the Axis, we were invaded by an army of V-I-P's who wanted to visit the General and Allied headquarters before returning to their respective homes. Unfortunately, Mr. Churchill failed to appear, although scheduled, and all of us were particularly disappointed that President Roosevelt hurried home without a visit to Algiers. But I did meet General Sir Alan Brooke again, warming to that friendly personality which always comes as a surprise to anyone expecting Colonel Blimp on being introduced to the "Chief of the Imperial General Staff." With him and General Eisenhower, it was "Brookie" and "Ike."

I also renewed acquaintance with the only one of General Eisenhower's friends or associates who never got around to calling him Ike—General Marshall, who invariably, despite their long and close association, talked to Ike as "Eisenhower." In retaining this formality General Marshall was in character. He always greeted me immediately and shook hands in outward cordiality, yet I never could quite overcome what amounted to a touch of fear of him. Perhaps it was because of his military bearing, his careful speech, his somewhat fatherly attitude toward General Eisenhower; perhaps it was because General Marshall was my Boss's Boss. Regardless, even though I came to know him quite well in the months and years ahead, I felt there was an untouchable barrier, a barrier unequaled among all the scores of celebrated persons I met during the war. Nonetheless, I shared the universal respect for General Marshall's military genius and found him always the perfect military officer, the perfect Southern gentleman.

And I respected him even more after General Eisenhower told me his Boss had *ordered* Butch to see that the Supreme Commander took better care of himself, that he pay less attention to extra-office-hours and more to his health, that he get a place in the country and try to manage some exercise. The entire staff worried over General Ike's health; he refused to work normal hours, he declined to bed down with a lingering touch of flu, he never exercised, he suffered from increasing insomnia, and he worked at a murderous pace.

General Marshall had returned to Washington by the time our missing Prime Minister showed up, revealing impishly he had sneaked away for a hush-hush conference with the President of Turkey. He stayed with Admiral Cunningham, whose villa was in the same compound as that of General Eisenhower, in order to permit joint security measures.

When we pulled into the narrow, palm-lined driveway of General Eisenhower's villa that day, I spotted the familiar siren-suit headed our way. The General got out to greet the P.M. effusively; I stood by quietly, unable to salute, as a civilian, certain he wouldn't remember a mere army driver. After chatting with Ike for a few moments, however, Mr. Churchill came over to the car, walking right up to shake hands heartily.

Using the inevitable cigar as a baton, he opened the conversation by remarking, "Well, Kay, thought I'd find you here. How are you making out, driving on the righthand side of the road?" He made me perfectly at ease, with his natural buoyancy; downright appealing in his obvious pleasure at this warlike vacation from Downing Street, he was a far cry from a man one might visualize as carrying the cares of the British Empire on his hunched shoulders.

With the P.M.'s arrival, General Eisenhower was talked into a luncheon to end all luncheons. The guest list was enough to terrify any Foreign Office veteran, let alone a ceremony-hating soldier like General Eisenhower. "I'm going to get myself into a real mess, Kay," the General remarked beforehand. "I'm militarily and politically outranked by half my guests!" Seeing that guest list, I realized what he meant: the Prime Minister of the British Empire, General de Gaulle, Admiral Cunningham, Sir Alexander Cadogan, General Giraud, Messrs. Murphy and Macmillan, General Anderson, Sir Alan Brooke, Nogues, Peyrouton, and Boisson.

But Butch, the General, and Colonel Holmes, the striped-pants authority, managed to work it out with sheer genius. Mr. Churchill was made joint host with General Eisenhower, which solved the biggest problem of all. General de Gaulle was placed to the right of the Prime Minister, who, after all, had been working very closely with the Free French in London; Ike was flanked by General Giraud, with whom he was more intimate, comparatively. This intricate arrangement ironed out most of the protocol wrinkles, except the table talk. I wish I could have been there.

Five days later, General Ike received his fourth star.

Driving up to the villa for lunch, which he, Butch, and I usually shared in a welcome atmosphere of informality, I offered congratulations. All of us on the staff felt the unspoken resentment in some quarters that the Allied commander should be outranked by some of his subordinates: Admiral of the Fleet Cunningham; Tedder, a full Marshal; even "Colonel MacGowan" Murphy had become a Minister. Ike, of course, was pleased at reaching full generalship; after all, he was only an unknown lieutenant-colonel when England entered the war. And it took him twenty-eight long years to climb from second lieutenant to the top rung of the military ladder. At the same time, Butch said the General was a little peeved because the BBC broadcast the report of his promotion before he or anyone at AFHQ knew about it.

He brightened when a cable from Mrs. Eisenhower confirmed the report. And he promoted, as his first official act, each of the house staff's enlisted men. Promotion was out of the question for Civilian First Class Summersby, but I joined the entire gang in beaming with frank pride that our Boss now ranked with the best. Ike gave vent to his own enjoyment in the promotion that evening when a number of us—including the five WAC's—joined him for a quiet celebration. His voice really rang with abandon as he chimed in with the phonograph on his favorite two songs, *One Dozen Roses* and *Roll Out the Barrel*. Then we settled down to a serious game of bridge.

It was the General's last carefree evening for many a week.

At seven o'clock the next morning we set out for Constantine, Tebessa, and the scene of what turned into the sad American defeat at Kasserine Pass.

This was my first combat drive, with no resemblance to piloting the General around rural England. We started out in protective convoy, accompanied by two jeeps, a spare sedan, and a weapons carrier. Once on the main highway, I realized the protection was planned for possible aerial attack. Some stretches of that route were as lonely as only desert country can be. Still, to me, they were absolute Heaven compared with the spots where we hit supply convoys traveling the Red Ball Express; the road was two-lane at best, with soft shoulders, and truck drivers hogged that center part with frightening insistence, despite our little group's horns, the siren on our car, the flags, and the four-star license plates. The solid, miles-long lines of huge trucks constituted a dangerous, exasperating obstacle course. With my valuable passenger in the back seat, and remembering the rumors of sudden paratroop attacks on the open stretches, I began to see that driving a General in wartime is far from glamorous. Chilly, rainy weather added a final hazard.

The General's sole concern, however, was the continual collection of grins, whistles, wolf-calls, and coarse remarks I harvested in this exclusively-male territory. He cursed and tried to look as stern as possible, muttering about the lack of discipline; I attempted not to smile, pretending that I neither heard nor saw the wholly natural reaction of these men to a woman, *any* woman.

Our party spent the night at Constantine; I billeted with a small group of nurses. We left there before dawn, for Tebessa, where we picked up an escort to show us the forest-hidden Command Post and to guide us through the surrounding lake of mud. My passenger conferred with General Anderson, the "Dour Scot," then talked the reluctant General Truscott into a trip right up to the actual front.

I went off in search of Dick, stationed at Corps headquarters. Female-like, I was a little surprised that a woman's presence this far forward caused so little attention; I attributed it to my appearance, hardly slinky, what with dirty slacks, battle blouse, and an old Air Corps flying jacket. Dick soon enlightened me: the battle situation was so fluid that Rita Hayworth wouldn't have drawn a whistle.

Things were bad, really bad. Dick himself was busy and we had only snatches of conversation; I sat around morosely, soaking up the contagious apprehension, well aware this was no time for feminine chit-chat with old acquaintances. Dinner at the mess was gloomy, almost wordless. A jeep driver braved the mud to take me to the evacuation hospital several miles away, where I gained a lasting admiration for front-line nurses, reserved a bunk, and then headed back to the CP for a few more precious moments with Dick. He and the others were so worried about General Eisenhower's whereabouts in the unknown battle that I, too, became nervous.

"You'd better stay right here, Kay," Dick said. "If things get any worse, I'd rather you'd be here than over at the evac hospital. It looks as though General Eisenhower won't be back till real late, anyhow. So we'll bed you in the V-I-P's tent. It at least has a dry pebble flooring." I agreed readily, happy to be near him if anything was going to happen, then climbed into bed fully dressed, just in case.

Awakening several hours later, I heard the sound of muffled voices and boots munching around in the mud; I was sure it was the Germans, already in our camp. Just then I heard Dick's voice: "Sir, we didn't expect you back so soon. Afraid we put Kay there in your V-I-P tent. But there's another empty tent right down here, if you don't mind, Sir." Their boots gurgled in the mud and the voices faded away. I tried to sleep. But thoughts of Dick and the battle not far away canceled any drowsiness. After an hour of tossing about, I got up, stepped out into the damp daylight of early morning, and doused my face in cold water.

When General Eisenhower and Dick appeared at mess, I learned the Germans threatened our lines with a full-scale break-through, if not a rout. The General, bundled to his ears, was a very, very tired man and looked as though he hadn't slept a wink. He said the trip up front had ended in near-disaster when his jeep driver, exhausted from the strain of moving that near action with a four-star passenger in the rear, had tossed them into a ditch. General Truscott added, unsmiling, "We got your Boss back, Kay. But I never want to take him up that far again, ever!" Obviously anxious to get rid of the responsibility for us, he provided another escort to Tebessa.

One officer mentioned that four German military police had been captured there that very morning, following their open entry into Tebessa on the assumption that the city already had been taken by the Nazis and required traffic control. If the Germans were that confident, I knew the picture was even more black than it seemed back at Corps headquarters. And I drove off in a frantic state of nerves, distraught over leaving Dick there.

General Eisenhower refused plane transportation on the grounds that the Air Corps insisted upon aerial escort and he didn't want to pull any fighters away from the battle area, where they were so urgently needed for combat. We returned to Constantine for the night and, after bucking convoy traffic for eight hours on that narrow, dangerous highway, returned to Algiers.

Headquarters had all the cheer of an empty funeral parlor. News from the front, starting with the licking we took at Sidi-bou-Zid, was increasingly bitter to swallow. The Americans in particular were downcast by this first real taste of defeat. General Eisenhower was so glum and weary with these worries, plus the first home-front criticism of his combat direction, that I couldn't bring myself to complain about my own health. I didn't know just what was wrong, except that I always felt fagged, completely whipped. My ever-present hunger disappeared as soon as I pulled up to a table, suddenly nauseous.

"You don't look so hot these days, Kay," the General said one morning, peering intently through his frame reading glasses. "You're a funny-looking color. Stand over here in the light; let's take a good look at you." I moved over obediently. "You've got jaundice!" he yelled.

Ethel confirmed the Boss' sharp diagnosis. I was in the hospital a week.

Moving around again after my release, I found things had changed for the better at the front. And General Eisenhower had finally surrendered to Butch's perpetual suggestion, prompted by General Marshall's direct orders, that the Supreme Commander take better care of himself. He acquired the use of a villa-farm about fifteen miles outside of Algiers, a secluded and rather run-down place which overlooked the sea and provided access to wooded land.

It was ideal for the horseback exercise General Marshall advised; General Arthur Wilson supplied the horseflesh. There were three of them, all Arab stallions, the first stallions I had ever ridden, chestnut in color and with the peculiarly short ears and flowing mane and tail of Arab breeds. If horses can be truly beautiful, these were beautiful. (The spahi guards at General de Gaulle's palace in Algiers were mounted on pure white Arab stallions, as picturesque as characters in *Arabian Nights*.) Our horses were near-perfect for riding. They had one defect; should a careless rider permit two of the stallions to touch noses, they immediately erupted into screaming, kicking, fighting beasts.

The General and I went riding frequently. It was a treat for me because I had loved and known horses since childhood and enjoyed the jaunts with my Boss. He, for his part, learned to accept riding as a complete relaxation and, I suspect, welcomed the change from the ever-present military. Whenever we ran into troops in training, however, I kicked my horse and galloped away. Although the General was dressed in smart riding uniform, from mirror-bright old cavalry boots to an overseas hat sporting four stars, I had only an old shirt and a pair of jodhpurs sent from the States. I looked the part of an Arab girl and it ill-behooved me to stick around and embarrass the General whenever he passed troops.

Duty permitting, we went out riding three or four times a week. Butch came along one day but retreated to Algiers half an hour later, muttering that he was a seafaring man. Peg Chase, an old friend from the Red Cross, was an occasional companion, as was Tex Lee. Tex insisted upon riding as he worked, *i.e.*, with thorough efficiency. He tried to plan the route, time our arrival at a predetermined destination, and generally attempted to over-organize a pastime originally designed to get the General away from scheduled life. On the other hand, both the General and I agreed that the real fun was to ride out aimlessly, choosing a sudden bypath for no other reason than an impulse.

Meanwhile, the Boss followed General Marshall's orders explicitly; he tried tennis on the farm's court, till his knee started acting up, and he spent fewer hours at the office, although still putting in a longer day and getting more accomplished than most of his staff associates.

When combat conditions permitted free evenings in Algiers, he exiled shop talk from his villa in the same informal style as that followed at Telegraph Cottage back in London. He buried himself in a mountain of Western magazines which Mickey managed to keep growing. And he enjoyed an occasional Wild West movie; true to form, he insisted upon being the last on Special Service lists for films and gave strict orders that any G-I request was to supersede his own booking. Some evenings were devoted to ping-pong, in which Butch was an accomplished master, with a slice that made most opponents, including me, wild with frustration. The major entertainment of those off-nights was, of course, bridge, with the Boss and me usually facing such old card enemies as Butch and General Clark, who often stopped by on trips back and forth. As the weather grew warmer, bringing out hordes of flies, horseback riding was abandoned.

Right after a visit by Archbishop Spellman of New York, Butch took off for a quick trip to the United States. The office force was further depleted when the Boss sent his junior aide, Craig Campbell, away to the Ninth Division for several weeks' infantry-life holiday. Inasmuch as the division was inactive, General Eisenhower thought Campbell, fed to the teeth with headquarters routine, might enjoy the change. But war can make changes in even a Supreme Commander's plans. The Ninth was suddenly ordered into action and, before Craig could be recalled, his entire company reported missing in action. The General blamed himself for the entire incident and openly said it was his fault that Craig was missing, possibly dead. (It was months before he learned the Texan had been captured; it was two years before the Russians liberated Craig's prisoner-of-war camp in Poland and sent him back.)

When Butch returned, I drove the General and Telek out to Maison Blanche to meet his plane. Butch was carrying something like 600 pounds of baggage, mostly parcels from army wives in Washington. One held special interest for our Telek: a wife!

Caacie, named by Butch's womenfolk from the initials of an imaginary "Canine Auxiliary Air Corps," immediately let Telek know what she thought of this transocean marriage arranged Chinese-style, without either of the participants' prior knowledge. She bit him, hard.

A heavy, low-slung Scottie with dark memories of apparently brutal kennel experiences, Caacie was as nervous as a whipped kitten and met all our friendly advances by whimpers. Once in the villa, she spent most of every twenty-four hours under the furniture, approachable only by the Inner Circle, who had patience to move slowly and to virtually ooze kindness. Beside Telek's bombastic, celebrated charm, unabashed by chiefs of state or chiefs of staff, she was colorless and empty of true personality. To Telek, however, she was companion, friend, lover, and wife. And he sired three adorable little puppies—a Daddy before his first birthday!

When the atabrine treatment hit North Africa, the Germans could have walked through our lines without even a fist fight or an unkind word. From the Supreme Commander down to the greenest buck private and civilian, everyone took the first dose

under direct orders. Line troops and headquarters staffs alike were
laid so low with nausea that the dose was cut at once to half a
pill every third day. I was among the victims, but only that
once; thereafter, I took advantage of my unique civilian standing
and secretly stuck to my bottle of quinine. I never had the slightest touch of malaria.

My same unique civilian status, however, led to trouble with
the Royal Navy. It all began one night when Lieutenant Dampier,
flag lieutenant to Admiral Cunningham, telephoned. "Kay," he
said, "I understand you play a good game of ping-pong. The
Admiral would like you to come to dinner tomorrow night."

It was a strange invitation. I must be the only girl ever invited to dinner with an admiral because I play ping-pong. Naturally, I accepted. But the evening was complicated by an earlier
invitation, which I had accepted, to attend the first party in the
wardroom of the *Maidstone,* mother-ship for subs. That bid had
come from Barney Fawkes, the charming British navy captain
who permitted us girls to bathe—secretly—aboard the *Maidstone*
whenever our water supply at the villa failed. Barney also kept
our spirits up on low evenings by having us down for luxurious
navy dinners. So I couldn't run out on that invitation.

In satiating compromise, I hurried down to the ship that next
night to join the other civilian girls, WAC's, nurses, and British
WREN's in a quick drink before the Admiral's dinner at eight
o'clock.

But an air raid sabotaged that plan. Sitting there in lovely navy
comfort, with amiable companions and a cool drink, I couldn't
bring myself to brave bombs and shrapnel in order to be on time
for Admiral Cunningham's dinner. Besides, I thought, I have the
car at the dockside and can make the trip in no time at all. I
relaxed and stopped watching the clock.

The raid went on and on and my nervousness increased. Bombs
or no bombs, I explained to Barney, I had to go. Being navy, he
understood the urgency of a dinner date with a full admiral second
in rank only to the First Sea Lord. But the boat which started

taking me ashore turned around quickly as part of the dock went up in flames.

Barney arranged for me to call Lieutenant Dampier and explain. Dampy, however, managed to convey the distinct impression that I was being very un-English in letting a little thing like enemy action delay me for dinner with the Admiral. The *Maidstone* party wasn't much fun after he hung up, growling they would go ahead with dinner.

The instant that raid ended, I hurried ashore—only to find a new catastrophe. The General's car resembled a refugee from a junkyard. Its glass windows were smashed, jagged, and gaping; shrapnel had dented fenders and hood; the inside was littered with piles of debris, dust, salt water stains, even seaweed and seashells.

A passing M.P. rushed me up to Admiral Cunningham's villa. I was more than two hours late, undoubtedly the first person who had so openly insulted him, socially, in his entire navy career. Yet he listened to my tales of woe with interest and even sedate mirth. He didn't say much.

That next day I arranged to have the car repaired in a hurry, no one the wiser. But Barney Fawkes called to break sad news *re* A.B.C., as they always referred to Admiral Sir Andrew Browne Cunningham. "You couldn't have chosen a worse time to be late for his dinner party, Kay," Barney chided.

"What's happened?" I asked.

"Well, even though some of the chaps and several of the WREN's were late on watch because of the air raid, we might have got away with the party." He paused. "But I guess your late arrival at the Admiral's place was the topper. We've *had it,* Kay. Old A.B.C. has just put out an order: no more women aboard the *Maidstone!*"

For weeks, I was the butt of not-so-good-humored wisecracks from WAC's, WREN's, nurses, and the submarine boys. And I don't think I've been late to a dinner party since.

All this doesn't mean daily life in those early months of 1943 was a gay social whirl. Most of my days were taken up with driving. Sometimes it was a visiting general or V-I-P. More often it was General Eisenhower; too often, a trip to Constantine.

I came to hate that Red Ball convoy route with a deep, wild passion—the mud and the dust and the trucks and the growing heat and the constant fear of air attack. ("If we're ever attacked," I told the Boss one day, "don't wait for me to open the door for you. It's every man for himself, then!") Even the sudden appearance of masses of lovely poppies failed to counter-balance the hideous cactus; nor did sun-tan uniforms compensate for the new desert temperature. That eight-hour drive to Constantine alone was sheer, unadulterated torture. I had nightmares of smashing into some truck convoy, maimed for life and charged with the murder of my four-star passenger. Above all, I had nightmares, daytime nightmares, of Dick in action.

That feeling was comforted by another example of General Eisenhower's natural kindness; on a trip to the front, in territory which General Montgomery banned to all females, even women correspondents, Ike arranged for Dick to meet his plane—and then invited me along. Dick and I had a wonderful half-hour alone in the big Flying Fort, humbly appreciative for the thirty minutes of just being together and talking together. It made the separation easier for a while.

A trip to Oran with Tex and several others of the staff, to bring back a shipment of new Buicks, eased the tension, too. That highway offered more interesting country and a welcome contrast to the forward Red Ball route. And a quick flight to Gibraltar resulted in lunch at the old convent which had become Government House, with Governor Sir F. N. Mason-Macfarlane a genial host; everything was in the old-time grand manner, with doors swinging open as one approached, service up to prewar par.

Then, amidst all the routine, things began to pick up. The Germans were forced off bloody Hill 609. Mateur was captured. On a trip forward I saw batches of Italian prisoners of war, happy and even jubilant that their war was over. I noticed, for the first time, growing groups of Afrika Korps prisoners. They were still filled with spirit and sang Nazi songs lustily—in fact, to a woman, they were attractive males, perfect physical specimens, bronzed, blonde, and very handsome if one could ignore their arrogance and warped minds. Their mere presence in increasing numbers gave warm promise of early victory. After one week of May passed, the Americans took Bizerte and the British captured Tunis, whereupon we all felt the African war was over. Four days later, Von Arnim was captured and it was only a question of days, if not hours. Yet the Nazis ordered senseless air raids, heavy ones, on Algiers shortly afterward.

Within a few more days I followed Tex off in a caravan to the advance Command Post at Sidi Athman. The weather was so hellish hot that we had to keep the car windows up, despite the oven-like heat, in order to keep the fiery winds outside. Telek barked madly at the Arabs, but soon fell back onto the seat, his tongue hanging almost to the floor; he whimpered continually. The water in the canteen lacked only bubbles to be boiling to the taste. Dirt and sand caked my throat, eyes, and hair.

It was an awful trip, but the last wartime convoy for me in the North African campaign.

On May 20 we motored over to nearby Tunis for the magnificent victory parade staged over General Eisenhower's objection, at French insistence. By a stroke of fate, I stood on the platform with Monty, the man who didn't like women anywhere in his vast battle area, let alone in his immediate vicinity. We all baked in the merciless heat, sizzling to the point of collapse, hour after hour after hour. The pageantry was as spectacular as any I was to witness throughout the war. I was especially impressed by the fact that Yank M.P.'s were razzed by the G-I's, and, more soberly, impressed by many of the weird-looking French colonial troops, who sent shivers up and down my melting spine.

Despite the white-hot heat, I was happy. The campaign was over. We had won. And Dick was safe—I thought.

CHAPTER VI

For me, that strange late Spring was filled with the scent of orange blossoms. I couldn't smell the ordinary jasmine, the poppy fields; I could neither see nor hear the war being readied against Mussolini. I expected to be married before June melted into the African summer.

Dick, now a full colonel, was in Oran with II Corps headquarters. General Eisenhower not only promised each of us at least several days' leave after our marriage, already approved by the Army after its usual ninety-day waiting period; he also offered, as a sort of refuge from the war, the use of his little farm outside Algiers. We would have a full-fledged honeymoon in North Africa.

Dick arrived in Algiers the last week of May, en route to General Truscott's Third Division headquarters at Mateur. "I've got a command, at last," he told me. "Got what I always wanted, a regiment and actual field duty." With his West Point background and his impatience at headquarters routine, he was as thrilled with the new assignment as a newly commissioned second lieutenant.

We had one day together.

It was a wonderful day, thanks to General Eisenhower. He gave me time off, plus a special present: "I'll make it a point to go out somewhere this evening. You and Dick can take over the villa and be alone for once; with this wedding coming up, you must have a lot to talk about. Sergeant Hunt'll fix you dinner. And tell Dick he's to be my guest for the night." He grinned. "Have a good time!"

We did exactly that. Swimming in the afternoon, dinner for two at the Supreme Commander's villa, and an evening of excited plans for our marriage—all in blessed privacy, rarest luxury in any army.

The next day, Dick left for Mateur and his new regiment.

I breezed through the next week or so. With the North African campaign over, Dick was safe, even at regiment level in a division. And with our wedding so near, I couldn't even worry about what his duty would mean in combat; war, a world of the present, doesn't encourage thoughts of the future. I knew only that I was in love, soon to be married, and very, very happy.

Meanwhile, Caacie had her pups; Telek was a racing, barking, boisterous father. Headquarters life picked up as the Navy and the Air Force blasted away at the little island of Pantelleria. And I heard back-seat whispers about plans for invading Sicily. But none of it belonged to my orange-blossom world.

This light mood continued until one lovely June afternoon when I drove General Eisenhower up to his villa. My airy chatter, I realized with a start, was going unanswered. He was quiet, unusually quiet for a man who, even during momentous operations, has the knack of storing away his worries and making small talk. So his strange muteness this particular afternoon drove me into similar silence. By the time we pulled in the narrow driveway, that silence was oppressive.

General Ike climbed out slowly, preoccupied. I left the motor running, ready to leave. But he called over his shoulder, "Won't you please come in, Kay? I'd like to talk to you."

I followed him into the villa, on into the library, where he sat and motioned me to a chair. "Cigarette?" he offered me one. I shook my head and lighted one of my own.

He stared at the floor. "Kay," he said finally, "I don't know how to tell you this . . . guess I better give it to you straight." He looked up and said, "Dick has been killed."

In one of war's tragic ironies, Dick was struck down *after* the actual campaign fighting was over, several weeks after the spectacular victory parade at Tunis. He had been with his new regiment less than a week.

Investigation showed that he and a friend of his, a captain, both engineers and intimately familiar with mines, had been walking across an area well-marked with the usual white mine tapes. Suddenly, the captain stumbled on a trip-wire. He was seriously wounded by the explosion. Dick was killed instantly.

General Truscott sent a personal message of condolence immediately, explaining the circumstances and offering his sincere sympathy. His note was dispatched right after the accident on June 5 but, by one of those horrifying examples of Army paper work, it was lost at AFHQ message center for almost five full days. Then a colonel mentioned the fact to Butch and Tex, assuming they already knew. Butch rushed into General Eisenhower's office; the General shouldered the sad task of telling me, even though weighted down with a million responsibilities connected with the imminent invasion of Pantelleria that very night. (I realized something of his personal pain at bearing such news when Dick's kid brother Bob arrived in Oran and then ended up in an Algiers hospital for a complicated appendix operation. I had to tell him about Dick.)

General Ike was kindness personified.

He offered to request release of my services as a civilian with the American Army, if I found the surroundings and the memories too strong to bear. "Why don't you take a couple of days off?" he suggested. "We can spare you. There's no one at the farm—go on out there for a while. You can ride and get away from everyone; I know that's what I'd want." He paused. "I guess there's not much I can say, Kay . . ."

The farm was a welcome haven. I wanted only to be alone; that was the place for it. I sat around at first in a stupor, then rode wildly through the wood, half-hoping for a merciful fall and oblivion. Pantelleria surrendered the next morning, but I couldn't have cared less.

There in the country, however, alone and able to think things out, I realized thousands upon thousands carried loads of grief as great or greater than mine in this war. And I knew I would have to stick, too. It was a natural decision: to stay with the Americans, and the war.

Possibly to divert my thoughts, General Eisenhower confided a super-secret. Our next V-I-P was to be none other than His Majesty, the King of England.

"I'd like you to drive me to meet him," the General added kindly, "if you feel like it."

CHAPTER VII

THE KING'S visit was so hush-hush that we drove to Maison Blanche airport just as usual, with only the motorbike escort to clear our way. No special guards were provided. At the field, we moved down to a distant corner and joined the British High Brass, including Admiral Cunningham and Air Chief Marshal Tedder. Butch whispered he would open the door for His Majesty.

The huge converted Lancaster came in almost immediately, taxiing down to our end of the field. Smiling and a trifle awe-inspiring to even the most sophisticated of his welcomers, the King stepped down to a volley of British, French, and American salutes. The British seemed to have trigger-arms; every time he turned his head, they responded with salutes which vibrated as vigorously as palm fronds in a gale.

On the trip through Algiers Butch and I pretended to be ear-less machines. But we couldn't help eavesdropping on the King of England. He was buoyant and friendly with General Ike, the first to admit his downright excitement at getting out of embat-tled England for the first time since war started. He and the General talked about the Tunisian campaign and the scheduled invasion of Sicily. The King displayed a unique familiarity with even the most technical points, obviously up to date on all de-velopments. Butch, I noted, sat back stiffly and drove himself into a tizzy trying to decide whether he should return the salutes of British troops who recognized their King in our car. After twitch-ing hesitantly several times, he gave in and returned the salutes steadily. The General later confessed to being just as troubled as

The General in his Buick in Tunisia.

Command Post, Portsmouth: D-Day minus one. Seated: Capt. Mattie Pinette, R. H. Winston Churchill, myself. Standing: Cdr. Charles Ralfe Thompson, Cdr. Harry C. Butcher, Lt. Col. James Galt, Adm. Sir Andrew Browne Cunningham, Lt. Gen. Eisenhower, Brig. Gen. Leslie C. Hollis.

Butch. I was probably the least worried of the three of us, long hardened to the responsibility for V-I-P's in the back seat and to concentrating upon the job of driving. At the same time, and as a Britisher, I found a certain little thrill in driving the King of England through Algiers, observing the respectful "high-balls" he garnered from surprised Tommies. And I looked forward to speaking with him a few minutes, just as I had with all visiting front-pagers.

But after we arrived at the British villa and pulled up before a parade-ground guard of honor with fixed bayonets, my anticipation collapsed.

Butch let His Majesty out, beaming happily as General Eisenhower presented his Naval Aide. I gasped as Ike then motioned to me and made an informal presentation. It was a moment of confusion: as a civilian, I couldn't salute; in uniform, I couldn't curtsy, as one does in formal court presentations. So I shook hands boldly, murmuring—quite incorrectly, I'm sure—"How do you do, Sir!"

There was no reply. "Your Majesty," General Ike prodded helpfully, "this is Miss Kay Summersby, who's one of your British subjects and now on duty at our headquarters as my personal driver."

The King smiled briefly in dismissal, then moved on into the house, leaving behind a very frustrated British subject.

That same afternoon, General Eisenhower shocked his staff by unveiling to press correspondents AFHQ's secret plans for the Sicilian invasion. He took the step to choke off speculation on the next Allied move. His gamble and his faith were justified; not one newsman broke the pledge of secrecy.

Before leaving on his Mediterranean tour, the King gave our Boss that most coveted decoration, the Grand Cross of the Most Honourable Order of the Bath; General Ike was as close as a foreigner could come to an outright title. His pride in this honor was such that he never appeared in public without the thick maroon ribbon among his growing collection. He was similarly impressed when General Giraud presented him with the Grand Cordon of the Legion of Honor, France's highest military award, and, in this case, the same medal General Giraud himself had received for combat action.

After a three-day inspection of Fifth Army troops engaged in realistic battle training, General Eisenhower found himself again embroiled in the seething politics of North Africa. Washington, apparently, insisted that he take on the near-impossible task of explaining to General Giraud and General de Gaulle just how the British and American governments insisted the two leaders get together, stabilize the murky political situation, and get on with the actual war.

Above all, I learned from office gossip, he was to insist that General Giraud retain command of the French military. The end result of these instructions was a conference one Saturday morning with the two generals. And the end result of *that* was inevitable: General de Gaulle left the villa conference within an hour after the three-way meeting started. (This touchy situation eased up a bit with Giraud's confirmation as chief of the French forces in North Africa, De Gaulle being head of the French Committee of National Liberation, as well as Governor of Algeria.

General Ike never discussed these affairs in public. In private, though, it seemed to all of us he was pretty fed up with the political end of his job. During this period in June he escaped such by-products of command by inspecting more troops, from those in landing exercises to those in formal review, from those at Division CP's to those at overworked airdromes.

About this same time, the King returned to Algiers from visits to Tripoli, Tunisia, and Malta, no longer the bright, enthusiastic visitor we had met a fortnight before. His entourage explained His Majesty was a victim of the most disrespectful enemy in North Africa, that scourge of the Mediterranean which Yanks derided as "the G-I's." The King was so morose when I drove him and the General out to Maison Blanche that the latter abandoned all attempts at conversation. And *I* was definitely hurt that the King, leaving for London, didn't utter a word or offer to shake hands in farewell to a homesick Briton surrounded by Americans.

The Advance Command Post at Sidi Athman had been unsatisfactory in every respect. In the beginning, we all lived in tents when stopping there; daily life was a depressing round of mosquitoes, dust, mud, heat, great swigs of paregoric, and weary drives to Tunis. The narrow highway, clogged with speeding convoy drivers who refused to give right-of-way to our siren, our flags, our motorbike escort, and our star-studded tags, seemed again a regular obstacle course. Butch and Tex convinced the General of what I knew all along, namely, that the forty-five minute drive over the highway to Tunis was tiring, trying, and dangerous.

Consequently, Tex toured the countryside and found the ideal spot for a new advance CP: Amilcar. It was a welcome change, with Tunis only fifteen minutes away via a road mercifully clear of convoys.

General Eisenhower's "White House" was just that, an attractive white structure with a beckoning terrace, a view of Cape Bon across the bright Bay of Tunis, and steps right down to the water. Furnished extravagantly by an Italian moved to a bleak cell block, it was large and comfortable in everything but sleeping space. The General's bedroom was the only one worthy of the name; the other three or four were so tiny they must have been servants' quarters.

From Amilcar we traveled to nearby La Marsa virtually every other evening, to visit either Tooey Spaatz in his plush villa or Air Chief Marshal Tedder in his caravan. The first few visits with Tooey set hot fires under Air Force discipline. Until Ike blistered the Spaatz headquarters, the "fly-boys" greeted his impressive car and even the General himself with a bored nonchalance which would have been incongruous in civilians, let alone the military. Strict orders, however, soon brought hands out of pockets and goaded them into salutes; sometimes, even a semblance of attention.

Three or four times weekly we visited Bizerte, some fifty minutes away, where the British operated their headquarters in rather primitive fashion amidst all the debris. That trip required a ferry ride across the harbor—a grim mass of half-capsized vessels, masts, and other flotsam of war. I hated that trip through the narrow, mine-bordered channel. But it was part of the job.

"My personal mail's getting so heavy it's almost a full-time job in itself," the General complained one day. Then, as though struck by an afterthought, he added, "How would you like to take it over, Kay?" I jumped at the opportunity. Nevertheless, this was no haphazard offer; General Ike thoughtfully believed the work might brush away some of my gloom and fill up the empty hours between motor trips.

General Eisenhower probably is the one great military leader in history who felt humble enough, even during crucial campaigns, to answer all personal mail. These letters began to trickle into AFHQ soon after the North African landings, numbered thirty to fifty a week by the time he reached Tunis, and attained the proportions of a paper tidal wave by the time he was on the Continent. He first attempted to answer only those from G-I relatives; then, after I took over, insisted that each and every letter receive a reply. "They have something important to say," he once remarked, "or they wouldn't take the trouble to write. So it's my job to answer them."

The mail was a constant delight. One letter might be from an Arkansas mother worried about her son wearing his long underwear. One might ask, in careful finishing-school script, that a certain young man be transferred from the wicked city of Algiers. Another might suggest a Rube Goldberg invention to win the war at one Superman stroke. Still another, stained with tears and written laboriously, would simply and movingly offer God's blessing. Quite a few noted the slowness of promotions. The range of problems and subjects was greater than that faced by any priest at confession, for it seemed half the Western world regarded General Eisenhower as father, son, boss, friend, and a sort of male Dorothy Dix. Their letters poured in from each of the United States, from Canada and the United Kingdom, written in everything from a sharecropper's scrawl to an executive's stiff but touching dictation.

Peculiarly, no writer ever blamed the General personally for a particular grievance, whether it be the Darlan fiasco or the Kasserine Pass tragedy, a wounded husband or a sadistic C.O. The far-flung correspondents seemed to sense his staggering load of problems and usually wrote apologetically, "I'm sure you'd take care of this, if you knew about it." Very few wrote him with awe; they were respectful but informal, in the style of correspondence with a favored uncle or a city councilman.

Requests for autographs were an increasing problem. Ike decided to comply, *if* the writer were engaged in some sort of war work, no matter how small. Those who mentioned such activity—blood donations, bandage work, Red Cross service, USO aid, paper or fat collection—received a signed letter in reply. In this way, even the General's autograph was put to work for the war effort. I got the most fun out of the letters from the youngsters, who reported tremendous feats of home-front war work and wrote all about it, often in unconsciously humorous fashion, to win that autograph of General Eisenhower, which they prized more than any box-top gift.

Naturally, the mail included scores of parcels of every shape and description. They contained cigarettes, hand-knitted scarves and gloves and socks, sun glasses, Western magazines, books, food, piles of home-made fudge. Although meant as personal presents, they were far too many for the General's use. We saw that they went to the spots where they were most needed, the hospitals and the rest centers and the front-line troops.

Handling this flood of mail drew me into the small office, where I soon became part of the real official family. Before, I had been among the outside, after-hours intimates; now I was in the "paper world," the official inner circle. And I acquired three new friends, Sue Sarafin, Margaret Chick, and Nana Rae, WAC's with whom I was to be associated for the remainder of the long, mobile war.

Meanwhile, all routine office work took second place to one priority objective: the gigantic build-up for "Husky," the invasion of Sicily. Patton's Seventh Army and Montgomery's Eighth trained in the field until their men were almost stale with fatigue. Headquarters became increasingly tense.

Five days before the actual operation, official observers began to arrive. Among them, I met one of the war's most glamorous men, Lord Louis Mountbatten. Sitting beside him at dinner that night, I found the Combined Ops chief as engaging, interesting, and handsome as the gushing press described him. Very few men live up to the "dashing" tag, but Lord Louis Mountbatten is dashing—a tall, noble, intriguing man with a romantic background which began back in the days when he was a distinguished London playboy. He got along splendidly with the General, to whom he referred as Ike; the latter immediately called him Dickie. Lord Louis, an obvious admirer of the General, often got so excited during conversation that he almost moved into his listener's lap; as one of his own staff put it, "Dickie could talk the leg off a race tout." All in all, I found him very handsome—especially in Navy whites—and refreshingly charming.

Before that week was out, our war flamed up in full fire again. On July 9, General Eisenhower flew to Malta to supervise the assault upon Sicily which began early the following morning. The Germans had sworn to make a bitter battlefield out of every inch of the island and we all watched the news apprehensively.

Sicily may have been a side-issue campaign back home but on the scene it was a huge, vital operation; none of the Big Brass bothered to hide his worry. After all, the staff planners had ordered about one thousand naval craft of every description and at least 150,000 men to take part in the invasion—more than assaulted North Africa itself. We all breathed easier when the landing went off all right. But the Americans at headquarters cursed that General Patton, who had the tough job in "Torch" operation, also ran into the stiffest opposition in this show.

Sicily, in fact, brought out more Anglo-American differences than anything since Kasserine Pass, when the British had made barbed remarks about cocky Yanks who couldn't win a simple tank battle, while the Americans themselves, hurt and shocked by their first real defeat, blamed it all on their irate Ally. Sicily was more of an American campaign and now there was widespread resentment at the way the press played up the accomplishments of the well-publicized Montgomery, although Patton was bashing through much stiffer opposition than Monty and later ran circles around him. This conflict reached a crisis when the Prime Minister announced several victories even before AFHQ knew about them. The heaviest blow at international and interservice unity came with rumors around Algiers that the Royal Navy had shot down twenty-three American planes loaded with paratroopers.

I mention all this only as an indication of what General Eisenhower was up against, constantly, in directing the first truly Allied command in all history. He handled these and other backbreaking problems with direct diplomacy. In this case, correspondents were given an exact picture of the fighting, which showed the true relation between the celebrated Eighth Army, which was, in fact, bogged down, and Patton's Seventh Army, which covered ground with a wild boldness later to be hailed in Europe. And press dispatches began to give a more rounded view of Sicilian combat, an *Allied* view.

As for the story that R. N. guns had shot down U. S. paratroop planes—anti-British feeling became so intense in some areas that Ike had to release the true facts: these troop carriers came over Sicily just at the end of an enemy air raid and, mistaken for unfriendly planes, were shot down by both the British *and* the American Navies. He also took immediate steps to make certain that no such horrible error could ever take place again.

The Churchill incident was straightened out at top levels and—
this is an important clue to the General's welding of nationalities
into a cohesive staff—the British at AFHQ were the first to decry
the undue emphasis on their own troops, the first to batter London with loud protests. The men at AFHQ were like that, so
filled with Allied *esprit* they often apologized for their own government's action.

Perhaps I don't explain this phenomenon clearly. It might
be better to say, simply, that men at AFHQ were a sort of "One
World" group. Their "One World" was the war. And they bat-
tled militantly for that single cause, even against occasional opposition from their own respective governments. Historians probably will agree that this was General Eisenhower's greatest achievement in World War II—this ability to submerge national pride
into an international determination to win the war.

The most encouraging evidence of success came when Europe's senior dictator, Benito Mussolini, quit.

Only homesick, weary troops felt the end was near. Everyone
at headquarters warned the Germans intended to save their holy
Reich by battling for every kilometer of Italian soil; the Nazis
backed up that threat by sending a solid stream of divisions down
from the North.

Still, collapse of the Fascist government in Rome brought new
problems. And our next V-I-P was there to discuss the Italian
situation; he was the aging American Secretary of War, seventy-
five-year-old Henry L. Stimson.

On the lighter side, I found it amusing that General Eisenhower, soon after this important conference with the Secretary
of War, went to the dispensary for a physical examination—a
checkup for his promotion to the rank of colonel. He seemed to
find it no more than whimsical that the Army was just getting
around to making him, an officer already accustomed to his fourth
star, a colonel in the *Regular* Army. Within a month, however,
the Army cast caution out the Pentagon windows and made

Dwight D. Eisenhower a major general, a permanent major general.

Meanwhile, the spotlight turned to another general: Georgie Patton.

It was the middle of August and Dick's old 3rd Division was in Messina. The Sicilian show was over. The curtain was going up on the Italian campaign. But, in the field and in all headquarters, talk centered upon Patton. The factual details remained foggy; correspondents still hadn't broken the story. Yet everyone in the Mediterranean knew General Patton had slapped a soldier at 93rd Evacuation Hospital.

Even his staunchest admirers declined to justify the incident. Enemies pointed out that slapping a soldier is a court-martial offense for any officer, let alone a general, let alone a general as famous as Patton. His friends agreed, but argued that "Blood and Guts" undoubtedly was the most valuable fighting general in America's European armies; would it serve the war effort to junk him, just to satisfy regulations and one soldier's pride? Hundreds of soldiers' lives—not just their pride and military rights—were frequently sacrificed for the bigger goal, winning of the war. Shouldn't this same principle apply here? Patton's enemies counter-attacked this argument by charging his retention would cause an angry storm of protest so overwhelming it might destroy public faith in the Army. Besides, they added, there weren't enough high-ranking officers in the area to try a lieutenant general; a trip home and the resultant stench of court-martial, Patton's friends contended, might very well result in an international scandal damaging to the Allies and their war.

After Drew Pearson cracked the story, these problems boiled over into the American press; in our own sector they were fought from headquarters to squad level. General Eisenhower, probably Patton's best friend and yet saddled with the responsibility for correction, wrote to his Seventh Army commander the most severe reprimand he ever had to compose in Europe. He also ordered a direct apology to all the men involved, as well as to the assembled officers of their regiment. (Funny enough, none of the letters General Eisenhower received at this time blamed him for the incident; every writer, without exception, including those who waxed hysterical in indignation, expressed a belief the Supreme Commander would handle the matter appropriately.)

Not long afterward, I got a chance to ask General Patton about the whole thing. He was at Amilcar for lunch and a discussion of forthcoming operations. By the time I arrived, he and Ike apparently had concluded any talk on the subject and the lusty Seventh Army chief was well into his great warehouse of risqué stories. As usual, he exiled me for the moment by remarking, "How about mixing me a highball, Kay?"

At lunch, he suddenly turned to me and asked, "Why don't you get Ike to bring you over to Sicily on one of his trips?"

I murmured that General Eisenhower was a whirlwind of business whenever he visited Sicily; also, a woman would be very out of place with a general inspecting troops.

"Nonsense," Patton replied. "You should know American soldiers well enough by now to know you'd be damned good for morale!" He turned to the General. "Ike, it's only a hop, skip and a jump over there—how about it?"

The next day Ruth Briggs and I piled into a C-47 and traveled to Sicily for a command luncheon with General Patton. He provided a nice touch by having his chief of staff, Hobart (Hap) Gay, at the airfield to meet our plane; after almost a year of greeting V-I-P's, I enjoyed being welcomed by a general.

The drive to headquarters revealed heavy damage to Palermo; the harbor was as bad as that at Bizerte, jammed with half-sunken ships, their masts spiking through the water. As for the Sicilians along the way—we agreed they were dirtier, if possible, than the Arabs. They also treated their animals with an Arab-like brutality. The overall filth, which seemed natural among the downtrodden Arabs of North Africa, was an unpleasant surprise in Sicily. Neither Ruth nor I had any desire to go sightseeing.

We found General Patton enthroned in a palace once occupied by the King of Sicily. The building was huge, ornate, and rambling; although only a few rooms were in use, they gave a grand, palatial air to the G-I equipment strewn around.

Ruth and I turned down the famous Patton 75, a suicidal highball of champagne, brandy, and possibly other disastrous mixtures. Lunch consisted of G-I food and shop talk. And most of that shop talk centered around the distantly burning ears of Bernard Law Montgomery. General Patton blamed Monty for the worst military sin in the Patton book of land warfare: caution. And he used every word in a docker's vocabulary—apologizing to us women with humorous regularity—to condemn that caution.

Afterward, he called us up to his room and remarked with a smile, "Here's something you can probably use." Each of us grabbed, most unladylike, at a thin box obviously "liberated" somewhere in Sicily. Tearing at the wrappers, we found a treasure more priceless than steak, diamonds, or perfume: silk stockings.

Before sending us back to Tunisia, the General acted as our guide to an old, old, medieval church—and, religious soul that he was beneath that flamboyant exterior, prayed humbly for his troops and his family.

As we parted, I simply had to ask him about the slapping incident. General Patton sadly remarked, "I always get in trouble with my gawdamned mouth!" At the same time, he shouted at the top of his squeaky voice, "But if this sort of thing ever comes up, I'll do it again!"

Back from lunch in Sicily, we learned that Beetle Smith and the AFHQ Intelligence chief, Brigadier Strong, were on a mission as secretive and dramatic as that of General Clark's submarine visit to North Africa before the invasion. The pair flew to Gibraltar, changed into civvies, and then boarded a plane for nearby Lisbon—to discuss peace feelers put out by a General Castellano, Badoglio's chief staff planner and himself an incognito visitor to Lisbon. The tireless and conscientious Beetle handled all negotiations.

Soon, with September only eight days old, there was a joint announcement of Badoglio's surrender.

"Well, Kay," General Ike said to me two days later as we drove to Admiral Cunningham's for lunch, "this is our first big surrender The Italian government's out of the war. One down and two to go—Germany and Japan!"

After lunch, he and Admiral Cunningham were going out into the Mediterranean to witness the Italian fleet's surrender procession. I couldn't go aboard the destroyer, being a woman. "Besides," the Admiral explained, "I've already refused some of the WREN officers." Later, I broke that tradition about women aboard destroyers at sea; this time, however, I saw the General and the Admiral off, then drove over to the shore near Bizerte to join General Alexander and the other "Red Tab" brass in watching the spectacle through binoculars. It was a real spectacle, too: two battleships, five cruisers, and five destroyers, all trailing meekly behind our escort vessels.

The next two months were a hodge-podge of the present, the future, and an incessant parade of V-I-P's.

The present, despite the Italian surrender, was dreary. Our campaign in Italy, off to a bang-up start and smokescreened by a false optimism which discounted German determination to keep the fighting in Italy, bogged down. Salerno was only a black prelude to bigger tragedy in the offing at Anzio.

The future moved into our present in the form of the first talk about an operation to be known as "Overlord," the long-awaited invasion of France. After a visit to the Italian beachhead, General Eisenhower was little cheered by the report that he might be sent back to the United States to become chief of staff; General Marshall, it was said, was to head the new A.E.F. now slated to hit Hitler's Europe by the following Spring. General Ike never talked about these rumors as far as I know, but the rest of us did. We felt it would be a slap at General Eisenhower's official face, after his molding of an Allied team at

AFHQ and his successes in the Mediterranean. Moreover, he wasn't cut out for the diplomacy required in the chief of staff's job in Washington; he revolted against politics, heatedly. Selfishly, all of us hated the thought of leaving the cosmopolitan, veteran, one-purpose atmosphere of AFHQ; we wanted General Ike to run an AFHQ for the French invasion—and we wanted to be in on it.

Most of this speculation about the future and the gloom over the combat picture, however, was washed away by a deluge of V-I-P's.

The Big Brass flood started with a visit on October 1 by the American Secretary of the Navy, Frank Knox. He was followed the next day by Mr. Donald Nelson, head of America's war production, and Mr. James Landis, the Harvard Law School dean who was handling American civilian defense. The *next* day, it was Lord Louis Mountbatten again, en route to India. Then came the Ambassador to Moscow, W. Averell Harriman; his arrival gave me a chance to renew acquaintance with his daughter Kathy, whom I had known in London. The day after their appearance in North Africa, we met Treasury Secretary Henry Morgenthau in the morning, had him and Ambassador Harriman to lunch, met Secretary of State Cordell Hull in the afternoon, had him to dinner that evening, and saw him and the Harrimans off for Moscow that night. It was a typical day in that V-I-P period, and, I must admit, a trifle heady.

About the same time the war in Italy ground to a near-halt, we had to say farewell to our old friend, Admiral Sir Andrew Cunningham. Although steeped in Royal Navy tradition and outranking the Supreme Commander himself, old A.B.C. had been General Eisenhower's staunchest naval supporter and a close personal friend. As he left to become Britain's First Sea Lord, we welcomed his successor, who bore the same surname; Sir John came to dinner just a fortnight after Sir Andrew left, a night when another guest was General Brehon Somervell, the American supply chief, then on his way to India for conferences with Mountbatten and General Stillwell.

If these were pleasant visitors, the nomadic politicians were real burdens. They made a point of collaring every G-I in sight, bellowing, "Where you from, Son? I'll be sure to tell your Ma I saw you when I get back to the United States of America!" Some of this was friendly and natural. But all too often it was brazenly political, nauseating not only the accompanying Brass but the soldiers themselves. They all knew a vote-grabber when they saw one.

Butch tried to talk General Eisenhower into having one group of Congressmen up for dinner; Ike blew his top, refused to have a formal dinner party, and reluctantly agreed to a luncheon. "I'm fighting a war," he yelled, "and a damned tough war. I'm not a politician, I'm a general!" That same day, he went to the dispensary for a routine checkup; the doctors postponed his physical exam because the politicians had sent his blood pressure skyrocketing.

The third contingent of V-I-P's consisted of show people, most of them big-hearted troupers anxious to give soldiers a little relaxation and quite good-natured over the difficulties in both transportation and staging. For example, there was Bea Lillie, who charmed the General with several impromptu after-dinner sketches at the villa. General Ike liked to have the headliners up for an evening, to show his appreciation of their efforts. Other welcome guests included Vivian Leigh, so lovely and petite one felt in the presence of an exquisite, fragile, Dresden China doll; Fredric March, who, unlike some of the male film and stage stars, was reserved, respectful, and well-acquainted with the war; Noel Coward, who executed a few fancy dance steps at AFHQ one day to show us he could do something more than write witty, sophisticated drama; Bob Hope, greatly admired by the General for his natural wit and his never-ending tours of battlefields all over the world; and a host of other fine persons.

Some of the USO people were quite different, ignoring the G-I's they were sent to entertain and concentrating upon the High Brass. Their chief concern was publicity. Their tag line usually ran, "It was little enough for me to do, to give them a few moments of smiles before they went off into battle."

The phonies and the politicians soon hurried back to America, though. And November of 1943 brought us the biggest V-I-P of them all.

CHAPTER VIII

ENERAL EISENHOWER told me about it as we drove down
from the villa, where I picked him up every morning, to
the hotel headquarters of AFHQ in Algiers. "It's a top-
level secret," he confided, "but I can tell you because you're in on
it." He smiled. "In a week or so you're going to be driving the
President of the United States."

Chauffeuring isn't exactly a glamorous job. But I knew from
past experience that the presence of a female in the front seat of a
car, in all the heavy maleness of war, leads V-I-P's to soften their
stiffness and become human for a few minutes. So I looked forward to meeting President Roosevelt and, possibly, to actually talking with him. As a person and as a dignitary, he interested me more
than anyone else to date, including the Prime Minister and the
King of England. And by the time General Ike flew to Oran to
meet the battleship *Iowa* and its Number One passenger, I had
caught at least a little of the official family's excitement.

General Eisenhower was bringing the President to the comparative isolation of our Advance CP in Tunisia, rather than into the
still somewhat explosive atmosphere of Algiers; I joined other
lesser lights in the advance trip to Amilcar. The journey was as
rough as a bad Channel crossing; Telek, although morose and
whimpering, was the only passenger aboard that B-17 without fits
of nausea. And the taut state of nerves at the airport was hardly
an antidote for any of us. American Secret Service men, sloppily
dressed and as tough-looking as characters in a gangster film,
dashed about on mysterious errands to set up airtight security for
the High Brass, who would include not only the Commander-in-

Chief and the Allied Supreme Commander, but also General Marshall, Admiral Ernest J. King, Mr. Harry Hopkins, Admiral William P. Leahy, "Pa" Watson, and a flock of other officials.

On the afternoon of November 20, our welcoming party assembled at the El Aouina airstrip. There was the usual waiting period; then, when we heard the nearing sound of engines, every neck stretched upward as five C-54's circled the field.

One cut in for a straight, swift landing. We all strained for a first glimpse of President Roosevelt, but it turned out to be General Marshall. Apparently the Secret Service was taking no chances on enemy fighters knocking off the Number One plane and their Number One boss. Tex, with new lieutenant-colonel leaves on his shoulders, bundled the general into a waiting car. The other four planes landed one right after another; two began unloading passengers and a third seemed to be an empty "spare." The Number Two plane taxied to our end of the field, and stopped. Several men rolled up a ramp. I drove my Cadillac over beside the plane and waited.

"*Hey, there!*" A burning Irish face appeared at my car window, distorted with anger. I recognized Mike Reilly, the Secret Service chief who had been very much in evidence at Amilcar. "You're not expecting to drive the President, are you, Lady?" he yelled.

"I certainly am. I'm General Eisenhower's driver and he instructed me to drive him and the President to the villa."

"But you can't!"

"And why not?"

He was on the verge of apoplexy. "No woman ever drives the President!" he shouted, thumping on the door. "No woman ever has—or ever will, as long as I'm Boss here. Certainly no Limey woman!"

Just as I started to elaborate on my own Irish background, with some very Irish temper, he ran toward the plane. I looked over and saw General Eisenhower standing on the ground. In the doorway was Franklin Delano Roosevelt.

His personality positively crackled, without as much as a word.
That famous smile magnetized every eye. Even General Eisenhower, usually prominent in the foreground, seemed to fade away
with the others into a gray backdrop which permitted the spotlight to shine on only one person. To every person standing there,
President Roosevelt was the only man on the airstrip.

But the show was lost upon me, as I spotted Tex leaving General Marshall's car and heading in my direction, followed by a sergeant. "It's all right, Kay," he whispered, reaching my car. "We'll
straighten out this mess afterward. I hate to ask you, but will you
show this man how to handle your Cadillac?"

Seething with insubordination and loss of face, I jerked the
new-type gears and gave the embarrassed sergeant instructions
how to run *my* car. Then I hurried away and climbed into another
limousine, positive that everyone there, including the President of
the United States, was laughing at the entire mixup.

But the comedy had just begun. A Secret Service man came
over as they put the President into my Cadillac and asked me to
come back to drive the big car. As I climbed into the front seat,
Mike Reilly's florid face reappeared. "It's all off again, Lady," he
whispered. "You can't drive—the sergeant will take over from
here!"

Going back to the other car, my heels threatened to shatter the
runway.

Butch walked up and stuck his head in the window. "Don't
worry about it, Kay. We'll fix everything when we get to the villa
. . . it's just one of those things." He motioned to his companions,
Admiral King, and Mr. Hopkins, whom I had met previously in
Algiers. "How's about going in this car?" he yelled to them.

Speeding blindly, I gave those three a ride they'll never forget,
back to Algiers, through the city, and up the hill.

The guard around General Eisenhower's White House, now
a temporary but very literal White House, looked as though the
American Army expected the Germans' return to Tunisia any moment. My passengers got out and disappeared inside. Mike Reilly

rushed over and said patronizingly, "It's okay for you to get back in your own car now. They've gone in the house."

I looked straight ahead and replied coldly, "I'll stay right here until I get further orders from my Boss. And no big gimp of an Irishman's going to move me!" He stared for a moment, lips set, then walked away.

"Miss Summersby?" It was an officer from the official party. "The President has asked to meet you," he smiled, beckoning me to follow.

Glancing in the rear-view mirror to check a shiny nose, I trailed along into the villa. The noisy group of men in the front room were little more than a blur; I was worried about leaving my hat on.

I walked into the library. General Eisenhower, who nodded encouragingly, stood by the fireplace. President Roosevelt sat by the window, half-hidden by his two sons, Elliot and Franklin, acquaintances from my African days. Admiral Leahy stopped talking as the General moved over and said, "Mr. President, this is Miss Kay Summersby, the British girl you asked about."

Shaking hands, I immediately lost any trace of nervousness. Mr. Roosevelt's grip was friendly, his smile warm.

"I've heard quite a bit about you," he said. "Why didn't you drive me from the plane? I'd been looking forward to it."

From some deep storehouse of the past, I produced a maidenly but maddening blush. "Mr. President, your Secret Service wouldn't let me drive!"

They all laughed.

Mr. Roosevelt looked up. "Would you like to drive me from now on?"

"It would be a privilege, Sir."

"Very well. You shall drive me then. I'm going on an inspection trip soon."

He turned to the lovely view out the window, which framed the Bay of Tunis and the Bônn peninsula beyond, and began talking of how he wished there were time to spend weeks in Tunisia, away from official worries, just resting.

I recognized a kind dismissal and took my leave. The front room was, by now, jammed with people packed around a temporary bar and buzzing with as much noise as a crowd at a London cocktail party. It seemed incongruous, with the President near by. I couldn't help but compare the scene with the hushed dignity which always accompanies the King's official party. And I was a little startled to see a number of Secret Service men, some without ties and with sleeves rolled up, lounging around the temporary White House.

Mike Reilly was bouncing around the driveway. I called *him* over this time: "I've just been presented to the President."

"Heard you were," he grunted.

"And no matter what you say," I added spitefully, "the President himself has asked me to drive him."

With good Irish humor, Mike surrendered. We agreed to bury the hatchet, as we'd be working together.

Shortly afterward, the President reappeared. They lifted him into the car with a quick efficiency which made the gesture seem wholly natural. His difficulty was ignored by common consent . . . it simply didn't exist.

"I'd like to go over and inspect Elliott's outfit," he told me. "It's quite near, I understand."

We drove to La Marsa, a short ten minutes away, where he transferred to a jeep and rode along the lines of surprised and proud soldiers of Elliott's photo reconnaissance unit. We were back at Amilcar before sundown.

As the President went inside, for a rest in General Eisenhower's bedroom, I started to leave for mess. Franklin came dashing out, however. "Just a minute, Kay," he grinned. "General Eisenhower says he's ready to leave—and, incidentally, you're invited to dinner here tonight."

Outranked from his own quarters and far from a mood for office work, the General asked me to drive him over to another nearby villa for a visit with Harry Hopkins. The latter and Butch immediately proposed a few rubbers of bridge, a welcome suggestion **to** ease the day's tension. When serving as dummy, I spent the time staring at Harry Hopkins, wondering just how he remained alive; clothes hung on his tall, frail frame as though it were a mere clothes hanger. General Ike and I won.

We were a trifle late for dinner, but the occasion couldn't have been more informal. The absence of General Marshall, Admiral King, even Butch, emphasized this was a dinner, not a dinner party. President Roosevelt and his sons joked and talked as easily and naturally as fathers and sons anywhere in the world. Ruth Briggs, an Admiral's daughter, and I comprised the female guests. "Pa" Watson, the presidential aide, was a delightful companion, fatherly and gently chiding about my initial clash with Mike Reilly.

Sitting only one place away from Mr. Roosevelt, who naturally headed the table, I was exposed to the fabled F.D.R. charm. But I had to admit it was just that, pure charm; he had it on full, with all stops out. He soon had me feeling quite at ease and talking about Blitz experiences, in which he seemed intensely interested. And that was followed by a volley of keen questions about the role of British women in the war, queries about factory workers, service girls, air raid wardens, and bus "clippies."

I asked a bold, direct question: "Mr. President, will there ever be conscription of women in the United States?"

His answer was equally direct. "No," he said thoughtfully, "I'm afraid not. The country would never stand for it."

After discussing plans for a battlefield tour upon which the President insisted as part of his visit before proceeding to Cairo, the party broke up. It was only 10:30 but the honor guest obviously was fatigued by the long day, which had begun aboard a battleship in Oran, continued through a plane flight to Tunisia, included a troop inspection and a shop talk with General Ike, and concluded with a lengthy dinner. He needed rest. Bidding the others goodnight, he turned to me and spoke in a tone I hadn't heard since childhood: "See you tomorrow, Child."

Elliott and Franklin stepped up as I moved away to drive General Eisenhower back to the Hopkins villa. "Come on back, Kay," Franklin whispered. Elliott nodded, "We're having a little party tonight and it might take your mind off things."

By the time I returned to the White House, leaving the General to a session with the indefatigable Hopkins, that party was in full swing. The President must be a very sound sleeper as well as a very tolerant father, I thought, stepping into a room as noisy, smoky, and hot as any nightclub. A stray colonel from headquarters already was folded carefully into a chair. "I'm surprised at you Secret Service men," I said, cornering Mike Reilly. "Here you are on duty and half of your men are tiddly. How can you do your job and still put away all this liquor?"

He smirked, "We're tough, Kay. Have to be." Then he launched a sober and serious discussion of the route to be taken on the battlefield tour. I succeeded in turning him against the idea of riding the ferry across to Bizerte. "I feel nervous enough when I'm driving the General onto that little ferry," I explained. "The car has to be backed on. And the channel is narrow. I, for one, shouldn't feel safe with the President riding that ferry—if anything happened to dump us into the harbor, he'd be a goner!" Mike agreed, aghast at the very thought.

Remembering the drive ahead, I left early, about midnight. The party was just shifting into high gear.

When General Eisenhower and I drove up to the White House next morning, a Sunday, we both stiffened in astonishment. The convoy for our quickie tour of the battlefields was practically an armored column. There were at least twenty vehicles, including two truckloads of M.P.'s armed to the teeth, armored cars, half-tracks, jeeps, weapons carriers—and a grim-faced Mike up front in a radio car, with an expression which revealed a life-long ambition to head an army into battle. He had been up all night planning his campaign and going over the route, we learned, without as much as a wink of sleep after the late-houred party.

With President Roosevelt in the Cadillac, smiling at the Reilly brigade, we started off. Telek barked happily in the front seat. I looked forward to the idea of a picnic, which the President had suggested.

The lead radio car led our bristling convoy slowly over the Tunisian countryside. I relaxed and listened to the talk in the back seat. It revolved around the late battles, the terrain, difficulties encountered, and some of the command personalities.

The President remarked that no one remembers the chief of staff after a war; fame comes only to combat leaders. "I am determined," he said, "that General Marshall shall not be forgotten after this war." I took it as a new indication the Chief of Staff would head the invasion of France, instead of General Eisenhower.

Telek decided to make one of his flying leaps. The General gasped and caught him in mid-air, just before the bundle of Scottie landed on the President's legs. "I'm sorry, Mr. President," the General apologized. Telek cried and struggled, eyeing the strange passenger.

"Come on, Boy!" Mr. Roosevelt laughed. Telek jumped and nuzzled all over the world's most famous owner of the world's most famous Scottie. The President played with him as one who knows and loves dogs. To Telek, he was just another nice man; a nice man who smelled faintly of Scotties.

Mr. Roosevelt talked of Falla and asked whether Telek were British or American. General Eisenhower told him the story of Telek's English birth and his American wife. Looking up in the rear-view mirror, he added, "Trouble is, he's more devoted to Kay than to me. She looks after him so much. Still, I guess I think as much of him, Mr. President, as you do of Falla!"

The President continued to play with Telek. Suddenly, he pointed to a rare grove of trees and remarked, "That's an awfully nice place. Could you pull up there, Child, for our little picnic?"

Nothing could have pleased me more. Mike, I knew, had already selected a special spot farther along the road; it was perfect for "defense." He would be furious at this change of plans. So I turned off the highway quickly, followed obediently and unquestioningly by all the vehicles behind us. Those in front continued merrily on their way.

By the time we pulled into the wood, Mike had discovered the loss of half of his convoy and came racing up in wild temper. He couldn't say much to his Boss, however, and, instead, busied himself setting up an impenetrable cordon of guards. They were posted in a wide circle, their backs to us, only a few feet apart, weapons at the alert. In this military, bellicose atmosphere, my passengers started their picnic.

"Child," the President said as I got out of the car to join the other drivers, "won't you come back here and have lunch with a dull old man?"

Startled but pleased, I climbed in back and sat down beside him. General Eisenhower remained outside to hand us in delicious chicken sandwiches prepared by Sergeant Hunt. Coffee was the only other item on the sparse menu, as the General was afraid to offer lettuce or other green vegetables to the President in this disease-ridden climate.

As back at the villa, I soon lost any thoughts of shyness and felt as though I had known this vibrant man all my life, as though he were a distant uncle I hadn't seen since babyhood. Mr. Roosevelt had that enviable touch of natural intimacy. Evidently the General had told him about Dick, for he remarked on the tragedy of war and offered condolences. Then he asked all about my family, about England, about life along the Mediterranean.

"Why don't you join the WAC's?" he asked as I told him details of their marvelous work in North Africa.

"There's nothing I'd like better!" I replied. "But it's impossible until I can become an American citizen."

The picnic ended, we took the President on a fast tour of areas where great battles had been fought. Then we headed home. He left for Cairo shortly before 11 P.M.

Lying awake in bed that night, I gradually realized what an unusual week end it had been, for an ordinary Army driver, a British girl at that, to be presented to the President and to participate in his ial life. In fact, the past day alone had been a page straight from "Lanny Budd" fiction—sitting in the back seat of a limousine parked on Tunisian battlegrounds, surrounded by armed guards and the Secret Service, served sandwiches by a four-star general named Eisenhower, enjoying a picnic lunch beside the President of the United States!

That afternoon, however, the conversation between an army driver and the President of a great nation had been so natural that I failed to realize the extraordinary nature of the occasion. It seemed only another unusual incident in an unusual service with General Eisenhower, one of a steady procession of unique events so unreal and so blurred together in the rush of war that there was little time for me to contemplate the fairytale nature of my life with the Americans.

And, as usual, the excitement of the latest experience soon was lost in a fever of anticipation over the next—in this case, a trip to Cairo and the Middle East.

CHAPTER IX

IG BRASS gathered for the Cairo Conference were concerned
B mostly with world-wide strategy. But they also wanted to
hear testimony on the war raging right there in the Mediterranean . . . so General Marshall dispatched a special C-54 to
bring the star witness.

Instead of flying over in lonely pomp, General Eisenhower
made a characteristic gesture. He invited about a dozen of his
lower-rank staff members to go along. "There's no use wasting all
the space in this big plane," he explained. "Besides, it may be the
only chance you'll ever get to visit the Middle East."

Everyone except the naval aide took him up on the offer. Butch
said he'd seen all the celebrities and could use the time to better
advantage by going to Italy to set up our new Advance CP. I accepted quickly, before the General could change his mind; so did
Ruth Briggs, and Louise Anderson, one of the five original WAC
officers and now secretary to the AFHQ Deputy Chief of Staff,
General "Jock" Whiteley. Even Tex abandoned his office worries.

We left late at night. The trip proved to be smooth and, after a
few rubbers of the usual Eisenhower bridge, the plane turned into
a snoring dormitory.

Awakening to daylight and humming chatter, I looked out the
window to see one of the world's most memorable sights: sunrise
over the pyramids. The massive monuments looked ridiculously
small from the air, but a scholarly member of the party reminded
us that the pyramids, which stretch some sixty miles along the
Nile, date back into dim antiquity. Some were built, he added

with sobering emphasis, two or three thousand years before Christ.

The rest of his lecture was lost in the excitement of landing at Cairo's Payne Field—and the shock of stepping into staggering, merciless heat. Our winter-weight skirts and jackets immediately felt like suffocating blankets, contrasting sharply with the smart sun-tan uniforms of the welcoming party. Heat rose from the airfield in shimmering, celluloid-like waves. Clouds of dust and sand churned through the air.

Riding into the city, we forgot the heat and the dirt, oggling like tourists the world over. Cairo was an oasis of prewar memories, filled with smart, well-fed people and *civilian* motor cars. "Look!" I cried, almost jumping out the window, "Bananas!" They were my number one postwar dream, the first I'd seen since war began. Ruth and Louise quickly drew my attention to other sights. "We can get all kinds of fruit this afternoon," Ruth chided in maternal tones.

Everything we saw through the car windows added up to one overall impression: peacetime luxury. After the shabby, empty shops of London and the chic but ghostlike stores of Algiers—and the rubbled debris throughout North Africa, all the way up to Bizerte—Cairo was a fabulous city of peace. Our fingers itched to browse through her well-stocked shelves.

The ride ended before a large villa reserved for General Eisenhower. "Big, isn't it?" he said sheepishly as we looked around. Then he seemed to realize we were "excess baggage" for the official entourage, with no assigned quarters. "Where are you girls going to stay?" he asked.

"Don't worry about us, Sir," Louise said. "We're used to taking care of ourselves. We'll find a place."

The General insisted we remain in his villa. "Butch isn't here and I'll be lonely in this little palace," he emphasized. "And I'll be away at meetings most of the time, so you can have the house pretty much to yourselves."

It was irregular, but well-appreciated. We had found a home in Cairo. An officer in charge of the General's arrangements moved three beds into a room on the ground floor section which had the added attraction of a private bath.

We had assumed that our visit to Cairo, sudden and unofficial as it was, would include hours of work at the conference. But it developed we *were* pure excess baggage; for the first time in months we had absolute leisure. The first stop, of course, was Shepheard's cocktail lounge, for the traditional coffee. Like many another visitor to the Middle East, we learned Turkish coffee requires an acquired taste. This was thick and syrupy, so much so that it held a spoon aloft. We used several tinkling highballs to wash away the taste. Then, although without much money, we went shopping.

Cairo was both deafening and wilting. The bazaar people shrieked in half a dozen languages, adding to the din set up by a constant thunder of motor horns pounded by Egyptian motorists with a zeal even greater than that of Parisian drivers. The heat was stupefying; it sucked at our energy, soaked our wool uniforms, pulled curls from our hair. But it was foreign, and fun.

All Egyptians, in contrast to Algiers' stringy Arabs, looked as though they had been living on the proverbial fat of the land, despite the war-parched landscape so near by. The fat, dully-clad women seemed to worship bright baubles even more than their sisters on Fifth Avenue, Bond Street, and the Rue de la Paix; their pudgy bodies sparkled with giant gilt earrings, necklaces, bracelets, and rings. Some carried earthen jugs on their heads, picture-book style, giving even the stoutest an enviable, graceful, proud carriage. Many of the men in this quarter wore Western costume, the tight European business suit, with an incongruous fez. We accepted the hordes of begging children as part of the Mediterranean scenery.

Most of our shopping consisted of window-shopping, if it could be called that in this madhouse of open-air shops. But we couldn't sympathize with prices—as much as sixteen dollars, for example, for a pair of silk stockings. Our only purchases consisted of fruit, piles and piles of fruit, mostly bananas.

General Eisenhower, at a Presidential dinner that night, was surprised by the presentation of the Legion of Merit.

The next day featured more sightseeing and more shopping-without-buying, plus an off-the-record visit to Mena House, headquarters for the conference and vantage point for viewing the pyramids, the Sphinx, camels, and all the other items familiar from Egyptian postcards. We also attended a mass "tea fight" which managed to draw just about every Big Name from the conference; we went as females hungry for cocktail chatter, however insipid, as an antidote to the strictly military social life of the past year. One of the milling crowd I thought worth notice was Madame Chiang Kai-shek, of whom I caught fleeting glimpses; tiny, attractive, and well-poised, she was an outstanding personality. "Looks as though she'd never miss a trick!" someone whispered.

All these incidents were mere preliminaries to the real thrill of our visit, which came when General Marshall, alarmed at the haggard, harried look of his Mediterranean commander, directed General Eisenhower to take a few days' rest before returning to the Italian campaign. The Chief of Staff, in fact, *ordered* General Ike to take three days for a complete holiday. Always the good soldier and well aware of his poor mental and physical health, Ike agreed —but where could he go for absolute change, privacy and rest?

Air Chief Marshal Tedder, long an Eisenhower intimate, came up with the perfect answer: Luxor. One of his personal friends was Major Emery, the noted archaeologist. Would the General be interested in a specially conducted tour of Luxor and the burial grounds of the Pharaohs? He could retreat several thousand years from the nervous Present. As further bait, Tedder offered the use of his own plane.

. General Ike, a lifelong student of history, leaped at the opportunity. And, ever unselfish, he invited along several of his party. Elliott Roosevelt, Tex, Ruth, Louise, and I accepted; I, for one, was frankly thrilled at this chance to see Luxor, Karnak, and a part of the past which had intrigued me since school days.

Tedder's C-47 was equipped with a huge picture-**window**

but few of us enjoyed the view, even though his pilot flew low to provide a close-up kaleidoscope of the countryside. We spent every ounce of energy fighting off nausea from the heat, which bounced off the desert and soaked into our oven-like cabin with all the devastating intensity of the fires of Hell itself. Bumpy air close to the ground added to our torrid discomfort.

Landing at Luxor in late afternoon, we found even the clouds of mosquitoes a welcome diversion from the roasting furnace which had been that plane. Nightfall brought a dry sort of coolness, together with misty moonlight; it was impossible to stay in the Luxor Hotel, with one of the world's greatest outdoor museums just outside. Like other conference visitors (almost every high official at the Cairo meeting availed himself of at least a one-day trip to Luxor), we strolled around through the tottering mementos of Egyptian history.

Modern Luxor and Karnak are built on the dust of ancient Thebes, which was already a fabled city as much as four thousand years ago. We saw everything which defied the dust—the broad, sprawling temples, the twenty-foot statues of Rameses II, the clumps of pillars and columns, some of them so thick it takes six persons to reach around their base, the remains of quays, the once-sacred lakes, the courts, the obelisks, and the several avenues lined by dozens of crouching sphinxes. It was apparent even to me, who make no pretense at scholarly knowledge, that Thebes was a city fully as lovely as any in old Greece or Rome. When we returned to Luxor Hotel, unusually thoughtful and quiet, our learned guide promised real sight-seeing during the day ahead.

He kept his word.

Next morning we crossed the legendary Nile—a disappointingly muddy, dirty little river—and crowded into several ridiculous motor cars which apparently dated back to the invention of the first horseless carriage. Then we steamed, quite literally, out onto the road. The heat, even for December, was so intense the antique vehicles often boiled over; we waited patiently each time, then

got out to push, invariably assisted by mobs of urchins. The road
at times was little more than a footpath, twisting up, down and
around the bleak hills; at other times, a broad surface barely recognizable on the vast plains. Finally, we turned into a rough path
leading straight into the hills. After a while the so-called roadway
turned sharply. Before us were two desolate ravines.

This, our archaeologist announced dramatically, was the Valley
of the Kings.

We spent the entire day there in the greatest cemetery in the
world, the fabulous graves of bizarre Pharaohs who ruled Egypt a
millennium or two before ever Christ appeared on earth. Dressed
in our modern uniforms and accompanied by the Supreme Commander of a great war in the Mediterranean, we felt the atmosphere of history more than ever. It seemed impossible to realize
that kings had been buried here over a period of ten centuries, that
a surprisingly luxurious civilization had flourished in Egypt thousands of years before we even started counting the years of Christian time. Although looted thousands of years ago and stripped of
their treasures, the tombs still commanded dignity and respect.
None of us, not even the usually bombastic Tex or the irrepressi-
ble Elliott, ever wisecracked in those hallowed vaults. We walked
and walked until our feet ached with pain, until our clothes
steamed with heat, above ground, yet I could have remained for
weeks; very few sights actually thrill one with a physical emotion,
but these did.

The tombs, wrought from stone with superb masonship and
decorated with queer pictures representing everything from devils
and demons to farmers and queens, would have been awe-inspiring
to us even as normal, gawking tourists. But, with the wise and
friendly major as our host, it was like walking right into those
musty times. For one thing, the hieroglyphics, fascinating in
their dumbness, were voices to him; it was exciting to hear him explain the background of a particular Pharaoh and his times. One,
for example, probably ruled five thousand years before Christ, a

literal god to whom all the lesser Brass of the world bowed four-
teen times in the dust at his feet—feet shod, incidentally, in exquisite golden sandals.

The archaeologist explained the human side of old Egypt, too.
Slaves may have carried out the heavy labor on the big pyramids,
he said, but they were workers with certain inalienable rights.
There is evidence that they often resorted to a supposedly recent
union device: strikes. Also, the masons worked with bronze saws
taller than a man, saws which had jeweled cutting edges; both
these and the jewel-pointed drills cut with a smoothness unequaled by the finest modern tools. The Major told us of one obe-
lisk higher than Cleopatra's Needle; it was quarried out of pure
granite, in one piece, without seam or joining. He mentioned a
blue paint, a special secret of those days, which, along with many
other colors on the tombs' walls, remains just as bright and fresh as
a contemporary painting.

We had lunch in a tiny inn perched on a dreary hillside, surrounded by sheep, goats, curious *fellahin*, and that ponderous
sense of history. Then we went back into the stone pages of that
history, strolling through long galleries, chambers, and hallways
which stretched without end through the barren valley.

I was particularly interested in the tomb of King Tutankhamen,
first of the Pharaohs' burial crypts to be found untouched, with a
wealth of priceless treasure so vast that it still is being sorted and
catalogued and studied. But I was surprised to learn that his actual
coffin is small, that he apparently was a boy-king, that he reigned
in a backwater phase of Egyptian history, for a brief time only, and
that he was a very minor Pharaoh. It also was a trifle startling to
find his tomb lighted by electricity.

If the Major was pleased at our rapt attention to his intriguing
explanations, he was astonished at the historical knowledge of one
of our party: Dwight D. Eisenhower. The two of them frequently
wandered off alone in pursuit of some dim fact; other times, we
looked around to find them far back in a distant chamber, discussing a point of ancient life as compared to one of today. General Ike

Supreme Commander Dwight D. Eisenhower and Deputy Supreme Commander Sir Arthur Tedder announce the unconditional surrender.

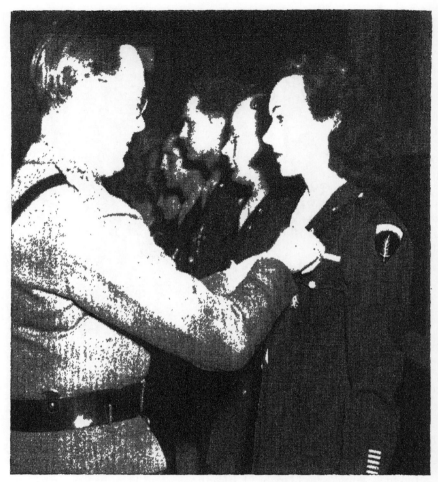

Prince Bernhard of The Netherlands awards the Cross of Orange-Nassau.

was as happy as a kid, making no attempt to hide his natural enjoyment, protesting frequently that we moved along too quickly.

Our guide, however, who knew every blessed inch of the ground, was determined we should see it all. So it was a tired, footsore, dirty party which returned to Luxor that night. But a happy crew. I, for instance, knew the day had given me a treasure chest of memories, I loved every minute of those hours. Everyone felt the same. The General was a different person, tired but mentally refreshed by the sights.

When we got back to Cairo next morning, General Marshall knew at once that his idea of a holiday for the Supreme Commander had been a corker. In fact, General Ike looked so rested and energetic that his Boss insisted upon another tour, if only a quick one.

"What are you girls going to do today?" Ike asked us in the villa after his session at the conference with General Marshall.

"We're going shopping," I said. "And maybe go slumming, see the real Cairo."

He smiled. "Well, you can go shopping if you want to. Or you can come with me . . . to Palestine!"

The choice was obvious as well as welcome. We were in the Holy Land within about two hours after taking off from Cairo. But the car ride from the Palestine airport into Jerusalem took ninety minutes, almost as long as the Cairo-Jerusalem flight itself.

This bad omen keynoted the entire visit. Bethlehem and Jerusalem were a complete let-down after the tingling atmosphere of Luxor. At the monastery in Jerusalem, American monks came trooping out as noisily as school boys; one of the brown-robed men, because he was from Kansas, hung onto the General's arm as though they were fraternity brothers at a class reunion. Every beggar in Jerusalem joined in the crowd which followed at our heels, demanding tribute. I was shocked to find most of Christianity's holiest shrines no longer Christian, but disgustingly commercialized tourist monuments exploited by the Moslems. This was true even at the Church of the Holy Sepulcher, where they hawked post cards and other items with all the blatant fervor of football game salesmen. We asked after the Mount of Calvary, thinking it would be several miles away and impossible to include in our hurried tour. But the guide dragged us to a spot close by, pointed to a circular hole, and said one could touch the rocks of the Mount by reaching down. It seemed as crassly sensationalized as our own Blarney Stone in Ireland. In Bethlehem, the Holy Manger turned out to be a marble, overly ornate monument wholly out of tune with the facts and one's dreams. Throughout all our tour, the General was plied with so many crosses, beads, post cards, and other objects that, despite his deep religious conviction, he whispered, "Guess I've got a free ticket to Heaven!"

There was one charming modern Christian church in Bethlehem, which was beautifully maintained. I was especially enchanted by the mosaic above its tall doors; the colors were alive, almost blinding in their beauty. Also, the Garden of Gethsemane proved to be as lovely and conducive to meditation as I expected; entrance was forbidden, but the General's stars secured us special permission for a stroll in its peaceful paths.

All in all, though, I couldn't help comparing the difference between Palestine and the Valley of the Kings. And in all conscience, even as a good Christian and an Irish Catholic, I couldn't convince myself that Christianity's "home" had even a touch of the dignity, art, impressive air, and downright excitement of the burial grounds of old Egypt's pagan Pharaoh gods.

Lunch at the ill-fated King David Hotel failed to lift my spirits. And the topper came when I borrowed enough money to pay twenty dollars for a full-length sheepskin coat ... which had such a vile odor that I've never worn it since. It's a good, appropriate souvenir of that trip.

CHAPTER X

ETURNING from Cairo to Algiers, I began digging away at
the minor mountain of paper accumulated on my desk.
Memories of Egypt and Palestine faded completely as I
worked late each night to reduce those piles of the General's "fan
mail."

Like everyone else at headquarters, however, I was still busier
on unofficial duties . . . working overtime on the old rumor that
General Marshall, not General Ike, would head the new American
Expeditionary Force building in Britain, and that Ike would go to
Washington to become Chief of Staff.

All of us were agreed that the Boss, now a veteran in the command of Allied armies in the field, should have the Overlord assignment instead of General Marshall, who was better qualified
for the role of handling global strategy, Washington politics, and
top direction of the American Army. Ike would be a misfit in the
Pentagon, a stranger to world-wide war, to chief-of-staff paper
work, and to Capital intrigue. Marshall would be lost in an active
AFHQ, baffled by the new job of combat command, by Allied ec-
centricities, and by taking orders from his old office. This reasoning seemed clear and logical. Yet the rumor gained new strength,
as unpleasant rumors will, which disturbed all of us who didn't
want to remain in the Mediterranean under a new boss. We
wanted to go back to England for the Big Show, under General
Ike.

The General himself was at first secretly hopeful of winning
the Overlord spot. He even said so, in hush-hush tones, to me one
day. Another time, in the car, I mentioned boldly, as only a woman

could have done, "Somehow, I've got a feeling you'll be Supreme Commander for the Continent, no matter what the rumors say!" He grinned, noncommittal. But as time went on he began to feel less hopeful. He hated the thought of going back to Washington as Chief-of-Staff, glued to paper work during the greatest battle in history. He emphasized he would rather, much rather, remain in the Mediterranean with a secondary command.

Finally, I heard him say he was resigned to being ordered back to take General Marshall's place; he went so far as to plan a "back door" route to Washington, via the Pacific Theater. The shock of this story threw our entire staff into gloomy moods. It looked as though we would lose General Ike, stay with a minor headquarters, and miss out on the big invasion of Europe.

But on December 7, the anniversary of Pearl Harbor, the message came through: General Eisenhower would be top boss of Overlord, the all-out assault upon Nazi Europe.

This happy news, contained in a vague message from General Marshall, arrived just as we were preparing for the return visit of President Roosevelt. So the normal excitement over General Eisenhower's appointment was lost in the bustle of readying Amilcar and the White House. The President planed in that same afternoon, more fit and energetic than the rest of his party from Cairo. In the evening he enjoyed a strictly G-I dinner supplied by son Elliott's mess gang. (I thought it a little strange, after Mike Reilly's super-security measures, that Italian prisoners-of-war were permitted to serve the meal.)

Next day, Ike accompanied President Roosevelt on a testimonial visit to Malta, accompanied by Harry Hopkins, Generals Smith, Spaatz, and Watson, Admiral Leahy and several other U.S. naval Brass. The group then flew to Sicily for a hurried inspection which featured the presentation of the Legion of Merit to Beetle and the Distinguished Service Cross to General Clark.

Meanwhile, back in Amilcar we received word the Prime Minister was due any moment. Concurrently, we heard that the President's big C-54 had mechanical trouble; instead of starting home, he was returning to the White House for another night with us. All this left the home guard at Amilcar in a complete flap: the General's big bedroom couldn't bed down the President of the United States *and* the Prime Minister of the British Empire, if both turned up at the same time. In addition, part of the heavy security detail had been withdrawn.

Happily, the P.M. failed to show. And I was up before dawn the next morning to drive General Ike and the President to the airfield for a dewy 6:30 A.M. takeoff. Mr. Roosevelt was just as friendly and natural as before. I stood aside, out of the official party, when they rolled out his special ramp. But "Pa" Watson walked over. "The President wants to say goodbye to you," he said, adding in a whisper that Mr. Roosevelt had mentioned giving me some sort of a gift.

(Later, General Eisenhower revealed that the President wanted to make it the Legion of Merit. My status as a British civilian apparently made such a gesture impossible. So when the General visited the States in January of 1944 and talked with the President, the latter gave him a photograph, one of my prized possessions, enscribed "To Kay Summersby, with warm personal regards . . . Franklin D. Roosevelt.")

Mr. Roosevelt complimented my driving, thanked me for "taking care" of him, and then smiled, "I hope you come to the United States, Child. If you do, please be sure to come and see me!"

We shook hands and he disappeared into the plane, which took off immediately for Dakar. It was the last time I ever saw him.

Two days later we were back at the same airstrip, greeting Winston Churchill. He was two hours late, having first landed at the wrong field. We forgot our planned gibes at his tardiness, as soon as he stepped from the plane. There was an abnormal slump to his round shoulders, his face seemed to sag, and even his eyes lacked the usual sparkle; the P.M. was nervous, tired, and not at all well. We didn't know it then, but he was headed for a real bout of illness within the week. And he helped to hasten the breakdown by insisting upon a vigorous schedule: conferences with General Eisenhower, as well as long sessions with Generals Arnold, Spaatz, and Alexander, Air Marshal Tedder, and Sir Alan Brooke, Chief of the Imperial General Staff.

Meantime, all eyes at headquarters were on Italy. The gossip had turned to one's chances of accompanying General Eisenhower to London, but all of us still were concerned with the bitter war going on in the Mediterranean. The General ordered a new Advance CP, in keeping with his oft-repeated belief that such moves, at frequent intervals, could keep sprawling AFHQ on the march; he disliked the idea of headquarters people "digging in" at any one location, particularly in a large, comfortable city, in a manner to create natural resentment among the foot-slogging combat troops. It was an unselfish idea and carried much military logic. But the more social officers always complained at being forced to uproot their comfortable after-hours lives. And the Signal Corps cursed at the steady extension of communication facilities, always considerable for the use of the Commanding General and his retinue. This time, there was more grumbling than usual. Ike was establishing his new CP in Italy itself. Some of the plushier officers didn't like the idea of Italian mud.

There were no beefs from me when we flew to Italy on December 18. I was anxious to see that country for the first time and to keep up with the war; I saw less and less attraction in the social life becoming increasingly important to many of the staff in Algiers. The weather was bad that day and the flight was long. No one complained about the weather; but Sue Sarafin groused about the long trip, observing pointedly that a four-star general's Flying Fortress should be equipped with a powder room.

Staff officers' worries about pup-tent life dissipated as soon as they saw the new Advance CP. Our headquarters was literally palatial, the Caserta Palace north of Naples. Once luxurious enough for the kings of Italy, it now offered a sufficient number of rooms and corridors for several military headquarters.

General Eisenhower protested vehemently when he saw his office: a sumptuous room big enough for a railway station or an airplane hangar, carefully conceived and decorated to impress and shrink the ego of any but the brassiest of visitors. It was adjoined by a mirrored, dwarfing, intimidating reception chamber. In short, nothing could have been further from the Eisenhower idea of a small, modest working office accessible to any member of his staff. He was especially irate over the giant potted palms, which added an extra, Tsarist touch of power.

We girls were assigned a suite so large that, as someone put it, rain clouds often formed in the distant ceilings. The kitchen was as spacious as General Eisenhower's entire office at Amilcar. The overall impression, in fact, was so eerie we moved our beds into one protecting room, for mutual comfort.

Butch, the inveterate trail-blazer, also had located Prince Umberto's hunting lodge on a nearby mountainside. I remember it particularly because it was the site of General Ike's memorable Battle With The Rat, which occurred in the bathroom the second night after our arrival. Despite our kibitzing—I roared unmercifully from the shelter of the doorway, while the others whispered good military advice—he had a perfect target; the quarry was cornered atop the toilet seat. But, let it be recorded for history that the Supreme Commander was a rotten shot. After three or four near-hits by General Dwight D. Eisenhower, head of the straightest-shooting army in the world, things were so bad that someone else had to come in and club the poor animal to death.

Talking with some of the records people, I learned Dick's young brother Bob was located in a Chemical Warfare outfit somewhere to the north of us. I mentioned this fact casually to the General during a conversation. Immediately, he suggested Bob be brought back to our place for a one-day rest cure. "The poor guy probably needs it," he added.

General Ike's kind thought turned into an order and Bob turned up shortly, muddy, baggy-eyed, nervous, hollow-cheeked, and weary. But a bath, shave, new uniform from the PX, and dinner in the rank-laden mess did wonders for his morale. He and I talked for hours, enjoying the reunion, talking about Dick and the war and the future. Still, I was startled when he showed no reluctance at getting ready to leave.

"Why don't you and Tex drive Bob back?" the General asked. We agreed, picturing a short drive to perhaps Corps headquarters. The front itself wasn't so very far away; we assumed the trip to a transportation point could be only a brief ride. In fact, it started out as nonchalantly as a picnic party, with Tex hustling Bob and me into the back seat and booming, "You kids take it easy and I'll drive. You've got plenty to talk about!"

At first, the highway was like a hundred others I'd seen throughout North Africa, narrow and dirty, filled with convoys interspersed with staff cars and other types of vehicles. The G-I's whistled and hooted at the sight of a female in the back seat of a sedan meant for High Brass. We all laughed at the sight of our first sign pointing to Rome, joking that we might pass through the enemy lines without knowing it and find ourselves in the Italian capital itself, thumbing our noses at German and Italian M.P.'s.

A short while later, my sense of humor began to droop. I noticed, with a driver's eye, that we hadn't passed a single staff car in miles; ours was the only sedan on the road. Instead of weaving in and out through convoys, we sometimes drove for long stretches without seeing another vehicle.

Then, passing a short convoy of mud-caked jeeps, I noted with something approaching alarm that none of the G-I's yelled wolf-calls, that none of them whistled; they stared, simply stared. I got the distinct impression that the presence of both myself and the long staff car constituted a freak sight. Tex, too, felt the difference in these surroundings. "Just how much farther is this outfit of yours?" he asked.

"Straight ahead," Bob said, returning to a long story about someone in his unit.

Tex and I looked at each other in silent agreement. Each of us had just noticed, at almost the same moment, that the only other cars on this road were jeeps—jeeps with the windshield folded down, combat style. Tex drove a little faster.

The idea of being captured by the Germans had never occurred to me before. Now it presented all sorts of horrible, nightmarish possibilities; there was no doubt we were well into the combat zone, our Packard as conspicuous as a Navy uniform in that region. The same thoughts, I imagine, were going through the mind of Tex, safer as a male and an officer, perhaps, but still an actual aide to the Allies' Supreme Commander. We two would make juicy prisoners.

Neither of us, however, wanted to appear in the least jittery; as headquarters staff, we had to maintain "face" before Bob, who acted as though this were a peacetime Sunday drive.

Personally, I was partially reassured by the little pistol in my handbag, loaded and ready for action. (I carried a gun throughout the war, in my purse or under my pillow. It seemed a basic insurance. My first was lost aboard the *Strathallen;* General Ike replaced it with one Tex picked up. The General insisted that I learn to shoot, which I did; he also insisted that I learn to load the weapon, which I got around by inserting a shell in the chamber and keeping it on permanent "safety.")

Both Tex and I were at the last fringe of self-control when Bob suddenly jerked up and pounded Tex on the shoulder.

"This is the place!" he shouted. "That's my unit right up there on the mountain—and the Germans are just above us."

He said it with all the gaiety of a guide pointing out an historical marker.

I looked at Tex, more thoroughly frightened than I had been aboard the torpedoed *Strathallen* or in the Blitz. We both had the same thought: our sleek Packard, obviously for High Brass, was an inviting sitting-duck target for an idle enemy gunner, sniper, or marauding plane.

As Bob waved for the last time, shouldered his pack and strode up into the war, we jumped in the car and took off with as much speed as a B-17.

I didn't breathe easily until we were back in Caserta.

That evening, we relaxed at dinner with General Clark in his

Fifth Army CP in the grounds of Caserta Palace. And it was a welcome, noncombatant role. Moreover, I had a chance to renew acquaintance with some of Dick's old Fifth Army friends. Neither Tex nor I mentioned our first taste of life at the front.

Early on the twenty-first, I drove General Eisenhower and Beetle across Italy to Bari, headquarters of General Montgomery. My passengers spent the entire time discussing who should get the nod for command of British troops in the French invasion, perhaps head all ground forces. Beetle, with characteristic clarity and lack of sentiment, outlined the relative merits of the two chief contenders, Generals Alexander and Montgomery. Time and time again they came back to the same conclusion: Alexander probably wouldn't be available. Taking that and other military factors into consideration, they settled on Montgomery.

At one of our own CP's, set in the edge of an orchard, a driver from the Montgomery headquarters took over and I got out to await the General's return, once again exiled by Monty's order forbidding women in his area. Sitting in the CP, cold and miserable, listening to the incessant rain outside, I thought spitefully of all the things I didn't like about B. L. Montgomery.

The one buzzing bee in my bonnet was all the publicity on how General Montgomery, a disciplined nonsmoker, often wound up troop visits or inspections by passing out free cigarettes with a gracious manner. It was one of Monty's trademarks. Yet I couldn't help remembering Monty *always* asked General Eisenhower for cigarettes he distributed without the slightest acknowledgment of their source. The whole business irritated me so much that I reminded General Ike, upon several occasions, that Monty was building up this personal romantic role on a second-hand gesture based upon American generosity. The General, however, sometimes tolerant to the point of maddening sainthood, apparently realized the folly of stooping to such trivialities. "So what?" he laughed.

(On the other hand, the General wasn't quite so tolerant when Monty slowed to a trot in the Sicilian invasion; I often heard him grumble, "Why doesn't Monty get going? What's the matter with him; why doesn't he get going?" He repeated similar remarks later, when Monty bogged down in caution on the Continent. Yet, such statements were made in careful privacy. They never tarnished Monty's press.)

One of the few times I really disagreed with the Regular Army viewpoint occurred one evening at General Eisenhower's villa. I was dining with Butch, awaiting the General's return for a little trip up to Caserta. Butch, with his civilian disregard of military discipline, asked Mickey to eat with us. It wasn't the first time we had done so in General Ike's absence and it was most natural, for the official family was very intimate; but I always felt a tiny fear General Eisenhower might return and bring the fury of West Point upon our heads.

This night, he did.

Walking into the house unannounced, he saw Butch, Mickey, and me dining in rather boisterous informality. The Eisenhower grin shrunk into a tight military line; his teeth ground so firmly that muscles rippled up each cheek. The storm warnings were up. "Butch," he said ominously, "I'd like to see you for a minute!"

They disappeared into another room. Poor Mickey muttered something about being finished, and fled into the kitchen. I picked at the food, cursing the war, the Army, and uniforms *in toto*.

Later, Butch told me that the General raked him over a thousand hot coals for having Mickey at the same table. Ike thought a lot of Mickey, who, in turn, adored the General. But Ike didn't feel—to put it mildly—that he or Butch could eat at the same table with an enlisted man, and then turn around and order him to do some necessary, but menial duty. General Ike emphasized it was bad enough around his quarters, with all the inevitable informality; incidents such as this, he added, only made ordinary discipline still more difficult. He concluded by stressing he didn't want to hurt Mickey like that again. Butch was left with the solid impression that another similar occasion might blast the earth right out from under his very feet.

The day before Christmas I was in on the murder of a tradition even stiffer than that of West Point or Sandhurst—the WAC's and I rode aboard a Navy destroyer at sea.

The ship was going to Capri, carrying General Eisenhower over for an inspection tour. Somehow managing to shatter this oldest of Navy regulations, he wangled invitations for us females. Luckily, he chose a gorgeous afternoon filled with bright sunshine and a soft breeze, the one clear day we saw during our entire visit in Italy. Yet, seeing Capri itself, it seemed impossible that the weather could be other than lovely, for the place is surely one of the most beautiful spots on this earth.

We toured the famed resort in jeeps, captivated by the indescribable color, the luxurious air of semitropical leisure, and the attractive, gay little villas.

General Eisenhower, however, spotted a villa which wasn't exactly miniature. "Whose is that?" he asked, pointing. "Yours, Sir," was the reply. The General reddened, then nodded at another house, so fabulous it appeared on loan from Hollywood: "And that?" "That one belongs to General Spaatz," our guide answered. Ike asked about several others, before erupting: "Damn it, that's *not* my villa! And that's not General Spaatz' villa! None of those will belong to any general as long as I'm Boss around here. This is supposed to be a rest center—for combat men—not a playground for the Brass!" (The villas were decommissioned within hours after we left, reserved for the men who really needed them.)

After a quick lunch at Red Cross headquarters and a visit to the picturesque, cliff-bordered villa of Axel Munthe, the famous Capri author, we headed back to the destroyer and to Naples.

That night was Christmas Eve.

We all gathered at the General's villa just outside the city, in a dreamy location overlooking the Bay of Naples and Mount Vesuvius. There was a small tree, bravely decorated with objects which included strings of popcorn supplied by Butch for communal popping. We gave each other silly things, just to keep the Yuletide spirit alive; General Ike gave Roman coins to all his "house" family. My own imaginative and expensive present to the Boss: a plain white handkerchief.

The General seemed relaxed and comparatively happy, although as homesick as all of us; it was a makeshift, make-do Christmas for everyone there, from four-star general to G-I waiter, from Red Cross girl to civilian driver. I wandered outside and enjoyed the view of the rainy city, thinking of all the dirt and damage underneath, all the death and despair; I thought of a lunch we ate in a restaurant where Caruso sang, a lunch sabotaged by the heartbreaking sight of ragged Italians digging in the slop and garbage for even a shred of palatable food. Perhaps that was why General Ike so admired the painting in his living room, a vivid view of the bay, the city, and Vesuvius, a view now banished to tourists' memories, a view never to be seen again. Going back into the villa, I took another look at that picture and knew why the General liked it so much. Soon afterward, the party broke up.

Around nine o'clock the next morning we flew to Tunis, General Eisenhower happy with his nicest Christmas present—President Roosevelt's official radio announcement that Ike would lead the invasion forces onto Europe.

The Tunis stop was made in order to permit a visit with the Prime Minister, recovering from an illness so severe that his wife was in attendance. This was my first meeting with Mrs. Churchill; she was charming, perfectly delightful, a wonderful wife to a wonderful man. I also liked their daughter Sarah Oliver, then an officer in the WAAF. And I was flattered when they included me in their invitation to General Eisenhower to stay for an intimate Christmas party; Ellen Ruthmann, a WAC dietitian overseeing the Churchill meals at Ike's suggestion, was preparing a luscious feast to be topped by champagne.

But the General smashed those dreams by insisting that he couldn't stay over any longer.

The P.M. accompanied us to the door, coming out on the steps dressed in his bathrobe and his initialed slippers; an alert photographer caught him in this bars-down mood, in a photo I still cherish. "See you in London, Kay!" he shouted.

On the flight to Algiers I cursed General Eisenhower most dis-loyally, if silently. Our Christmas dinner consisted of a cold, taste-less, depressing Army K-ration.

Headquarters was split into two distinct camps: the happy staff members slated to go to London with the General, and the down-in-the-mouth people staying behind. I was pleased to learn that all the household staff and the official family were coming along, in-cluding Mattie Pinette, one of the original five WAC officers, now assigned to our office for the first time.

But there was some difficulty about others in the official family, namely, Telek and wife Caacie. It looked as though they would be imprisoned in quarantine for six months as soon as they arrived in England. Even General Eisenhower couldn't get his dogs by the laws which keep Britain free of rabies; it's easier to get away with murder in the British Isles than to smuggle a pup past customs. Besides, half the photographers in London would be at the airport to shoot "human interest" pictures of the famous Telek—already second only to Falla in canine popularity—and his Anglo-American family. The General bowed to regulations.

At the same time, poor Butch again suffered the rare Eisenhower wrath for breaking regulations.

He walked in one day and presented Ike with that painting from the Naples villa. Instead of embarrassed appreciation, Butch re-ceived a warning stare. "How did you get that?" General Ike asked.

"Just cut it out from the frame," Butch said, bewildered. Loot-ing, in one form or another, was so widespread among the armies it failed to attract attention any more. Butch probably hadn't done anything more than obey an impulse; he knew the General liked the painting, so he sliced it out without further thought.

But General Ike didn't give him time for any explanation. "You probably meant well," he yelled, "but I don't care what you thought. I don't approve of looting in any shape, any time, any where. And I don't want to hear any more about this—you just get it back to that villa as soon as you can!"

I felt sorry for Butch, who had the same expression as a tomcat startled by the expression on his master's face when he brings in a very dead mouse.

On the last day of 1943, General Eisenhower departed for the United States. He left behind a headquarters filled with the sounds of moving and farewells. The latter were brief and unusually quiet; those of us who were leaving didn't have the heart to gloat over the stay-behinds, who slipped through the halls with funereal gloom. I was glad when our time came to leave.

Our last stop in North Africa was Marrakech. It couldn't have been a lovelier spot in which to leave both tragic and happy memories. And the storms at sea co-operated by weathering us in there for two days. We shopped, buying Moroccan handbags and other gifts sure to be welcome in tightly rationed England. We sunbathed, luxuriating in the balmy weather, acquiring a slight tan to be lorded over the January-white girls in London. We soaked up the tropical beauty of Marrakech, storing it against the coming grayness of English winter. We stared endlessly at the snow-tipped Atlas Mountains, then at the gushing sea. We ate, and ate, and ate. And one night we toured the native market, refusing to join in street suppers but watching wide-eyed as dark beauties danced in the moonlight; then, as one of our group described it, we wandered from one smell to another.

If Marrakech gave us a pleasant farewell, General Eisenhower's new B-17 promised a nice trip. Brand-new and smartly decorated in rich leather, this Flying Fort offered the last word in aerial luxury: a Comfort Station.

Despite the new fear of German fighters from Europe, the trip North was smooth, fast, and uneventful.

Staring out the window I suddenly saw land under the clouds—green, cultivated fields, as smooth and patterned as kitchen linoleum. This must be England!

A large airfield came into view, crisscrossed by tiny paths which became huge runways as we circled and started in for the landing. I began powdering my nose, excited at the thought of seeing Mother, being in London ...

CHAPTER XI

SUDDENLY the plane shot upward, roaring away from the airfield. We all smashed back against our seats. "Maybe the wheels won't come down," someone said in a small voice.

Snuffy Nixon, the navigator, stuck his head in the cabin and broke the silence. "Don't worry, folks. I just got mixed up in my figuring and picked the wrong country."

"Not *France!*" we cried.

"No," said Snuffy, "it's not France. But it's not England, either." He grinned over at me. "This is Kay's home. We almost landed in southern Ireland!"

We relaxed and sighed with relief as the plane straightened out and headed for England. It would have been sticky trying to avoid internment by the neutral Irish; sticky, and a horrible way to wait out the war. I joined in a bridge game started to while away the time. The girls talked excitedly about the contrast between North Africa's barren country and the green, well-tended fields below. Although one of the engines had conked out some time before, the other three droned on quite efficiently and the remainder of the trip was pleasantly uneventful.

As our plane dropped onto an American base in southern England, Sue pointed out the window and yelled, "Look! There's a Russian officer!"

I looked—and laughed. She was pointing to an ankle-length gray overcoat which could only belong to an officer of the crack, legendary Scots Guards. And the man inside that overcoat was about as Russian as the House of Lords: Lieutenant-Colonel Jimmy Gault, General Eisenhower's Military Assistant. Jimmy waxed hot enough whenever some Yank called him a mere "aide," which the British use to describe an aide below the rank of major. I'd like to have heard the Military Assistant's reaction at being called a Russian. Sue was most contrite.

While the crew repaired the B-17's engine, we piled into the base mess for the first of many meals to feature that little horror of the British wartime ration, Brussels sprouts, which Americans came to despise as much as the rain.

The next and last stop was Bovington Airport, where, while Tex and the girls tried to hide our Moroccan fruit from awed station personnel, I telephoned my mother. When she came on the wire, both of us tried, unsuccessfully, to be very casual about the whole thing; it was our first talk in more than thirteen months. A lot had happened between December of 1942, when I left England, and this day, January 14, 1944, the day of my return. Dick, the torpedoing, Algiers, Tunisia, lunch with President Roosevelt, Cairo, Luxor, Palestine, Sicily, Italy . . . I tried to cram it all into that brief telephone conversation.

Riding into the city, I was that happiest of Britons, a Londoner coming home. Only a true Londoner can appreciate the emotion. The capital was just as scarred as ever, it looked drab after the color of Algiers, Cairo, Capri, and Marrakech—but it was London.

And the red-brick of 20 Grosvenor Square, despite its very American air, seemed an integral part of London. Mattie and I went into the billeting office, where an obliging officer assigned us to a flat in the Park West and agreed that Ruth Briggs could share it when she arrived from Algiers. Outside, there was a deep fog, which Mattie found as intriguing as any pictured in mystery movies about London; I found it a bother, for I had to leave Mother's place early that evening in order to find my way back up to Edgeware Road.

Next morning, Mattie and I stepped outside into a damp, gray, blurred world.

"Now you're seeing the grandfather of all fogs," I told Mattie, who was bewildered and a little frightened. "This is a pea-souper, a real London pea-souper!"

It was, too. The sun was little more than a fuzzy spot high up in the dark fog. All lights blazed at the office with nighttime strength. Everything was topsy-turvy, being readied for the General's arrival.

"The Boss is coming in tonight," Tex explained. "Fog's so bad that it's impossible to fly down from Prestwick. Gault's up there with a special train." He looked questioningly at me. "They're due in about 11 P.M., Kay. Sure you can drive through this fog—or will it lift by then?"

I laughed. "Lift? This is a pea-souper, Tex. It'll be worse by tonight, if anything. But I should know London well enough to drive it blindfolded . . . which is what it will amount to."

That night, I had my doubts. Even leaving early enough to allow plenty of time, I had to ease the Packard through Mayfair and down through Kensington at a snail's pace. Traffic was piling up, cars and taxis abandoned right in the streets. I saw a double-decker bus inching along, the driver leaning out his window to watch a man walking in front with a flashlight, one hand on the fender, leading the bus as carefully as a farmer with a blind horse. My own car lights were useless, melting into the murkiness a mere two feet ahead. The job of driving was something like trying to swim underwater at night, with one's eyes open.

Apprehensive that a bus or lorry might bear down without warning, I stopped and got out. I had to stoop and feel along with my hands to learn if the car were on the right side of the curbing, on the street proper or on the sidewalk.

Then, reassured, I coaxed the Packard down to Addison Road Station, the same place from which General Eisenhower left for North Africa.

General Ike looked very well indeed, refreshed by his visit home. But he and the entire party, including Butch and Mickey, gasped at the fog; it was impenetrable and slightly terrifying at first sight. "Now I know I'm back in London," the General smiled, adding doubtfully, "Think you can make it, Kay?"

I nodded with more confidence than truth and we set out.

Stalled vehicles now were scattered all along the streets, making obstacle courses out of even the broadest of thoroughfares. They loomed up in the fog unexpectedly, forcing me to brake often and hard. But there were no complaints—no talk, in fact—from the back seat. I drove strictly from memory, making each turn blindly, half expecting to run straight into a building.

Arriving in the general vicinity of what appeared to be Grosvenor Square, I decided to get out and determine exactly where we were; the blind-man's-bluff route might have landed us anywhere from Berkeley Square to Bryanston Square, blocks away. Once again I had to bend over and feel my way along the street's surface, groping for the sidewalk. A dim light glowed several feet away at some sort of doorway . . .

"Here it is!" I was shouting, holding fast to the blast-wall headquarters entrance. "This is 20 Grosvenor!"

While I exulted in the fantastic luck of locating the building, right on the nose, in the middle of a real London pea-souper, General Ike went inside for a quick check on incoming cables. He reappeared within a few minutes.

Jimmy Gault then directed me down toward Berkeley Square, to Chesterfield Hill, where we stopped before a dim building on the corner. This was Jimmy's pride and joy, Hays Lodge, an attractive and nicely furnished town house which was to serve as the General's home and headquarters in the city. It was pleasant, after the fog, to step inside and collapse into the plush chairs. General Ike inspected the upstairs and the basement and then announced, to his Military Assistant's satisfaction, that he liked it very much. "But I'd still rather live in Telegraph Cottage, out of town," he said wistfully.

Within the week, we were settled into the same old 20 Grosvenor offices left behind in 1942.

I, for the first time, had a corner in which to start whittling down the surprisingly large pile of "fan mail," already beginning to split almost equally into letters from Americans and those from

Britishers. Ike was busy assembling his staff, handing out assignments, and getting reacquainted with pre-Torch friends, from headquarters guards right up to the King of England. He made his first friendly call upon His Majesty several days later, rather touched when the King asked for an Eisenhower autograph for a royal relative.

(Upon another occasion, the King also asked if he might be eligible for the European Theater ribbon. Planned to cover American campaigners anywhere from North Africa to Germany, the ribbon already was a sore point with Mediterranean veterans who scoffed at London troops wearing the same award given to those in combat—and the English thought it humorous that Yanks got a decoration for just being in England. The King, however, wanted that ribbon. He was, of course, the technical chief of Britain's armed forces and he had been in Africa. So Ike, leaning mightily upon General Marshall's Washington prowess, arranged the details. Field Marshal Jan Christiaan Smuts was another Empire leader who requested and received the little E.T.O. ribbon. The King always wore his with pride, but I thought it strange he received the decoration without a whisper of publicity; it wasn't even mentioned in the all-inclusive Court Calendar.)

The day after Anzio began, I drove General Eisenhower to an important Sunday meeting of the Allied commanders at Norfolk House, a tall and spacious building originally owned by the family of the Duke of Norfolk, premier Duke of England. Norfolk House, which served as AFHQ before North Africa's invasion, now was stiff and formal with its new importance as the Overlord planning center. Even parking space was numbered in strict accordance with military protocol.

Heading our plain olive-drab Packard toward the Number One spot, however, I saw it was occupied by the flashy, shiny, black Rolls Royce which could belong to but one man in all of England: General Montgomery. I was furious, as only a rank-conscious army driver can be.

"That's okay now," General Ike said soothingly. "Don't say anything. It just doesn't matter."

After he got out, I made it a point to remark, ever so sweetly, to Monty's driver, there must be some mistake. And when Ike emerged from Norfolk House, *his* car was in the space, his driver beaming a purely feline smile.

The General wasn't interested in such trifles. He was quiet on the ride to Grosvenor Square and, back in the office, I learned why. Firstly, Overlord had been moved up from May 5 to at least the end of May. Secondly, the British (Mr. Churchill in particular) were offering bitter objection to his vehement championship of the plan for "Anvil," invasion of southern France. Thirdly, he didn't believe Overlord invasion plans called for sufficient shock troops.

He sent a message off that night to his Washington bosses, the Combined Chiefs of Staff, and wrote in my office diary the next morning:

> Last night sent my conclusions, as to strength of Overlord attack, to C/CS.
>
> Whatever my orders are, I'll carry them out—but I am convinced that the original plan does not carry enough strength in the control wave. Since I earnestly hope to preserve "Anvil" —the message I sent puts a terrible additional burden on resources.
>
> But if we could have them (principally LST's, LCT's) until Aug. 1, I believe we can win quickly!

This somber side of headquarters life was relieved shortly by the arrival of Telek, en route to six-month quarantine in Hackbridge Kennels on the outskirts of London. I, especially, had been miserable without him; Hunt, Moaney, even the General himself all remarked frequently that Telek was the "something missing" at Hays Lodge. But our pleasure in having him back in England was sullied in the sickening flood of feature stories and photographs dripping with sentiment; one would have thought our little Scottie was a movie star headed for concentration camp. General Ike was thoroughly disgusted with press treatment of the whole episode.

Even so, we sneaked away for private visits with Telek, driving out secretly to avoid correspondents. I slipped away more often, two or three times a week, to offer the unhappy prisoner some juicy scraps from the General's mess. He was particularly joyous when Ike showed up to romp with him in the yard.

Press attention shifted to Caacie when she arrived, and when a real key-holer learned that she was pregnant. Alone, Telek and Caacie whined happily at each other through a wire-covered hole cut in their adjoining wall. But Caacie, always abnormally shy, threw fits whenever photographers attempted to trick her into posing. The publicity furor which flared up when she gave birth sent her into a pitiful nervous breakdown. The puppies went unfed, and died.

I was furious, not only at the crowds who virtually murdered Telek's offspring by frightening Caacie, but also because their pups could have been taken out of quarantine immediately. And all of us were equally resentful when the kennel owners, who charged General Ike an exorbitant (for England) four dollars a week, had the bad taste to ask him for a letter of recommendation.

Beetle, incidentally, who brought Telek up to London from North Africa, placed his own black spaniel in Hackbridge Kennels. (Historians researching this particular period probably will be more interested in noting that January 28, 1944, saw the two-star general and future Ambassador to Moscow become *Lieutenant General* Smith.)

I was spending my off-duty hours during this time in getting reacquainted with the new London, which was a stranger to the one I knew in 1939 and the chins-up, bloody London of the Blitz —even different than the hesitant, bewildered London of 1942.

Official histories miss this very human point, that London was to the second world war what Paris was to the first: a gay wartime capital. When the armies got to Paris this time, something was missing; it was as though they tried to copy their predecessors in World War I, as though they wanted to ape the champagne idea exactly, however desperately. London didn't have this precedent which bogged down Paris in 1944–45. So, almost like a discreet matron carried away by far too many drinks, London became —probably for the first and last time in her career—a playgirl of a city.

Part of this new era was inevitable, with the scores of Allied headquarters scattered in and around the capital. But most of it stemmed from the city's magic as a magnet for troops on leave; London was *the* leave city.

Perhaps it was the airmen who set the pace, beginning back in the days when The Few of the RAF flocked to London for forty-eight hours' worth of precious escape, when the Canadians and the Eagle Squadron boys began partying with a wild vengeance. Regardless, the huge Canadian Army, which stayed in Britain so long awaiting Dieppe and the Normandy invasion, kept the kettle boiling even faster. And the Americans' mass arrival really blew the lid off.

The center of this leave-world was Piccadilly Circus, dirty, damaged, boarded up, and blacked out, but still a sort of Times Square for soldiers and officers looking for fun . . . Poles, Czechs, Canadians, Free French, Dutch, Belgians, New Zealanders, Aussies, Scots, Indians, Yorkshiremen, Welsh, Norwegians, Irish, South Americans, colonials of every color, language, and uniform. And overwhelming all others by sheer weight of numbers were the Yanks, hands in pockets, leaning against the walls, flirting with anyone in a skirt, looking for guided tours, or just plain loafing with all the careful, superb nonchalance of the American with time on his hands.

With darkness and the blackout, Piccadilly became more boisterous, more alive. One felt rather than saw the tidal waves of song, drink, love, and loneliness. Strange languages lashed out in the wake of passers-by. The night was filled with giggles, yells, curses, laughs, and fights. Doorways became temporary love-nests. Flashlights bounced around in the darkness like fire-flies. Busses, taxis, cars, and lorries jangled along the street unnoticed, winding in and out of the crowds spilling over the sidewalks. Sometimes a siren would scream, followed by the long fingers of searchlights grabbing at the sky; neither ack-ack nor bombs emptied Piccadilly, however—only the ugly light of morning did that.

General Eisenhower was perturbed at the reckless spending of American troops, who, like the Canadians and the Australians, were semi-millionaires alongside the comparatively poor British. It made me ache to see Yanks drinking double-whiskies while their home-bound Allies sipped silently at watered beer and watched the well-heeled Americans walk away with their women; this condition, not quite so blatant in the vast stretches of Tunisia, caused more damage to Anglo-American relations in England than any other single situation. Ike, right after his arrival, ordered all U.S. commanders down to the smallest units to encourage their soldiers and officers to send home as much pay as possible, in the form of money orders, war bonds, and savings. But no medicine was quite strong enough to cure this incurable, chronic ailment of Allied warfare.

There was another London, aside from the Piccadilly London. This was the world of theater, of movies, Hyde Park soap-boxers, quiet pub-crawling, serious sightseeing. This was the wonderful world of American Red Cross clubs, where women gave unstintingly of their time and humor and patience, where G-I's found the next best thing to Home. This was the universal world of Allied friendships, of dinners in private homes, of love affairs which blossomed into marriage. Then too, there was the normal, ageless day-by-day London of the business world. And the military London of headquarters life. Yet, all in all, the London most veterans will remember is the after-dark London.

Fresh from Africa, I got a tremendous bang out of every part of this new, 1944 London.

I liked seeing the curious crowds of Britons gathered around a Yank softball game in Hyde Park, only yards from anti-aircraft guns and grim-faced Tommies on duty. I liked seeing G-I's and

ATS or WAAF girls strolling the parks and sidewalks, holding hands unashamedly. I felt a surge of pride in the absence of iron rails and fences, all gone into the melting pot forging Britain's all-out war effort. I liked the fierce pride of the Cockney, the taxi driver, the bus "chippies," the confident and swaggering paratroops. I liked the way tight-belted Englishmen, even the poorest, hurried by American PX's and ignored the Yanks loaded down with cigarettes, sweets, and other treasures—it was a welcome contrast to Africa, Sicily, and Italy.

I knew what "Allies" meant when I walked into the cleaning shop and saw as many as a dozen different nationalities' uniforms on the rack, when I saw British and American officers gabbing at the mess, when I saw RAF men with tired eyes and Polish or Czech patches on the shoulder. I knew what the war was about when I saw all these foreigners gathered in London, when I saw tight-lipped rescue workers digging in bomb debris. I liked the cosmopolitan air of the "bottle party" nightclub, the international friendliness in the dirtiest pub. I liked the feeling of importance, the quiet air of excitement of just being in London, the atmosphere of pregnant and forceful action. I liked . . . well, I loved it all, this 1944 London.

General Eisenhower loved it, too. Of all the worldly honors the Allies bestowed upon him, I think he was most moved by the occasion when, after the war, London gave him the cherished Freedom of the City.

But, as Supreme Commander in early 1944, he also knew London's distractions. I noticed he spoke more and more of his distaste for having a headquarters in a major city, let alone London. He wanted SHAEF chucked out into the country, at least in the outskirts, where his staff could buckle down to hard work.

Beetle agreed, emphasizing that London was becoming more and more of a military target. He was particularly perturbed over intelligence reports which warned the Germans were building mysterious platforms along the West Wall, presumably to bombard England with secret rocket weapons. Beetle foresaw, as did many others, a real danger to headquarters and morale if our bombing failed to destroy the new emplacements. Moreover, Hitler was beginning to send "retaliation" bombers over London; they were small flights, compared with those of the Blitz, but they caused continual, terrible damage. And one big bomb landing anywhere around Grosvenor Square, for example, where Americans and records were jammed in every building, might seriously impair invasion planning. (One did hit near enough to Norfolk House to smash some windows there; another knocked out a part of the American Army Group's Bryanston Square headquarters; Admiral Cunningham's office was bashed about a bit; there were continuing, worrisome reports of such incidents.)

Knowing General Eisenhower and his love for shifting headquarters, I assumed the inevitable. The conniving of staff officers well-entrenched in the social Battle of London left me cold; I'd seen this same useless maneuver in Algiers, just before we headed for Caserta.

We moved. All of SHAEF migrated to buildings formerly occupied by the Eighth Air Force, the post known by the none-too-subtle code name of "Widewing." The place itself was a group of temporary buildings and tents in Bushy Park, near Kingston and not far from Hampton Court, the lovely Thames-side palace retreat of England's kings. Part of the area was enclosed by a high wall; all traffic entered or left through gates meticulously guarded by the "Snowball" M.P.'s. Lumbering khaki-colored busses and other vehicles maintained a regular shuttle service into London.

Widewing gave SHAEF its first family atmosphere. Instead of being scattered in far-flung billets, as in Algiers and London, the officers were quartered together and approached a more ideal state of friendly intimacy. This buddy-feeling increased with the introduction of an afternoon tea ceremony in most offices; official reserve broke down, and informality accomplished far more than conference-table logic. A few sections, striving for neat balance, served coffee in the morning "break" and tea in the afternoon; it provided a nice Anglo-American touch. General Eisenhower moved back into his beloved Telegraph Cottage, soon to enjoy its gay gardens of everything from roses to violets. I moved into a nearby house with the five WAC officers; top Brass located in the same general neighborhood.

Nissen huts, cement structures, tents, and shacks housed messes, PX's, supplies, and troop quarters. And headquarters itself was encased in long, low buildings covered with a camouflage net intended to give enemy airmen the idea this was no more than a dirty brown hill.

Our offices in "Building C" were the most spacious to date. The aides occupied one room; for the first time, I had one to myself. Mine was the only one through which special visitors—such as Beetle, the only person permitted immediate entree without preliminaries—could go into the inner office. Even telephone conversations were halted at that barrier, pending verification; I always answered, "General Eisenhower's office, Miss Summersby speaking," and then stepped in to ask the General if he could talk to the caller. This method did away with the nuisance of switching calls and spared him the nerve-jangling screams of telephone calls.

General Eisenhower's office was, as usual, plain and unpretentious, shocking visitors who expected grandeur in the Supreme Allied Commander's inner sanctum. He laughed at the American idea that an executive's worth is measured by the number of telephones on his desk; he had but two. One was the old "Red Line 6," his personal, super-service wire with the same designation as that in North Africa. The other was nothing more than the accessory "scrambler," common in Britain as a means of foiling line-tappers who, should they cut in, would hear only a meaningless jumble of Donald Duck sounds.

There was a dark brown carpet; ordinary chairs and sofas fringed the wall. The room was devoid of any hint of a solemn conference table. General Eisenhower's desk, flanked in the rear by British and American flags as well as his red four-star general's flag, was unimpressive and excessively neat. An "In" basket was placed on one side, an "Out" basket on the other; unlike the overflowing receptacles of most headquarters offices, these were always kept at low-water mark. Stray papers never cluttered the desk top, which featured framed photographs of the three most important people in the Eisenhower world, his mother, his wife, and his son John. Scattered ashtrays awaited cigarettes stored in a desk drawer. On the walls were a few autographed portraits of such respected friends as President Roosevelt, Mr. Churchill, General Marshall, and Admiral Cunningham. There were two extraordinary comforts: (1) a swivel chair, in which the General often leaned back in order to prop his feet on the desk, thoroughly relaxed, while pondering some tremendous problem or talking with a real intimate, and (2) a private toilet.

Ike had buzzers for his British Military Assistant, for his Naval Aide, for his Texas Aide, for me, and for Mattie, his Captain-stenographer. Perhaps the most important item of equipment in the office was the General's fountain pen, indispensable for the steady chore of official signatures. But I still thought more of my own, part of a very special Parker pen and pencil set matching those Ike presented to his topmost commanders in North Africa. Like theirs, mine was inscribed:

Kay—for service in Mediterranean A.F.H.Q. D. D. E.

I was extremely proud at being included in these honors, so much so that I kept framed on my desk the letter which he wrote to accompany the set:

29 March, 1944

Dear Kay,

I am sending you, along with this note, a fountain pen which I hope you will accept as a personal present from me. Nine of this particular type have been made up specially for me and I have given them to persons who have been of particular assistance to me during the time I have been an Allied Commander. The others have gone to the officers that served as Commanders-in-Chiefs under me in the Medi-

terranean, and to four others. In your own most important
sphere your services have been of inestimable and constant
value.

I thank you very much and hope that this little pen will
remind you of my gratitude.

Sincerely,
(Dwight D. Eisenhower)

In Algiers, the General once walked into his office to find one of
the stenographers filing her fingernails, puffing away at a cigarette like a woman in her boudoir. The resultant storm was such
that I never smoked in my office from that day on. It was an
order, if not a direct order, and I never disobeyed it. Nor did I
smoke while on duty in the staff car.

Likewise, I once heard the General remark that he disliked red
fingernail polish. He never mentioned it to me, but I adopted
natural, clear polish thereafter.

There was no resentment on my part in sticking to both these
rather unusual ideas. General Eisenhower was a militant cham-
pion of women in war and I had no wish to let him down by presenting the picture of a night-club woman at the very door of
his office.

The official day in our part of Building C began, usually around
8 A.M., with General Ike poring over the maroon, leather-cov-
ered logbook which contained all hush-hush cables and correspondence, intelligence digests, staff summaries, and the like.
Meanwhile, I started the previous day's load of "fan mail," often
enchanted by the latest gift of one of Ike's favorite admirers, a
Mrs. Chambers, who sometimes gave up her few chickens' production in order to send the Supreme Commander a dozen precious fresh eggs. Barring inspection trips or visits to other headquarters, the day then settled into a never-ending routine of phone
calls and High Brass visitors. Lunch might be a sandwich or hot
plate, served at the desk. The real breather came sometime after
four in the afternoon, when the mess sent up tea service and I
carried it into the General's office.

"Bring yours in, too, Kay," he would say occasionally. "It makes more of a 'break' to have someone to talk to."

It seems no exaggeration to say that General Eisenhower, with his historic role, faced problems of such heroic range that they required the judgment of a Solomon, the military mind of a Napoleon, the diplomacy of a Prime Minister.

One hour, for example, he might be on the giddy heights of international politics, discussing with Under Secretary of State Edward Stettinius delicate problems expected to arise in liberated Europe. The next hour, he might be bawling out a chastised General Patton for making a chance public remark (highly resented by hard-pressed Russia) that America and Britain would have to rule the postwar world. The next, Ike might confer with Monty, listening to complaints that several U.S. generals were not up to their jobs; with a War Department colonel intrigued by the General's suggestion for a special award or insignia to designate infantry troops who had been in combat; with a general from South Africa, bringing greetings from Field Marshal Jan Smuts; with an Intelligence officer worried because a report warned the German V-weapons might wipe London off the earth; then, with another Allied officer who believed the V-weapon stories to be a gigantic hoax to attract and waste our bombs; with Harvey Gibson, the American Red Cross boss, Before lunch, after such sessions, General Ike might discuss anything from lower-echelon promotions to the possible disaster at Anzio, from agreements with the Dutch government to the high rents being paid by American officers for their London billets.

Lunch? One day it was a snack in the office; the next, playing host to the entire British War Cabinet, out for a look at Widewing and future plans. And, usually at least twice a week, there was the strain of lunch with a Churchill full of new ideas on old arguments.

There was the period to which I referred grimly in my appointment book as The Hanging Hour. This was the time when the Judge Advocate General came in to give General Eisenhower the final, awful responsibility of individual life and death, as op-posed to the equally weighty responsibility of mass life and death in future operations. General Ike must have re-lived those court martial decisions a thousand times, aching with that power of God-like judgment.

Yet, no decision he made in that office was an easy one. The mere fact a problem reached his desk indicated that only he could make the decision. Beetle, working himself into ill health, shoul-dered the intermediate responsibilities; smaller problems and smaller decisions were cleared away at lower levels. The Supreme Commander received only the toughest of problems and had to make the most momentous of decisions.

General Ike could battle for an idea till blue in the face. Once proved wrong, he could about-face and battle, with equal vigor, for the very same plan he had opposed so bitterly. He took some convincing, of course. Mr. Churchill had this same blessed quality and I'm sure it was one of the major reasons for their mutual re-spect and admiration.

Most typical of the Eisenhower will to push an idea, once au-thenticated, was his championship of the airborne operation in connection with Overlord. Many of the highest Brass, including Air Chief Marshal Sir Trafford Leigh-Mallory, opposed the plan vehemently; they believed, conscientiously, the odds were so great as to produce an appalling aerial disaster. General Eisenhower, despite these arguments, sided with his planners in the argument that the whole thing was necessary to the invasion and therefore, on his sole responsibility, had to proceed as scheduled.

Actually, one of the major problems of this period was that of air power itself. New enough to offer uncharted strategical hori-zons, but old enough to pepper arguments with precedents, it was a principal, continuing headache.

Ike, an advocate of unification at even that early date, fought a consistent battle to control the badly-split air command for at least the initial invasion phase. "I'll fight for that with everything I've got," I heard him remark upon one occasion. In addition, there were the questions of bombers' role in assault, of long-range fighter uses, et cetera, et cetera. More political but still very military, there was the question of air raids over France. The British argued for concentrating upon European oil sources, to avoid the possibility of French hatred from Allied bombings; General Ike insisted upon destruction of transportation centers in France as a key part of the invasion plan.

At the same time he was worried over the one problem which had plagued him and his planners since North Africa and its recurrent invasions: landing craft. A good part of his time and energy was spent—from the time he made that cryptic comment about LST's and LCT's in my diary upon landing in England in January, right up to the time just before the invasion—in pushing, shoving, pleading, begging for the vital landing vessels.

I was continually appalled at the weight and the variety of the problems which this man was called upon to solve. Were we prepared to use gas, if the enemy should use it in desperation? How should air combat troops be rehabilitated? Were they, as rumored, getting poor hospitalization? Were some of the routine Theater regulations working hardships on combat troops? Did detailed planning in lower units come up to that in higher echelons? Just how much should the press be told? What about winter combat equipment? Would German secret weapons endanger England before the invasion?

With all this, the General could take in his giant's stride the tinier questions. For example, he ordered that an expensive, antique, mahogany table be taken from Hays Lodge and replaced with a plainer piece. He jumped Butch for ordering extra-soft sofa cushions, flew all over a well-meaning mess officer at Widewing for using reverse Lend-Lease to purchase special silverware. He abandoned the small swagger stick from North Africa, lest it brand him as too pro-English in mannerism. He agreed with Admiral King that SHAEF needed more U.S. Navy staff officers. He clamped down on officers' personal use of Army vehicles and impressed that same restriction on members of his personal staff.

Ike expressed deep concern, upon his arrival in London, over
a Theater regulation which forbade enlisted WAC's to go out with
officers, except on special pass. He believed that woman's official
role in the war had little to do with her after-hours life and he
deplored the London attitude that a non-officer WAC could travel
only in an enlisted world. In short, he was incensed over the preva-
lent idea that WAC's were sent over as companions for enlisted
men; Ike maintained that the WAC contingent arrived solely because it had an official job to do, that its social life was a private
affair. The regulation and the attitude were too well solidified,
however, to permit change.

Even then, he was bothered with the now-familiar cry that the
Eisenhower name be permitted entry into political circles. A Chicago correspondent, for instance, brought him a veterans' group
message re the Presidency. The General answered negatively, emphasizing he was a soldier, not a politician.

On April 12, just before leaving on an inspection trip in the
North, he was so upset by all the Stateside talk that he dictated a
personal memorandum to get it off his chest. He said then, years
before the huge draft-Eisenhower movement in America, he did
not approve of soldiers seeking nomination for office. And he made
it quite clear that Dwight D. Eisenhower absolutely was not interested in politics. He had a war to fight, a big war.

Another page of my office diary shows typical problems the General faced in early 1944, a typical Eisenhower day. It is a sample
Monday in April, when General Ike:

Staged a meeting of his top commanders to discuss "capability
of air in support of land operations" . . . Lunched with the Prime
Minister . . . Considered involved plans for the invasion of southern France . . . Held a long conference on the complicated Free
French situation . . . Talked with leading newspaper correspondents . . . Approved plans for improving the American PX . . . Ordered co-ordination of Special Service facilities among the Allies
. . . and, with Kay Summersby, won eleven shillings that night
in a bridge game at Telegraph Cottage.

Another stabbing worry was the ever-present fear the entire invasion might be compromised, with deadly effect, by one little security slip-up.

The Eisenhower temper really came to a boil when an Air Force officer—a major general—gabbed about the invasion date at a cocktail party. Even Tooey Spaatz finally agreed to the punishment for that major general: reduction to his permanent rank of lieutenant-colonel; plus a trip home in reprimanded disgrace. A Navy captain also was sent back to the States for "loose talk." A soldier misaddressed secret invasion data to a civilian Chicago address. An American correspondent tried to leave England, reportedly threatening to publish a fantastically foolish "scoop" on the real invasion date. A British carpenter inadvertently saw invasion maps on a London headquarters wall. A careless officer left secret papers in a London club's cloakroom; another tossed some into a railway trashcan.

(I got so I was afraid to go out, breaking into a cold sweat at the very thought of giving away some super-secret in a chance cocktail remark. Even when Wes Gallagher, the Associated Press correspondent and an old friend from North Africa, called to suggest an evening of the Lunts and dinner at the Savoy, I warned him against any sort of shop talk. He laughed and promised not to pry. But Wes was a good newspaperman; while the evening was still young he began asking leading questions, fishing for unofficial hints. I froze so completely that Wes apparently thought me as much fun as an Egyptian mummy. He never asked me out again.)

General Eisenhower had far less social life than the most lowly member of his staff.

The lunches with Mr. Churchill were hardly carefree or remotely social. Anthony Eden was considerably miffed when Beetle showed up at one function, substituting for Ike, who reserved his precious free time for such command affairs as a Tunisian Victory Lunch and a dinner at Ascot with the Dominion Prime Ministers. And it was only at British insistence that he finally attended a football match at Wembly one afternoon, receiving a wild ovation before the Chelsea *vs.* Charlton match and later presenting the winner's cup. On the inspection trip to Scotland, he managed to get in an entire day of salmon fishing at the lovely estate of Colonel Ivan Cobbald, a SHAEF officer doomed to a bombing death in London.

Normally, however, any leisure was spent at Telegraph Cottage, where bridge was the major indoor sport. Once in a while General Ike would look up from his desk, hounded by nerves, and suggest an hour's horseback riding. Upon such occasions we accepted the standing invitation of Sir Louis Gregg at the Air Ministry and hurried out to enjoy trails in Richmond Park, which was closed to the public because it contained false-front "factories" as decoys for enemy bombers.

When the General did have a dinner party, it was informal and intimate. I was especially pleased one night when he included my mother and me in a party of about ten invited to Hays Lodge. Among the other guests were Jimmy Gault and his wife, some people from the Red Cross, and General Patton. The latter was in good form that night—on good verbal behavior which impressed my mother no less than me. As usual, he kidded Ike about wanting some more medals. "You haven't done anything yet," General Ike chided. "Wait till you get on the Continent!"

During the war I heard, with nauseating repetition, many chairborne staff officers cry how they'd give anything "to be in the field" and "to be with the troops." One of the very few I believed sincere in this familiar headquarters wail was the Supreme Commander himself.

Seeing and talking with soldiers in the field was more pleasure and more relaxation for him than anything London's social planners could devise. Also, he thought it vital that the Supreme Commander be seen, that he become a person instead of a vague signature on orders, that he try to obtain firsthand evidence on conditions in the field.

This interest wasn't false, for General Eisenhower never was happier than when he cleaned up the paper work and headed for open country. Nor was it exhibitionism, for he was genuine, dignified, but never patronizing in his attitude toward troops; more important, he fumed angrily whenever reporters tried to follow him around, or listen to his off-the-cuff remarks. He felt the visits were personal, likely to be endangered or formalized by correspondents' presence.

And he always insisted, often with downright temper, that he arrive on time for every inspection. He didn't want to keep troops waiting for the Brass. When weather or traffic delayed us, I sometimes bore the brunt of his tirades; nothing was as important, he insisted, as keeping on schedule.

In all truth, I doubt if in military annals there is anything to equal Ike's record of a general's non-stop attempt to visit all his troops before an impending operation of such magnitude.

Despite pressing headquarters problems, he launched this ambitious campaign within a fortnight after reaching England. We went by train to Plymouth on February 4, spending that Friday and Saturday inspecting the Fourth and Twenty-ninth Infantry Divisions.

A week later we traveled to Sandhurst for special ceremonies at the "passing out" of cadets at Britain's West Point. General Eisenhower presented traditional Sam Browne belts to the two cadets with top marks; if those two men survived the war, they probably still cherish the Eisenhower autograph enscribed on their honor belts. General Ike also made a speech that lovely February afternoon, speaking from steps and inspired by the scene. (At least a dozen persons crowded around me afterward to demand copies of his remarkable address. They did everything but call me a liar when I maintained there was no written speech, that General Eisenhower always speaks from a well-ordered and wealthy mind.) Within another fortnight, the General was off for an inspection of the famous Scottish Highlanders, and the American 2nd and 3rd Armored Divisions.

From then on, the pace was relentless.

He took twenty or thirty SHAEF officers to Salisbury to peek at the performance of the hush-hush weapons. The very next day he was out at Bovington, part of a parcel of Allied Brass anxious to see the new B-29 hidden in a far, roped-off corner of the field.

Less than a week later we journeyed to Newbury for a thrilling mass airborne demonstration by General Maxwell Taylor's 101st Airborne Division. I say "thrilling" advisedly, because it was just that. I stood on the reviewing platform and gawked excitedly as hundreds upon hundreds of paratroopers bailed out in the clear sky, followed by equipment dangling from parachutes of every color. Mr. Churchill added to the occasion by delivering an appropriately bombastic speech. (I was pleased when he bowled through the crowd, like a tank, to come up and shake hands with me. This time, I wasn't with the General and I thought it further evidence of the Churchill greatness that he took time to say "hello" to even the smallest of his acquaintances.)

The Prime Minister was honor guest that night in the smart blue atmosphere of the Supreme Commander's special railroad coach, the Bayonet. General Ike was the perfect host, obtaining champagne for the P.M.'s special pleasure. And, unlike many generals who reserved V-I-P's for themselves, he invited everyone possible to share in the experience of dinner with Mr. Churchill. In addition to Jimmy Gault, Mattie, and me, he asked General Taylor, General Charles Corlett of XIX Corps, General Watson of the Third Armored, and Mr. Churchill's daughter Sarah. Talk centered around the day's exercise, the war, landing craft, and the invasion. The Prime Minister devoted most of his attention to General Corlett, who had considerable service in the Pacific; it was one of the few times I heard of Mr. Churchill acting the sincere role of listener.

Next morning, March 23, we traveled to the 2nd Armored Division CP, where General Ike, as usual, traveled from group to group delivering extemporaneous talks—never, to my continual astonishment on such occasions, repeating himself. Waiting for the next inspection, we played bridge, then headed for units of the 9th Infantry Division between Andover and Winchester.

There General Ike joined the Prime Minister for a ride into Winchester, where the car became so engulfed by crowds that both he and Mr. Churchill had to alight and acknowledge the ovation. The P.M. gave a speech which caused more pandemonium and applause than old Winchester had heard in centuries. He was the General's guest at dinner again that night, buoyed by the troops and by the crowds. He told Ike, with suppressed emotion, that the Supreme Allied Commander could count on Britain's support "with everything I've got!" General Ike, of course, had new commanders in to dine with the Prime Minister that night— General Bradley, then commanding the First Army, General J. Lawton Collins of VII Corps, and the 9th Infantry Division's General Manton Eddy.

Even aboard the train, General Eisenhower was in close touch with SHAEF headquarters. A special, direct line was plugged into his coach at every important station, permitting him to keep right up to the minute on latest developments in London and Washington.

During the month of April we traveled to still more divisional areas. Ike inspected the American 1st, 28th, and 29th Infantry Divisions, among others, plus their V Corps, as well as the Polish 2nd Armored and the British 52nd, in Scotland. He also viewed the 4th Division's amphibious landing exercise on beaches near Darmouth. These were built up to carbon-copy actual landings expected in France. The reviewing stand was a seaborne infantry landing craft. But the maneuver went sour; bombers, navy vessels, airplanes, and special units fouled up in everything from timing to orders. One or two landing craft were sunk, with casualties numbering several hundred.

Between all this, the General managed to visit various hospitals as well as a number of British and American air bases. At one of the latter, the pilot of a brand-new Lightning invited Ike up for a spin in his funny-looking "Droop Snoot." It was the General's first fighter flight but he stayed up almost ten minutes, while

Tooey watched the plane apprehensively, without smiling or speaking. Tooey's forces had lost sixty-four bombers that day.

On a trip in the vicinity of Tenby that month, we drove about 120 miles in one day, a lot of mileage for England. The rain was incessant; General Ike insisted on every stop, on time, and ended up with a bad cold.

As these incessant inspection trips indicate, the British Isle was loaded—loaded with troops, arms, and ammunition. (By June 1 there would be over 1,500,000 Americans alone on the island.) The current joke maintained that only Britain's barrage balloons held up the overcrowded island and kept it from sinking into the sea.

Endless convoys roared through the countryside day and night, traveling over narrow, all-clear roads, headed for the coastal "staging areas." Secret weapons—flame throwers, tanks with flailing arms and plows to furrow up mines, the amazing amphibious "Ducks," fog-dispellers, rocket-equipped airplanes, concrete and steel breakwaters, "Mulberry" and "Gooseberry" artificial harbors—all these and hundreds more were sneaked into port areas.

Britain tightened her Tight Little Isles still further. Civilians had been forbidden to travel between Britain and Ireland since early February; the German Consulate in Dublin had many ears. Civilians also were banned from the entire "staging area" along the coast, where a ten-mile military zone was enforced. The most unusual step of all came when the British Government bottled up all diplomats and couriers in the British Isles and even did away with traditional immunity of diplomatic communications. About the same time, British military scheduled to participate in the invasion had all their mail subjected to strict censorship. Late in May, Americans' mail was held up for ten days; they couldn't telephone, or cable, to the United States. General Ike asked the War Department to keep its usual V-I-P's in the States. Immigration and emigration halted, except for the small body of Allied intelligence agents with last-minute information. The security net around Britain was skin-tight.

With May growing old, London was drained of its leave troops. Barmen, theater owners, movie ushers, taxi drivers, and night-club doormen commented on the poor business. Staff officers due to travel in the invasion fleet disappeared one by one from their offices, without explanation. Headquarters staffs were strained, touchy to the point of ugly temper. American military personnel were restricted to quarters for a twenty-four-hour period so M.P.'s could root out AWOL's. Hospitals dismissed all but the worst bed cases; laundries received instructions to make hospital linens a top priority. Travelers found few trains; hundreds of engines and coaches had been shunted to military service.

Everyone in the British Isles—and probably in the German General Staff—knew the invasion would pop any day. But only the necessary few men knew it was scheduled for June 4.

General Eisenhower attended the final Big Brass conference three weeks before, on May 15, at General Montgomery's Twenty-first Army Group headquarters in old St. Paul's School. All the rank were there; the King, the Prime Minister, Field Marshal Smuts, Air Chief Marshal Leigh-Mallory, General Bradley, Admiral Sir Bertram Ramsay, glamor-generals Monty and Patton, the whole scintillating line-up. It was the last grand session.

In the next taut fortnight, Ike stepped up his field inspection schedule, taking quick last looks at everything from U.S. Infantry Divisions and Navy ships in North Ireland to a Guards outfit and the First Canadian Army. Two typical entries he penned in my little blue diary:

> Both 5th and 8th Divisions impressed me most favorably. Training appears to be excellent. Witnessed a divisional exercise practice this afternoon under General Pickering. Very good indeed!
>
> Visited 8th British Corps., Lt. Gen. O'Connor, Guards Armored Division, 15th Scottish and 11th Armored. They're all in good shape.

Then, all our attention focused on the South Coast, now choked with invading armies straining at the leash.

Hesitant to bother any of the active headquarters with his presence, General Eisenhower set up an Advance CP at Southwick, six or seven miles north of Portsmouth. His office was a trailer; I had a tiny desk in one corner. The whole CP was set in a wood where sunshine was exiled, where rain soaked our entire canvas headquarters days on end, giving everything a damp, musty odor; it was a long jump from London or Algiers. The Prime Minister and Field Marshal Smuts were headquartered on a special train parked at Southampton.

Nerve-ends were so exposed, security so exacting, that even the Supreme Allied Commander had to carry a pass. Everyone topside was jumpy over our Other Enemy: the weather. The area was alive with weather experts, meteorologists, and plain second-guessers—all studying, figuring, worrying about the weather, key to the whole invasion.

On June 2, the Prime Minister was unable to hold himself in any longer. He and the inevitable Smuts showed up at headquarters. Someone said Mr. Churchill was in a stew because the King, Ike, and all military-political advisers absolutely refused to let him ride on an invasion ship. He played grumpily with a cat at mess, feeding it milk from a saucer on the table.

The nightly weather conference failed to lift anyone's spirits.

On June 3, Messrs. Churchill and Smuts reappeared, their famous faces immediately slipping into the general gloom evidenced around headquarters because the weather was "off."

Late that night General Eisenhower gravely decided to postpone D-Day at least another twenty-four hours.

June 4—supposed to be D-Day—undoubtedly was the longest day of 1944. The Prime Minister came down for a comforting visit, leaving as downhearted as the most pessimistic man in the office. Another visitor was General Charles de Gaulle, who raised maddening political questions at this late hour and displayed interest only in those phases of the invasion which might affect his Free French; he was not informed of exact target details.

There was another weather session that evening. All who attended were agreed D-Day could not be delayed much longer.

So the final, decisive conference was set for the next morning, at 4 A.M. Everyone went to that meeting with the full knowledge that a decision had to be made this time. Further postponement, even another twenty-four hours, would endanger the entire expeditionary force. On the other hand, cancellation of D-Day meant a complete rescheduling of the whole invasion, weeks, perhaps months, later in the summer.

The duty for the frightful decision belonged to General Eisenhower. Even knowing him as I did, I had no idea what was passing through his mind.

"If it goes all right," I remarked to him afterward, "dozens of persons will claim the credit. But if it goes wrong, you'll be the only one to blame."

Fifteen minutes after going into that meeting in the damp morning of June 5, General Ike made the historic, staggering decision.

It was his decision, his alone. Barring his death, no one else could make it. Not another person on the face of the earth could make that decision at that time and place.

The invasion was on.

And by nightfall not even he could stop it.

General Eisenhower got a little lift of spirits when I drove him to an inspection of a British unit and the assault troops yelled, over and over again, "Good old Ike!"

His next official action was a ninety-minute press conference for the four correspondents chosen to be the eyes and ears of their respective professions: little Ned Roberts (UP), for America's press associations; Stan Burch (Reuter's), for Britain's; Red Mueller (NBC), for the American radio chains; and Robert Barr (BBC) for Britain's radio. Two U.S. Army men were there to take the initial photographs and motion pictures. It must have been a memorable occasion for each of those six.

That evening around 6:30 I drove the General to Newbury, where, ten weeks before, we had witnessed the spectacular dem-

onstration by the 101st Airborne troops. This time, Ike had to look
these troops straight in the eye, knowing that he, only he, was
responsible if they and the men of the 82nd Airborne encountered
sheer disaster.

Air Chief Marshal Sir Trafford had warned casualties probably
would be, in cold military language, "prohibitive." The gigantic
aerial armada of more than nine hundred planes, most of them
towing helpless gliders and without armor or leakproof tanks,
were headed for one of the most alert and heavily fortified areas
in the world. General Ike had the full responsibility.

Now, he stepped out of the car, ordering the four-star license
plate to be covered, that only one staff officer accompany him
on his rounds. This was no time for ceremony.

The 101st paratroopers, faces black with night paint and decked
out in full, bulky combat kit, sent tingles up and down my own
spine. I wondered how Ike felt. I wondered how these men, soon
to jump or glide right into Hitler's Europe, felt at seeing their
Supreme Commander.

I needn't have worried.

They went crazy, yelling and cheering because "Ike" had come
to see them off.

To unit commanders' surprise, he ordered each group to break
ranks and forget about military formalities. Then he said a few
words to them. I could hear the new roar of cheers, chain-fashion,
as he progressed from group to group.

We covered three separate airfields before night fell.

Back at 101st headquarters building, General Ike nodded wear-
ily to the few staff officers. They were pathetic in their chagrin
at remaining behind. Coffee and doughnuts killed a little time
and substituted for conversation. Then we all climbed onto the
roof.

The night was lovely, clear and filled with stars.

Aircraft took off near by, climbing up to join the massive for-
mations gathering in every direction. Their blinker signals winked
ominously.

Then they started off for Normandy.

General Eisenhower turned, shoulders sagging, the loneliest man in the world.

Without a word, he walked slowly toward the car. I hurried; we had to make the Southwick headquarters before 1 A.M., D-Day.

"Well," Ike said quietly. "It's on."

He looked up at the sky and added:

"No one can stop it now."

CHAPTER XII

THE rest of that day is history.
Personally, I spent it praying for the invaders . . . and, like the rest of his official family, aching with sympathy for our apprehensive Boss.

General Eisenhower stood the appalling strain for another day. Then, in the early morning of June 7—it was 0720 hours, just twenty-six hours after H-Hour—he left for Normandy's beaches.

I fled to the lonely comfort of our trailer-headquarters. Working on the General's "fan mail" never seemed so difficult, so unimportant; but it helped smother worries.

He returned to our Southwick CP shortly before ten o'clock that night, quietly excited by his on-the-spot survey and obviously pleased that all was going according to plan. He hadn't been able to go ashore, but the destroyer on which he traveled provided a close-up view of the actual beaches. The General told me he was worried about the landing craft smashed up there; he thought, however, they could be repaired. Generals Bradley and Montgomery had come aboard ship for a long, satisfying talk with the Supreme Commander, who now felt he had a better grasp of battle progress.

General Eisenhower was especially pleased the airborne operation justified his insistence that it be included in the plan. Air Chief Marshal Leigh-Mallory even wrote to acknowledge casualties, although heavy, were far, far less than feared. Instead of the outright disaster predicted, only some 29 or 30 of the C-47's in that vast flight of about 950 had been lost. One of Ike's major command decisions was safe in posterity.

He showed considerable worry the next day when reports from English ports and the beachhead itself indicated something of a tangle in shipping problems. Loading and unloading operations were behind schedule. General Ike took time-out for a meager press conference that afternoon, then went into a huddle with Gen. John C. H. Lee ("Courthouse" Lee to the staff, "Jesus Christ" Lee to his not-so-adoring troops), Deputy Theater Commander and overseer of the supply network.

Suddenly, only three days after the invasion, General Eisenhower had to turn from the beaches back to the worrisome routine of London, staff problems, the Prime Minister, and V-I-P's.

For me, this meant a return to the front seat of that four-star staff car, driving back and forth between London and Portsmouth until every curve and bump in the road was as familiar as London's West End.

We made our first trip to London the morning of June 9. The General immediately set to work on such diverse headaches as promotions and the sentence of two G-I's convicted of rape. The afternoon brought Winston Churchill hurrying out to Widewing, where he shoved his entourage into the map-covered War Room and then cornered Ike in the office for a long chat. The General told me afterward that Mr. Churchill was again vociferous in his demand to make a trip to the beaches. He also told General Ike he was happy to pass along "Uncle Joe's" heartiest congratulations upon the invasion; Stalin promised an offensive on the Leningrad front two days later.

America's highest Brass—General Marshall, Admiral King, General Arnold, et al.—arrived in London the next day for a look-see at the European war and a meeting of Ike's Bosses, the Combined Chiefs of Staff. But the General himself was more interested in the battle of Normandy; I drove him down to Southwick for a conference at the headquarters of Admiral Ramsay.

The following day, a Sunday, was equally full. Shocked at reports the wounded were being evacuated too slowly, he hurried back to London for a series of meetings which demanded full priority for these operations and all others concerned with loadings. After a staff conference on the best use of Mediterranean forces for the invasion of southern France in August, he then jumped into the car and we started on another evening London-Portsmouth trip.

Monday, June 12, was a big day for General Eisenhower. Leaving our CP before six o'clock in the morning, he took the visiting V-I-P party to Normandy. And they went right onto the beaches—the Supreme Commander's first step onto Nazi Europe. (The impatient Prime Minister also picked that Monday for his first visit to Normandy, followed the next day by General de Gaulle; two days later, by King George VI.) General Ike came back about 8:30 P.M., feeling chipper that he had got ashore at long last, invigorated by actually visiting the troops, and happy that everyone's spirits seemed so high.

In addition, there was another, unofficial reason for his happiness—a reunion with his son. Graduated from West Point on D-Day, Second Lieutenant John S. D. Eisenhower was en route to England to spend leave with his famous father. General Ike had dispatched Tex Lee to Prestwick to meet John.

That same Monday was memorable for all of us in England: it marked the first V-1 attack on the British Isles.

Only three or four out of two dozen actually hit London the first night. The official communiqué was rather tardy and therefore failed to dam back the flood of rumor which always follows first use of a secret weapon. London, although well baptized by bombing, was somewhat frightened by wild stories of a "pilotless plane" which dropped its bombs and then returned to Europe for another load. This so-called robot bomber was the sole subject of conversation, even overshadowing progress of the invasion.

Within an incredibly short time, the V-1 was an accepted part of daily life in London and southeastern England, much as heavy fire and high explosive raids had been during the Blitz. "Pilotless plane" stories evaporated as thousands learned, firsthand, the new

V-1 was not a robot bomber but a self-propelled bomb. And it became known, in exacting slang, as the buzz-bomb.

As they rained down with increasing frequency, the V-1's caused extensive damage and horrible casualties. Their blast was so powerful that windows disappeared even more quickly than in 1940, shattering glass for hundreds of feet in all directions whenever one landed. Residential areas were hard hit, one bomb often demolishing an entire row of houses. Defense was all but impossible, although fast fighters tried to shoot them down in open country and ack-ack batteries kept up an almost continual barrage in the area outside London. The V-1's kept coming, more and more of them, day and night.

Nerves were the greatest casualty. All of us froze whenever the drone of a buzz-bomb approached. I dreaded it much more than the Nazi bomber; the latter, at least, was subject to human error and fear—and we had the satisfaction of hearing our own planes, our own ack-ack, at work in defense. The buzz-bomb, however, was a *machine*, inhuman. The nearer it traveled, the louder it became, the nearer the danger. Even worse was the horrible silence when its engine cut off. That meant the huge bomb was headed down, perhaps straight down, perhaps in a long glide in any direction. One could only wait, terrified. There was a very selfish relief in hearing the explosion, elsewhere, just as there was a relief in hearing the Thing continue on overhead, to land somewhere else, *any*where else.

To me, the buzz-bomb was the most dreadful, impersonal, dangerous, and nerve-wracking weapon of the war. Above all, it never stopped, day or night. Everyone in London became touchy-tempered from lack of sleep and the incessant strain. London office work was disrupted many times a day as the "imminent danger" signal sounded, warning of at least one V-1 headed straight for that particular area. At Widewing, that meant running out to blast shelters, clutching at Secret papers, listening with every pore and nerve, tight with the eternal waiting, waiting,

waiting. Quite a few landed in the section around Bushy Park, indicating a German interest in our headquarters. One hit a London base command building, one hit a crowded hotel just off Piccadilly Circus, another hit the popular Lansdowne restaurant. Actually, hardly a section of London was spared; some sectors were reduced to rubble. (One of the most tragic incidents occurred when a buzz-bomb fell flat on a truckload of G-I "casuals" just leaving to help dig Londoners out of V-1 debris; these men, awaiting assignments and volunteering to do their bit in London, literally disappeared.)

The situation soon became so dangerous that Allied bomber targets were shifted to V-1 platform sites in France, ordered to erase as many as possible, as quickly as possible.

Meanwhile, I was busy driving General Eisenhower between Widewing and London, between London and Portsmouth. The buzz-bomb was but one of many of his pressing problems. He went over to Normandy several times. He fought until the shipping situation began to straighten out, until experts promised to have Cherbourg in working order within ten days. He introduced his son to historic figures, sat up till late talking to John about memories, present headaches, and future plans. He set up an A-1 priority on combat troops and ammunition. He saw General Marshall and his party off to North Africa. He worried about the weather, de Gaullist complications, a delayed attack in Normandy, supply shortages, incompetent commanders, manpower.

Throughout all these gigantic harassments, General Ike carried on a running duel with Mr. Churchill over Mediterranean plans.

(As the Prime Minister was one of the few figures who outranked my Boss, the telephone protocol was staggering and amusing. A secretary at Downing Street would call me, I would tell General Ike that Mr. Churchill was calling, Downing Street would put The Prime's private secretary on the wire, I would put The General on the wire, and, finally, the secretary would get Mr. Churchill on the wire.)

The Prime Minister and a large part of His Majesty's military and political forces were strongly opposed to "Anvil," the invasion of southern France. Ike, most of the Americans, and many of the Anglo-American SHAEF staff were just as adamant in their insistence upon the operation. Mr. Churchill carried the fight to General Eisenhower, via telephone calls, lunches, late-hour meetings, and every voluble argument in his celebrated mind. The General was just as dogged, and, of course, eventually won the battle, with Mr. Churchill becoming his most fervent supporter.

In the month after the invasion of Normandy, however, the constant bickering over "Anvil" consumed much of General Ike's time and energy. The office diary made note of it almost daily. On June 22, for example, less than three weeks before D-Day in southern France, General Eisenhower mentioned a meeting with General "Jumbo" Wilson's Chief of Staff for AFHQ; Eisenhower postscript in the diary: "Told him I want an Anvil, quickly. Am against an attack into Hungary via Trieste." The next day I noted in the diary that the Boss went into London for a conference with the Prime Minister and told the latter he was flatly against any move into Trieste. And a note on June 27 quoted Mr. Churchill as being absolutely set on the capture of Trieste.

Two days later, I lost all interest in Trieste, "Anvil," even the Prime Minister.

General Ike, still worrying about rain holding up action on Monty's front, had several of us out to Telegraph Cottage for dinner. John, he said, was fretting because the West Point graduation leave was almost over; he was due back at Fort Benning.

"I'm sending John home in my B-17," the General explained. "Tex is going along. So are Mattie Pinette and Sergeant Farr." He looked at me. "There's a spare place and I know you're anxious to meet Dick's mother. How would you like to go along?"

I promptly forgot the war and entered into a little war of my own—an exit permit to leave England. My final attack on official lethargy was in the form of a telephone call from the Supreme Commander's office. The permit came through immediately.

Our send-off from the Germans was a buzz-bomb. It landed several hundred yards away and rattled the car windows as we drove out to the airport.

All of us breathed a sigh of relief when London and the airport were far behind. In an airplane, the thought of being struck by a V-1 is particularly frightening.

Prestwick, major airport for transatlantic flights during the war, was muddy, windy, and rainswept. But without the steady purr of buzz-bombs, it was beautiful. The bar and the civilian-airline atmosphere of the dining room created an appropriate atmosphere for our take-off to the United States.

Iceland, first stop on our long trip over the North Atlantic, proved to be as dull, dreary, and unexciting as everyone proclaimed. The Colonel who rushed out to greet General Eisenhower's B-17 and the General's son immediately made quite a fuss over our second lieutenant V-I-P and invited us into the Senior Mess. John, with an endearing insistence upon being treated like any other second lieutenant, refused the gushy attention. We did, however, take the only sight-seeing tour offered by that lonely base, a wild, bat-out-of-Hell drive over bumpy roads to lava beds. The latter were as disappointing as the barren landscape, the fields fertilized (and odorized) with masses of fish. Wartime duty in Iceland was, as any veteran will bear out, maddening.

"Where are the trees?" we asked our driver, a G-I who talked with all the intensity of a prisoner who has been in solitary confinement. "Trees?" he mused. "Trees? What are they? I've been in Iceland *two years.*"

On the flight to Bangor I got to know John Eisenhower a little better. Taller than his father, slender, and clean-cut in appearance, he seemed excessively modest, leaning almost too far backward in his anxiety to avoid unfair use of the Eisenhower name. He had an absolute horror of Brass. I noticed in London that he and his father enjoyed a unique relationship, more friendly than soppily sentimental, more chummy than most fathers and sons; it was an adult relationship. John, incidentally, had the General's flair for writing and expression. And even an idiot could see he adored his father.

Our B-17 landed at Bangor in beautiful weather, with Mattie shrieking ecstatically at setting foot once more in her native state of Maine. I was no less thrilled at my first step on American soil. Even more thrilling was the PX, stocked with hundreds of items long forgotten in England. All of us—Tex, Mattie, Sergeant Farr, and I—immediately ordered great quantities of milk. Within a short time we taxed our stomachs with everything from chicken to raw butter, every scarcity of which we had dreamed in England and Africa.

En route to Washington, the heat and our gorgings combined to make most of us nauseated: I was sick, plain sick, overwhelmed by the rich food.

Circling over America's capital, I could see the planned beauty of the city, great circles with avenues jutting out like spokes in wheels, great parks studded with magnificent buildings, midget bridges spanning the Potomac and leading into suburban Virginia.

The white buildings actually seemed dazzling as we came in for the landing. I thought of London's gray, wartime drabness, aged beside these bright new structures.

But the heat was even more dazzling. I found it more humid and intense than anything we encountered in North Africa, worse than the Egyptian desert. Stepping out of the plane was like stepping into a giant boiler room. The sun's glare was blinding.

Two women rushed up to welcome us to Washington. One was Mrs. George Allen; the other, Mrs. Mamie Eisenhower. I found the General's wife an attractive, petite woman, her bangs the hint to a vivacious, friendly personality. We all chatted excitedly. Then Mrs. Eisenhower and Mrs. Allen went off to town, with John in tow, promising to call.

Tex, bless him, had arranged hotel reservations in overcrowded

Washington. Despite the handicap of conducting these negotiations from London, he had obtained rooms in a downtown hotel.
We started out, with everyone pointing out the sights to me. I
was intrigued by the absence of bomb damage, the whole and un-
shattered window glass. Peculiarly, perhaps, I didn't feel the
slightest bit of resentment at this vast, luxurious, unbombed but
wartime United States; I could only bask in the peacetime atmosphere, the air of plenty.

With my driving background, I was amazed at the thousands
upon thousands of civilian cars. I gaped and gawked at those
autos; of all sizes, shapes, and colors, they poured through the
street in a terrifying procession of traffic. Everyone in America
must own a limousine, I thought, absolutely everyone—and the
petrol ration must be a myth.

Also, I saw for the first time what Yanks abroad meant by the
word "block." Washington's streets and avenues were straight,
crisscrossed as perfectly as lines on an accountant's ledger. A
"block," I could see, is a definite distance in the United States;
in London and most European cities, where streets curve and
wander without plan or sense, a "block" might be 10 feet or 100
yards long.

Tex, Mattie, and Sergeant Farr were amused by my first impressions of this New World. Amused, but not too interested,
they were busy reacting to the thrill of being home—and they
didn't lose much time heading for their respective states.

Next afternoon, I went up to the fashionable Wardman Park
to visit Mrs. Eisenhower, who greeted me at the door with a welcome, tinkling, orange-filled Old Fashioned. Her cordiality helped
me to meet the wives of various friends around headquarters,
men I had known in North Africa and in England. In the beginning, I felt strange and foreign, much too British and much too
militarized for this forgotten social side of femininity. But their
natural friendliness soon thawed my embarrassment. Moreover,
we had mutual interests, mutual friends: their husbands. I enjoyed meeting the wives of overseas friends, putting flesh on the

name-skeletons rattled so continuously by lonely husbands abroad; they enjoyed meeting someone who knew their husbands, who could tell them how their husbands looked, how they felt, what they ate, where they lived, et cetera. It was a lovely afternoon and I enjoyed it thoroughly.

The noise in Washington early the morning of July 4 seeped into my dreams; I awakened in a cold sweat, half-awake, shaking with fright which took me right back to the London of 1940. Even after the hotel management explained July-the-Fourth celebrations, I jumped nervously each time a firecracker exploded with bomb-like noise. The day seemed much too long; the strain left me limp by sundown. Then, however, I sat enthralled by the Technicolor spectacle in the skies, a fireworks display far surpassing anything in England on Guy Fawkes Day. The night was simply gorgeous with exploding color.

Second Lieutenant Eisenhower guided me around the tourist Washington, explaining points of interest with a clear, factual, interesting manner similar to that of his father when discussing future operations at a staff meeting. He was the perfect guide, the perfect gentleman, almost apologetic that neither he nor the city had felt war.

We saw every building from the impressive Lincoln Memorial to the stately Capitol, from the White House to the Jefferson Memorial. We even traveled to the top of Washington Monument, where the view gave me a final conviction that Washington is one of the world's loveliest of cities, very reminiscent of Paris.

The heat was all but unbearable, worse than anything I had experienced from Marrakech to Luxor.

I saw the female side of Washington with one of Tex's friends, a girl who now is one of my very best friends. She mothered me through the initial shock of American department, grocery, clothing, and drug stores.

Coming direct from rationed, wartime London, where peace and peacetime goods and peacetime courtesy were only memories almost five years old, I needed some mothering.

"Would it be possible to get a bottle of fingernail polish?" I asked a friendly salesgirl in a huge department store. In war-born humility, I gushed without pride, begging shamelessly. "If you could only spare one bottle . . . just one little bottle . . . ?"

She laughed, then added kindly, "Of course, as many as you want! You're English aren't you? We get quite a few of your countrymen in here." The smile faded. She leaned on the counter, all sympathy. "It must be terrible over there. I've been reading about those horrible buzz-bombs. You're all so brave! Sometimes I wonder if New York or Washington could . . ."

The experience was typical in so many ways. The abundance of merchandise, the friendliness of everyone in America, and the universal sympathy, the rather humble respect for people actually feeling the cold brunt of warfare. I was embarrassed, often, at the constant remarks about how brave we were to stand up to the bombs, and now, to the buzz-bombs. Actually, I felt a sheepish heroine, for I knew many of these people's own relatives and friends were the real heroes that very moment, anywhere from Normandy to the Pacific.

Most of my first impressions are familiar to anyone entering the United States for the first time: The clean, smart appearance of the people . . . The wonder, the miracle of drug stores, their overly stocked shelves, their soda fountains . . . The goods in all windows . . . The precociousness of American children . . . The hordes of civilians . . . The large, streamlined taxicabs, as compared with the tiny, ancient hacks of London . . . The friendliness of Americans, whether cab drivers, soda-fountain waiters, store clerks, or hotel porters.

Amid all this excitement I tried to get in touch with Dick's mother at her home in New York State. Innumerable telephone calls (which impressed me with the speed and courtesy of long-distance operators in America) disclosed Mrs. Arnold to be en route to Florida. No one knew exactly how she was going, where she would stay down there.

So when John suggested a quick sight-seeing trip to New York,

I jumped at the chance. Perhaps I could get in touch with some of Mrs. Arnold's friends, who could furnish more details; I didn't want to leave the United States without seeing her.

New York, strangely, wasn't half the experience that Washington was, probably because the former is so similar to its likeness in story, song, and films. It seemed only right that the skyscrapers be so tall, so bizarre; the crowds were as dense as a European would expect, just as hurried and rude and energetic as I'd heard. The nicest view was that from atop the Empire State Building, with Manhattan a mere toy island-city far below. John thoughtfully arranged for me to see a typically American musical comedy: "Oklahoma!" It was as lavish as any Hollywood musical; I was especially struck by the large number of males in the cast, which would have been impossible in wartime London.

The telephone failed to help me locate Mrs. Arnold. But I did learn that she was driving down South, alone; I got a description of her and the automobile. Then, back in Washington, I got in touch with some of my Secret Service friends who had been with President Roosevelt in North Africa. Could they help?

They could . . . and would . . . and did. Mrs. Arnold's description was given out to hundreds of highway patrolmen north and south of Washington.

Eventually, however, even the Secret Service gave up. No one of that description, driving alone, had been seen anywhere along the highway.

Once again I called New York, over and over, until a call to Mrs. Arnold's attorney finally obtained her Florida address. I telegraphed immediately.

Two days before our party was due to head back to London, she called from Florida, distraught at driving right through Washington, unaware I was there on a visit. She laughed at my Secret Service dragnet, then explained that, instead of making the trip alone and following her planned route, she had taken along a friend and wandered along an entirely different highway. The Secret Service couldn't be blamed.

"But you must get down here somehow, Kay," she said. "We simply must get together somehow!"

This time, General Marshall's aide was my fairy godfather. He provided passage on a beat-up C-47 cargo plane, with a "White House" priority which insured I wouldn't be "bumped off" for higher Brass.

I had a wonderful day and a night with Mrs. Arnold, collecting a bad case of sunburn in Miami . . . and, more important, a new, close friend.

And I didn't have to ride back in that bucket-seat C-47. Our old B-17 showed up in Miami. Captain Larry Hansen, General Eisenhower's pilot, had a double reason for coming down: firstly, we were due to leave for England the very next day; secondly, his wife lived in nearby Coral Gables. We took off for Washington that afternoon.

The B-17 developed engine trouble just as we landed that night at National Airport. We would have another day or two in Washington.

I really went shopping then, thankful—in that heat—for the one civilian dress I owned. I toured every store and shop in the downtown section. I bought hose for myself, blouses for Mother, girdles and other queer items for some of the girls back in London. (The list they gave me before leaving was exceeded in length only by my "call" list; I'm sure I telephoned anxious parents and wives in half of the United States, each time going to great detail to explain why a British girl was calling. It was fun, though, and very, very warming.)

Washington, I realized with surprise, was jammed with women, certainly four or five to every man. Fresh from London, I was wide-eyed at the smart uniforms of various services; the Marine auxiliary wore quite the most attractive I'd ever seen on women at war, despite a musical comedy touch to the hat and the high heels which seemed incongruous with the WAC uniform, stern and military in comparison.

Some of the Army wives I met this time left a bad taste in my memory. A few seemed so calculating, so cold. They gauged each other purely by rank, more so than the most rank-conscious West Pointer; all social and personal attention centered on those whose husbands carried more Brass. And, I'm afraid, a shocking amount of that attention was focused on the ranking leaders with but one of two ideas in mind, sometimes both: a promotion for the husband, and/or a transfer to better duty, preferably in the United States.

I was hurt, then angered at the slander of WAC's overseas. The girls in London and Algiers had told me about it, but I still didn't believe such selfish venom existed until I ran right into it in Washington. Some of the most social Army wives made it quite clear—crystal-clear—they regarded any uniformed female overseas as a mere "camp follower."

I looked at these Washington wives in their smart frocks, nibbling luxurious foods, making cocktail talk, safe in one of the world's few unbombed cities. Then I thought of the WAC's working long and thankless hours overseas, often living in tents or buggy barracks, anxious about loved ones in battle, still carrying on. I thought of Red Cross girls who got up before dawn to drive their Clubmobiles onto isolated airfields, distributing coffee, doughnuts, and good American cheer to airmen taking off for possible death over Europe. I thought of the mutilated men I'd seen in hospitals, of the American nurses who worked day after day with those wounded, drawing upon a personal courage almost holy in its selflessness. I thought of the nurses I'd seen in the waters around our torpedoed *Strathallen,* the nurses staggering through the mud in Tunisia at the time of Kasserine Pass.

How, I wondered, how could these Washington gossips have the colossal conceit and self-deception not to see their own shameful images? How could they lump all overseas service women into one dirty group and then jab it with woman's cruelest weapon against woman: moral slander?

Being human, I was even more upset at learning my own reputation was lost. In addition to being a woman overseas, I was a *foreign* woman—and I traveled with the High Brass. Therefore, I was a Bad Woman. This was fact, gleefully acknowledged and established fact. These women didn't—and don't—leave any loophole for doubt; they didn't—and don't—give any opportunity for defense. Nothing I could say or do would change this attitude. I was classified, labeled, and filed.

This all-out assault upon my character hurt; it hurt terribly. After the hurt came resentment; after the resentment, anger. I thought bitterly of my ambulance days in the Blitz, of my torpedoing in the Mediterranean, of my driver's life in North Africa. I thought bitterly of Dick. I thought of my day-to-day work, small but directly connected with the war. And I thought of all the kindness, the gentlemanly and understanding kindness shown me by some of these wives' own husbands; it wasn't fair to those men, let alone to me.

My wounds soon hardened into scar tissue destined to stay inflamed the rest of my life. Practically every woman who served abroad in uniform bears this wound. It's the one thing we'll never forgive, never forget. It's the most painful wound of all, for a woman—and it didn't come from the enemy.

(Nor has it stopped with the return of peace. A small, wicked voice inside cries out: "Next war, My Girl, you may as well do all these things of which you're accused; they'll *say* you did, anyhow!")

Tarnished but slightly by this one experience, the Washington visit drew to a close. I spent most of the last hours stuffing piggishly, covering everything from milkshakes and orange juice to meat, salads, and fresh vegetables, all the delicacies I'd miss in London

At the same time, I noticed a growing impatience with this selfish holiday. I wondered about the buzz-bombs, about Mother. I wondered about headquarters, about the official family, about

Normandy. Tex, Mattie, and Sergeant Farr admitted to the same emotions.

That old war-born sense of urgency surged through all of us as the B-17 took off, circled the lovely city of Washington for a final salute, and then headed "home" . . . back to the war.

CHAPTER XIII

AFTER a long but uneventful flight across the North Atlantic from Newfoundland to Prestwick, we found ourselves back in that war in a hurry. It was waiting for us right in London.

In the fortnight since our departure, Widewing and the surrounding area had become a primary target for flying bombs. One bomb exploded within five hundred feet of our own office wing, injuring four or five persons, lifting the roof from Beetle's secret corridor to General Eisenhower's office, and blowing glass out of windows. Stories on the damage in London proper were downright frightening.

Mattie stopped off at our house to give the girls some firsthand news of the United States. Tex and I hurried over to Telegraph Cottage to report on our American tour.

We found the General entertaining a few close friends, with champagne donated by a British admirer. But we couldn't get our tourist talk into the conversation; these people were interested only in flying bombs.

One had landed so near Telegraph Cottage that an upstairs room lost some of its ceiling plaster. General Ike and his entire household staff frankly confessed to spending several nights in the big shelter nearby.

My own fears returned with a rush when a buzz-bomb suddenly roared overhead, its chugging, putt-putt motor drowning all conversation. Everyone froze when it cut off. There was a dreadful silence—then, an explosion in the distance.

I spent that Saturday night in the shelter.

Back in the office, I worked extra hard and long to make up for my American holiday. The General's "fan mail" gave my desk the appearance of a post-office table. Looking into the office diary, I saw he had maintained the day-by-day notes from June 30 to July 15. They gave some indication of his activity:

Bradley attack to south now postponed to July 3. How I suffer! . . . Arrived in France about 6:15 p.m. . . . Learned our new anti-tank equipment and our 76 mm. in Sherman are not capable of taking on Panthers and Tigers. Sent long wire to Bedell to begin investigation . . . Attack goes very slowly. Bad weather handicapping air. Selection of artillery targets most difficult in this close country . . . Went with Bradley to artillery battery while he pulled the lanyard on a Long Tom as part of a scheme for celebrating July 4th. The orders were for every gun to be fired at German positions (1 round) at exactly noon . . . In fairness to all troops it must be said that swamps, hedges, bad weather all combine to make great difficulties . . . 2nd British Army at long last begins a rather ambitious attack. Preceded by bombing by 500 heavies . . . Dinner with Secretary of War . . .

Little notes here and there indicated the Eisenhower personal touch:

Must go to Portsmouth. Wish I could get time to see Telek. Butch's friends to dinner. Tried to play bridge. Awful.

The entries also touched on flying bombs:

In shelter 5 times today on "imminent danger."
Buzz bombs chased us to cover about 6 times during the afternoon and 3 or 4 after going home.
Large number of "buzzers" at Portsmouth last evening.
Went to Stanmore for air conference. Long discussion of use of air, including attacks on "buzz-bombs" and rockets.

I knew, aside from personal experience, the flying bomb danger must be great, if General Ike, who preferred death to the personal indignity of going to shelter (he approved construction of that shelter only on condition it be big enough for everyone in the neighborhood) could take up this much space in his sparse notes to mention the bombardment.

The full extent of England's danger came home to me less than two weeks later when I saw secret reports covering the weeks of damage since the buzz-bombs started: all in all, well over sixteen thousand persons killed or seriously injured. In purely military terms, that would mean the equivalent of more than a division wiped out in only five or six weeks. London, already well into a housing shortage after the Blitz destruction, was receiving almost half of all the V-1's sent over England. And the new weapon already had damaged a staggering total of more than 700,000 British homes; approximately 15,000 had completely disappeared. The V-1 was far from a last-ditch weapon.

Atop all this, I heard staff officers whispering in the General's office about a V-2. This was another secret weapon, reportedly able to climb so high, so fast, that nothing could stop it. And the V-2 was supposed to have a far greater blast than the V-1. Hearing such speculation and, at the same time, running out to shelter or slit trench several times a day, I began taking a personal interest in reports on the bombing of V-weapon launching sites.

At least the worry of Telek shivering alone in a kennel during these raids was over. I drove out to get him a week after we arrived in London; he seemed as happy as a human being released from prison. (Caacie got out of quarantine shortly afterward.) Telek hated the buzz-bombs as much as the rest of us, although after the long incarceration in his kennel, he obviously was thankful for human company during the alerts. He needed it and demanded it. There were twenty-four "imminent danger" signals the very day he came out to Widewing and things got worse, instead of better. Telek jumped up in Sue Sarafin's lap, for comfort, whenever she came into my office to take dictation.

Meanwhile, General Eisenhower was beset by a thousand worries. The Prime Minister maintained his barrage of objections to the invasion of southern France, he insisted on touring the battle area, he called for all-out assaults to destroy the Nazis, he pressed for heavier air attacks upon V-weapon platforms. The General fretted, alternately, about difficulties holding up General Bradley's attack and Monty's push. He was forced to take demotion action aginst a general officer for failure in battle. Privately, he sank into the depths of despair when the Air Force messed up a co-ordinated assault by dropping its bombs "short," killing some of our own troops, including Lieutenant General L. J. McNair, a high War Department observer who had been wounded previously in Tunisia.

Inevitably, the General suffered several bad headaches, complained about his blood pressure and, in a rare mood of fatigue, spent one morning in bed. His only social engagement during the rest of July, outside of frequent bouts with the Prime Minister, was a luncheon in Portsmouth aboard Lord Nelson's old flagship, *The Victory*, built about 180 years before the "V" became a symbol for victory in our war. Several times, General Ike drove off from the Southwick CP in a jeep, by himself, and took short flights in an L-5 observation plane to "get away from it all . . . and you all."

Always, the General had Monty gnawing at his nerves.

As a patriotic Briton, I shared the universal British respect for General Montgomery's historic success in the desert. As a woman and as a civilian, I didn't pretend to understand his military troubles, such as the concentration of Germans on his front, the lack of replacements, and the like. *But*, as a SHAEF staff member, as part of the official family, and as secretary-driver to General Eisenhower, I grew to dislike the very name of Montgomery. In my personal opinion, he gave the Supreme Commander more worry than any other one individual in the entire Allied command.

It wasn't a question of nationality. Some of General Ike's best

friends and open admirers were crusty Britishers such as the
Prime Minister, Admiral Sir Andrew Cunningham, and Air
Chief Marshal Tedder. Dwight Eisenhower was the one man
available in the Western armies who could mould AFHQ, then
SHAEF, into closely knit Allied headquarters which rose above
national rivalries and characteristics to win the greatest war in
Europe's history.

It wasn't a mere question of temperament, for Ike handled the
explosive General Patton with kid gloves lined in mail—and Patton invariably offered the closest of co-operation, despite his
occasional bad-press flurries. (Just after General Marshall approved Patton's promotion in August, General Eisenhower gave
out orders that any future statement by Blood-and-Guts could be
struck out by censors. Correspondents understood.)

Monty, Britain's most glamorous and successful general to
date, simply couldn't be sacked. That was the simple, unspoken
truth, in my opinion. His retirement from European action would
have kicked up a storm in Britain big enough to smash Allied
unity.

My own guess is General Ike knew that, all too well. He had
no scruples about replacing officers who didn't measure up to his
yardstick of efficiency; he reduced generals right and left. One
was a good friend and a West Point classmate; when this man
failed in combat, however, Ike decided the Supreme Commander
couldn't afford the luxury of friendship at the expense of the
war effort. He reduced the divisional commander to a colonel.
(This particular officer was pure gold. He took the demotion
gracefully, begged not to be returned to the States in disgrace,
stayed on in action as a colonel, and eventually won his stars
back—the hard way.) Regardless, the fact remained that Monty
was in the line-up, for better or for worse.

Unfortunately, I thought it was often the latter.

The June day we left for Washington, for instance, General
Eisenhower entered in the diary: "Saw Tedder who is just returned from the beachhead. Monty momentarily expecting heavy

counter-attack which he is confident of defeating. Meanwhile he is just waiting."

Six days later he added: "Wrote letter to Monty urging all-out offensive to break the deadlock and get elbow room."

By the middle of July, Monty's delay in attacks, his excessive caution, and his reluctance to attack until he had a force as powerful as that at El Alamein, had many officers against him. General Ike went over to France on the twentieth; returning, he said Monty seemed quite satisfied with his own progress, as though it were up to Bradley to go ahead. Next day, Air Chief Marshal Tedder sent in a letter upbraiding Monty—the tone indicated Monty actually might be unsuitable for his job. Tedder agreed with Ike the idea of "limited attacks" was all wrong. A week later, the General wrote Monty that he just *had* to keep going.

Throughout the campaign in Western Europe, it seemed to me that Monty plagued the General with this same sort of worry, the cries for more men and supplies, the excuses for not taking bold, Patton-like action.

(To be specific: on August 20, Monty was fearful he had insufficient troops to move into the Pas de Calais area. Three days later, he wanted ten U.S. divisions to help in that sector. On the twenty-fifth, British and American air generals dining with Ike complained that Monty was the only planner against use of airborne troops around Pas de Calais; as one remarked, "Monty just doesn't understand airborne operations." On September 5, Monty messaged General Ike proposing a single advance to the Rhine while American troops, in effect, were to stay put. Five days afterward, the General went off to Brussels to see Monty, who demanded all kinds of supplies.

(On September 11, while I was in London getting supplies from Widewing, General Eisenhower wrote in the diary: "Discussions covered entire field of next month's operations. Bradley (as always) most co-operative. Patton has just started across Moselle . . . Ramsay came out in P.M. Much worried because Monty seems unimpressed by necessity for taking Antwerp approaches." General Ike added, the next day: "After discussing ways and means of supporting left flank, sent Beetle off to see Monty to find out just what we had to do. Monty's suggestion is simply—give him everything. This is crazy . . ."

(One message from Montgomery on September 20 requested all available supplies; another requested permission to keep the airborne divisions. Two days later, another pair of messages: he wanted more supplies and he wanted the battle line altered.

(October was just the same. On the eighth, Monty advised Ike he was not strong enough to accomplish feats SHAEF expected of him. He must protect his flanks. After General Eisenhower insisted for weeks upon all-out assault of Antwerp, it wasn't until October 10 that Monty's directive placed the port's capture in highest priority. Et cetera, et cetera, et cetera.)

In late July, however, Monty was but one of General Eisenhower's multitudinous problems. Most of all he was interested in getting an Advance CP set up on the Continent.

On July 29 I flew over with him in a B-25 escorted by fighters. We landed on a muddy airstrip known simply as "A-9." It was my first visit to Normandy and my first step on liberated Europe. I saw no civilians, no dead Germans, no bomb damage. In fact, it was no different from an Army area in rural England. The only point of interest was a cow, fat and healthy, in sharp contrast to the scene in Italy, where the Germans shot all cattle. We stayed only a few hours and then returned to England.

For three days General Ike was so depressed by the delays in attacks, the Prime Minister's worries about V-2's, and other SHAEF problems that he suffered from high blood pressure and headaches. Then, on August 2, the news that Patton was loose in Brittany jacked up his spirits and his health. Even the noise of buzz-bombs that night—when almost 100 got through—failed to dampen his ardor. He made his eleventh trip to France the next day, returning with a demand that offices cut down on the use of personnel and not be so extravagant with precious manpower.

The Prime Minister came down to our Southwick CP for lunch on August 5 and—just ten days before the invasion of southern France was to take place—spent the whole of the time arguing against it. Mattie and I enjoyed his classic language and marveled at General Ike's refusal to back down as much as an inch from his opinion that "Anvil" was necessary to the main operation in Normandy. A message from the Combined Chiefs of Staff in Washington the next night gave the go-ahead signal for "Anvil" on August 15.

Characteristically, with this old political battle over, Ike promptly turned again to the future. On August 7, he conferred with Secretary of the Treasury Henry Morgenthau on monetary problems which might arise in Germany. He chose a temporary CP for SHAEF on the Continent, named Granville as the next headquarters after that, and, in keeping with his unification policy, decided to bring naval and air staffs into our new headquarters on the Continent.

That night his official family moved right behind him into Europe.

"Shellburst," our new CP in a Normandy apple orchard, was no different from a hundred other command posts in France. Mickey, Hunt, Moaney and the rest of the household staff, having learned tricks of the trade at our Southwick CP, soon had the entire tented area running smoothly. General Eisenhower worked out of his trailer, as usual. We girls camped in a nearby field reserved for women only and guarded as carefully as ammunition. Actually, we found Normandy a sort of rustic, pastoral retreat. And, free of the buzz-bombs, we had our first good nights of sleep in weeks.

General Ike's spirits soared visibly at being on the Continent, able to visit commanders and troops on the spot once more.

The morning after our arrival I drove him to see General Bradley at St. Jean de Daye, where the pair immediately set out on a tour. Even after the damage in London, I was amazed at the terrific destruction; whole villages were reduced to little more than rubble. There were few civilians.

The following morning General Eisenhower had to fly back to London. There, his principal order to Beetle demanded that SHAEF offices and staff members be pushed into France as quickly as possible, that a *real*, complete headquarters be established right behind the troops. Beetle agreed wholeheartedly. Before coming back, the General managed to inspect both the 82nd and 101st Airborne Divisions, to which he distributed a number of decorations after receiving a tumultuous welcome.

In our CP, he set about re-establishing the bridge games which gave him such relaxation. General Bradley teamed with Mattie against General Eisenhower and me soon thereafter; from then on, the lines were drawn. The Eisenhower-Summersby team won that first night, starting new banking difficulties in the conversion of francs into pounds, still our monetary basis.

Then, as later, I found General Bradley a peaceful, charming, alert companion. Speaking with a quiet tone which belied a fighter's heart, he endeared himself to all of us in the official family as much as he did to his own First Army G-I's. Then—as throughout the rest of the war—I regarded him as the only other General in either the British or American armies under whom I would enjoy serving.

That, I know, is a sweeping statement; especially when it comes from one who met just about every famous and infamous general in the Allied armies. But it is typical of the sort of respect, admiration, and loyalty Omar Bradley commands from those who know him. All of us were happy when, three days after that bridge party, a message came in from Washington verifying the rumor that General Bradley was to become a permanent two-star general.

Most of August was filled with headline combat news. The invasion of southern France cracked German defenses wide open and troops poured into Vichy country up as far as Grenoble, taking such spots as the vital Marseilles port, Avignon, and Toulon. Troops from our area spilled over a great part of France from Le Mans and Orleans up to Chartres, and from Rouen to Rheims to Verdun.

But General Eisenhower, to whom these names and operations had long been familiar in planning, was looking ahead once more. For one thing, he was concerned about a long-discussed and much-debated assault upon the Pas de Calais area, which General Montgomery regarded as so impregnable that he constantly demanded more troops, more supplies, more planning.

Also, General Ike was still eyeing Germany itself. When British Foreign Secretary Eden and his party came over for lunch, the one topic of conversation was that of postwar German boundaries. General Eisenhower, even at that early date, said he believed the Russians would go ahead and do what they wanted to do, regardless of any Western decision. And, he added, as the Supreme Commander of SHAEF he felt quite definite in the view that western Germany should *not* have separate French, British, and American boundaries. This advocacy of an over all Allied boundary apparently took Secretary Eden by surprise; he admitted he hadn't thought of an Allied occupation in that sense; he thought it worthy of Cabinet discussion.

(A fortnight later, the General was so disturbed at the thought of separate boundaries in Germany that he mentioned it while bed-bound with his bad leg. I had taken some papers in for his signature, when he started off on views valuable enough for inclusion in my diary entry for September 3. The General said he would not permit SHAEF staffs to put American, British, and French boundaries on paper. He emphasized that division of western Germany into such zones could only divide the Allies; defeated Germany must be administered just as the war had been fought against Hitler Germany, on an Allied basis similar to that of SHAEF. Otherwise, he concluded, the former Allies would be at each other's throats.)

General Ike had his standard assortment of minor headaches. The British press attacked him for relieving Monty of over-all ground command. The American press attacked him for permitting "British interference and domination" despite the majority of U.S. forces over British troops. The Supreme Commander replied to all this by explaining that Monty's command was planned only for the beachhead invasion phase; now Monty had to lead 21st Army Group forces while Bradley took over 12th Army Group operations. He emphasized the Allied nature of all command and deplored the stress upon nationalities.

A message from the French offered definite evidence of widespread looting by troops, ranging from liquor hauls by privates to a silverware theft by a brigadier general.

General de Gaulle wrote to underline the importance of taking Paris, which Ike wanted to by-pass in order to save troops and supplies for use against the Germans. The French General argued that rioting and looting would become rampant in the capital, that Paris was of utmost political importance to the Allies, that Parisians faced a winter without much food or fuel.

Still, General Ike never appeared downcast, disheartened, or even disappointed in public. Occasionally he let down his guard around the inner office and in the evening bridge sessions. "You're one person," he said to me one day in a low mood, "who ever sees me with my hair down. I don't have to keep up pretenses—because you're not after rank, you don't blab to the press, and you don't gossip with staff members."

There was a trickle of V-I-P's during this period: Lord Louis Mountbatten; Generals de Gaulle, Juin, and Koenig; a group of labor leaders who got the Supreme Commander to record a speech asking for still more production in the United States. General Brehon Somervell and the War Department's Mr. Robert P. Patterson dropped in to talk about distribution of petroleum and to urge another call for more home-front war production. The man destined to head America's peacetime armed forces, Navy Secretary James Forrestal, came over for a visit. (As a personal favor he asked that Ike let him know about the progress of a relative, a lieutenant; I wrote regularly once a month, each time receiving a personal letter of appreciation.)

Between times, there were inspections and visits to other headquarters, such as those to the CP's of Generals Montgomery and Bradley.

On August 26, I drove the General on a long, tiring trip all the way to Chartres. The most memorable portion of our route ran straight through the Falaise Pocket: it was a soldier's nightmare of retreat and defeat. German equipment—splintered wagons, smashed tanks and lorries, banged-up and burned staff cars—jammed the sides of every roadway so tightly that it spilled over into the adjacent fields. Horses, swollen in death, covered the area, each in a grotesque position. The litter, the gigantic, awful litter, was unbelievable. Hundreds of distorted German bodies testified to the sudden power of the Allies' trap; some covered the ground for hundreds of yards in all directions, others hung limply from tanks and lorries; some were only gruesome parts. I was glad when we emerged from the Falaise section, leaving the sickly odor and sight of death far behind.

Arriving at General Bradley's headquarters in Chartres, we found the very air vibrating with one magic, romantic word: *Paris.*

An Intelligence general, somewhat giddy, walked up and sighed, rolling his eyes, "I've spent the night in Paris. It's wild, just plain wild, a Mardi Gras and a battle! First time I've ever been shot at—and kissed—at the same time!"

At this and other stories from men just back from Paris, the correspondents yelled up such a storm that General Eisenhower said they could go into the city that night. I begged to go along but the General said he couldn't be responsible for my safety.

Everyone at headquarters agreed that the Supreme Commander himself should go into Paris, for psychological reasons. The city needed a show of strength, of Allied unity; collaborationists still were active, unconvinced the Occupation was over, really over. He acceded, asking General Bradley to accompany him and, always the SHAEF diplomat, messaging General Montgomery to ask if he wanted to come along to represent Britain. Monty declined the honor.

Our convoy started out for Paris, the war's Shangri-La, early the next morning, a Sunday, August 27. I drove Generals Eisenhower and Bradley.

With the Versailles approach described as "dangerous" by reconnaissance patrols, we had to spend more than two hours on the slow route from the south.

Entering Paris that beautiful August day of Liberation was one of the most thrilling events of my war.

On the surface, the city looked just as it had when I left there in August of 1939. The tree-lined sidewalks, the unbombed houses, the broad thoroughfares . . . all these were the same.

But many a street was blocked by crude barricades, where the people of Paris had started their own liberation. Along some areas were burned, overturned German vehicles. The only cars were those operated by mad-eyed F.F.I. men who careened through the streets with a speed matching anything in an American cops-and-robbers chase, firing their guns whenever the spirit (or a new bottle) moved them. Tanks and other armored vehicles of General Jacques Le Clerc's force roamed the avenues with a festive air immediately contagious to new arrivals; soldiers and officers alike were ecstatic with wine, women, and excitement. British, French, and American flags hung from thousands of windows, sometimes joined by crudely painted welcoming banners. The sidewalks were packed with crowds who shouted and threw kisses at our convoy. Some held gifts of wine, fruit, or flowers.

A million bicycles wound through the streets, ridden, it seemed, by a million beautiful women. No producer could have staged that parade of cycling beauties; no writer could describe it. Every male in every vehicle stared shamelessly as the girls pedaled and waved—oblivious, as only Parisian women could be, to the tufts of wind tugging at their full skirts, which often ballooned up over their waists.

All this—the undamaged city, the French troops on happy orgies, the signs, the flags, the gutted German vehicles, the people's barricades, the shouts, the odors, the bottles, the trees, the wide avenues, the women, the bicycles, the skirts—this was the Paris of every foreigner's wildest dream. Certainly, it was every soldier's dream. And I, a pallid female wallflower in Gay Paree, thrilled to it as much as anyone.

General Eisenhower first stopped off to see General de Gaulle, then Generals Giraud and Koenig.

Duty calls over, he followed his heart to the Arc de Triomphe. As I drove up to the circle and the huge arch, people began to recognize him for the first time. The one word *"Eisenhower!"* roared up in growing symphony. By the time he and General Bradley got out of the car and paid their respects to the Unknown Soldier, the Etoile was a shoving, shouting mob of near-hysterical Parisians.

General Bradley climbed into a jeep. General Ike, warned against possible crowd action, jumped into the car.

We headed down the Champs Elysées, four stars gleaming on the license plates. Proud British, French, and American flags streamed from the radiator cap.

The boulevard seethed with people. Men and women alike surged up to the open windows of our car, reaching in from their bicycles to try to kiss the General exuberantly, even to touch him.

Police barely kept the crowds in check. I had to ease the auto along in low gear.

We moved slowly down the Champs, past the famous shops, and on to the Place de la Concord.

Then we fled to the open country.

I'm sure General Eisenhower, one of the century's most honored men, will remember to his dying day that spontaneous salute by liberated Parisians.

I shall. And I was only the driver of his car.

I hate lofty, dramatic words. But there in Paris that August day—a Paris still resounding to liberating gunfire, a Paris absolutely wild with mass happiness over something intangible called Freedom—I knew exactly what the war was all about.

CHAPTER XIV

LESS than a week later General Eisenhower had one of the narrowest escapes of his wartime career. We almost lost our Boss; the Allies almost lost their Supreme Commander. His inhuman, non-stop schedule was the cause.

Just three days after the Liberation parade in Paris, he had to drop everything and take off for London. The Prime Minister wanted to smooth some wrinkles in the Mediterranean command. And the press demanded a conference to explain why Monty had been "demoted," as London papers put it, from Allied ground commander to a 21st Army Group chief on an equal basis with General Bradley and his 12th Army Group.

To save time, he ordered his staff in Normandy to move the Advance CP in his absence.

"Shellburst" was set up in the Norman seaside resort of Granville upon his return. Even so, he was enraged to find G-I's stringing up barbed wire to make a secure compound; our CP would be moved forward before they could finish the job, he emphasized. He was, however, pleased to find his mess equipped for the first time with running warm milk; the equipment consisted of two placid Norman cows. He also seemed pleased with his new quarters, an attractive little house located several miles outside Granville right on the water. Almost at the same time he heard of General Montgomery's elevation to a Field Marshall, General Ike learned that his house bore the name of "Villa Montgomery." The view rivaled that of his villa set above the Bay of Naples; here, he could look out to the picturesque old abbey of Mont-Saint-Michel, a travelogue island at high tide.

General Eisenhower didn't spend much time studying the view. On the first day of September he worked on plans for moving the main body of SHAEF from London to the Continent: the new headquarters must be north of Paris, he said, not in the city, where distractions for his staff would be worse than those of either Algiers or London; besides, he didn't relish the idea of combat troops seeing SHAEF dumped right into delicious Paris. He also spent considerable time with the personnel section, writing regulations which would forbid fraternization in Germany.

Most of his interest centered on the battle picture. The Canadians, with a fine sense of justice, had taken Dieppe. Fighting in the Brest peninsula was so heavy that one report listed some four thousand casualties to date. Patton bragged of entry into Verdun; the very name of Verdun evoked nostalgia among World War I veterans in our Advance CP, but General Eisenhower had no leisure for sentiment. "I'm going up and give Patton hell," he said, worrying because the Third Army's spectacular advance stretched supply lines to the snapping point.

The General flew up to Versailles the next morning for a long talk with Bradley. He said he would be back in a couple of hours.

Back in Granville, we watched morning fade into noon, then into afternoon. The weather was terrible. We had word the General had left Versailles, but tea-time came and went without any further message. We called airfields—only to learn the great Allied army had no trace of its own Supreme Commander.

As I later learned, Ike had insisted upon leaving Versailles that afternoon despite an ugly storm covering most of France. The pilot, hardly one to argue with a four-star General, shrugged grimly and took off.

The plane went sour shortly afterward. They had to land in isolated Chartres.

There, instead of stopping for repairs to the plane or proceeding by car, the General required that he continue on by air, at once. The pilot therefore located one of the tiny, one-passenger

Cub liaison planes with which Ike was already familiar—and they took off in the rain.

The little L-5 brought them through to Granville in comparatively good shape, but they couldn't find the airfield. Their petrol was running out.

The pilot took a calculated risk: he headed for the narrow beach near Villa Montgomery. Although the beach might be mined, they couldn't land in the water, or on the foggy airport.

They made a perfect landing.

The next worry was the plane, threatened by rising tides. General Ike pitched in to help the pilot move the ship onto dry land. Pushing and pulling through the soggy sand, however, he twisted his knee, his so-called "good knee."

Then, with the plane safe, the two of them, dripping and muddy, staggered almost a mile cross-country to the road. The first vehicle to pass by was a jeep, driven by a G-I who stared incredulously at the sight of an air-force pilot and a limping four-star general. The soldier rushed them down the road without asking a single question.

Ike was welcomed to Villa Montgomery like a man risen from the dead. He got *extra-super*-service that night from the household staff.

When I took some papers in for his signature next morning, he was laid up in bed, the twisted knee in a rubber bandage, the leg stiff as a rifle barrel. He took up such subjects as the occupation of Germany, the disposition of the invasion forces knifing up through southern France, and the selection of a new public relations officer for SHAEF. And he wailed about the injured leg, which threatened to keep him home-bound at Granville for several weeks.

But within three days, he was off again on his travels.

On September 8 he left for Paris to make an address, place a wreath on the tomb of the Unknown Soldier, and participate in a ceremony which resulted in the SHAEF patch being added to the Arc de Triomphe. That afternoon he traveled to the VIII

Corps headquarters outside Brest, due to fall eleven days later with thirty thousand prisoners of war.

That same day, the first two V-2's fell on London. Fantastic rumors poured into our headquarters; unable to lay hands on a factual report, I was ill with worry over my mother back in London.

Knowing this, General Eisenhower suggested that I take over the two-day job of gathering up supplies we needed from main headquarters at Widewing. Typically, he thought of this even while leaving for Brussels to tell Monty why he couldn't strip every other army in the field in order to give the new Field Marshal all the supplies he demanded.

Soon after landing in London I realized that scare stories about V-2 were false. The new secret weapon was terrible, it came down so quickly that even radar failed to record the flight, it ripped deep into the ground and then blew a hole about twenty to thirty feet across. But the fact that it arrived without a sound, without warning, gave Londoners a perverse, grim pleasure. They far preferred this new V-weapon to the nerve-shattering noise and suspense of the flying buzz-bomb; both were deadly, so it was much better to do without the chug-chug motor of the V-1. That seemed to be the general psychology in London; the occasional, sudden explosion of a V-2, muffled and only momentarily frightening, failed to create half the furor of nerves caused by buzz-bombs. London was taking the V-2 very much in stride.

Feeling at least a little better about the whole thing, I went back to France on the thirteenth. General Eisenhower was happy about Patton starting across the Moselle, unhappy because Monty couldn't work up any excitement—without the bribe of a complete priority on all supplies—over the order to take the vital port of Antwerp.

More personally, General Ike was bothered by his bum knee. He started keeping a journal of sorts, to justify the few short hours he "wasted" when confined to bed. A note he made in my absence also indicated a new awareness of his spotlighted role in World War II:

> Dictated all P.M. Have started to put down some of the things that might be appropriate for me to say in a personal account of the war. Good way to occupy myself when flat on my back.

His most violent gripe in this period was over the way in which Paris had been invaded by Communications Zone ("Com Z") supply headquarters.

Hours after the Liberation, sections of this headquarters began a sudden movement to the capital. The emigration from Valognes, in Normandy, was so complete that virtually every Com Z office was already set up in Paris by the time General Ike heard about the unauthorized move. Knowing that combat troops would burn with resentment at Paris, Mecca of the war and Europe's ideal leave-town, being occupied by rear-area supply troops, he really howled with anger over this violation of his hard-fast rule that no Army headquarters should locate in a large city. General Lee's staff not only had taken over Paris, they also had grabbed off the choicest, lushest spots. At the same time, Paris was so shaky in its adolescence of liberation that General Juin asked, as late as September 22, for permission to take two entire divisions out of the Army to keep order in the capital.

General Eisenhower held a number of blistering parleys with General Lee, also in disfavor because his supply troops were unloading only seventeen thousand tons per day instead of the thirty thousand demanded by operational plans. Moreover, Com Z had been warned that a slow, unescorted boat to the United States awaited the man responsible for the muck-up of signal communications.

Hardly a day went by without a new order from the Supreme Commander: Paris would be barred to all unauthorized military personnel, regardless of rank. Hotels would be returned to the French, who complained with understandable bitterness: the

Americans had taken over so many buildings the French Army itself was without sufficient accommodations. No one under the rank of lieutenant-colonel would have a private room in the capital. Supply offices would be scattered to the outskirts as much as possible.

General Ike was particularly put out at Com Z because his own headquarters was avoiding Paris, moving into Versailles.

We took our Advance CP up there in late September, joined by the main staff from Widewing in England. For the first time in months we had a complete headquarters—near the same spot where the Allies had signed a treaty with Germany a little more than twenty-five years before. None of our forces moved into the place, however; even the Germans, still rankling from 1918–19 indignities, hadn't violated Versailles Palace.

Supreme Headquarters occupied the famous Trianon Hotel. The Commander's office was separate, in an annex apparently used previously for special entertainment. The office was so huge and cavern-like that he ordered a special partition, which, since it didn't reach the high-altitude ceiling, gave me shameless opportunity to hear as much as a whisper in his sanctum. Thus, the official side of my job was made easier, for I could tell immediately when the General was available for interruption, I could write down the day's business in the diary without asking him what had transpired. And, as a normal female, I thoroughly enjoyed the luxury of eavesdropping on conversations in the Throne Room.

This time General Ike's British Military Assistant found him a house lately occupied by enemy Brass. He and Jimmy Gault moved into the large, comfortable house which had belonged to none other than General von Rundstedt, who apparently insisted upon making the building still more homey by the addition of a giant air raid shelter, which, as far as I know, the new four-star tenant never bothered to inspect. Fifteen or twenty minutes from the Trianon, Von Rundstedt's house offered comparative isolation and privacy.

The WAC girls and I lived in Versailles above a garage. Parts of the headquarters were set up in stables once used by French royalty's favorite horseflesh. Tex bedded down in a small apartment over our office-annex. Butch was in Paris trying to untangle press complications.

Within a fortnight, of course, General Ike was so worried about us "settling down" in Versailles that he announced another advance. We then trudged up to Gieux ("Goo" to the G-I's) and set up a new "Shellburst" where the Boss could live in his favorite super-trailer, a present from Tooey Spaatz, and escape the monotony of headquarters routine; we females took over rooms upstairs in the Gieux country club. Life here was a pleasant cross between that in the Normandy apple orchard and that in quiet Granville.

Whether in Versailles or Gieux, General Eisenhower's time, energy, and abilities were concentrated upon duties which fell into three distinct categories: (1) command problems, (2) trips, and (3) V-I-P's.

The problem of supplies was both constant and overpowering. Stretching straight down across Western Europe from the North Sea to the Mediterranean, the front line was a long, long distance from the main ports of Cherbourg, Le Havre, and Marseille. The task of hauling all the vast material used in modern warfare was dangerously close to impossible; drivers drove themselves into complete fatigue.

At one time things got so bad that vehicles were stripped from new or resting divisions, even bombers became aerial trucks, making expensive hauls of ammunition and petrol whenever weather permitted such make-do, unorthodox shipments. These superhuman efforts were necessary. For example, General Patton once messaged Ike he needed at least *three million gallons* of petrol for his next attack.

General Eisenhower spent a good part of his waking hours trying to keep supplies en route to the advancing armies, trying to fulfill field commanders' every request. Again, Patton is a good example. Upon one occasion in November, when trench-foot was causing more casualties than the enemy, the Third Army chief called desperately for wool socks and dubbin. The socks would permit G-I's to keep their feet dry, the only preventive measure against trench foot; the dubbin would toughen foot-sloggers' boots. Patton called the night of the twelfth and, after I put him through to General Ike, explained the situation. Minutes afterward, General Eisenhower was on the phone to General Lee at supply headquarters, with an or-else priority for woolen socks and dubbin. Twenty-four hours later, Lee called back to report the shipments on their way to Third Army units.

Aside from supplies for the fighting armies, the Supreme Commander had to worry over supplies on the political fronts. One day he took up the subject of re-arming the French Forces of the Interior; the next, the subject of how to get arms away from the reluctant Belgian Forces of the Interior. The French had to be told transportation facilities were so strained in supplying the combat troops that the Allies could give France only one-third as much coal as that furnished by the Germans during their occupation. Political and economic advisers emphasized the Dutch soon would face actual starvation unless large shipments of food could be supplied by the Allies.

Sometimes General Eisenhower's troubles sprouted right in his own backyard. For instance, he wrote a note in the diary on September 12 which typified numerous difficulties with Washington:

Arnold suggests our heavies (U.S.) be moved to France. This is a typical suggestion from someone who doesn't know the problem here. It's fantastic.

With all the pressing contemporary issues, he also had to make decisions on the future. What sort of uniform would be worn in Germany, what sort of currency issued? Who would be a good commander in Berlin? Shouldn't we stop sending prisoners of war back to the States? Could we risk civilian administrations in postwar Germany?

The Quebec Conference ended General Eisenhower's dreams of a truly Allied, SHAEF-like occupation of Germany. He was told to plan for national boundaries, Russian, British, French, and American. His bosses also warned he might remain in Europe for a considerable length of time after the war. Aching for the end of the campaign and his job, homesick for leisure and his family, General Ike had to steel himself to the idea that he probably would command the occupation zone in Germany.

No question was now too small to be side-stepped by lower echelons and bucked on up to the Supreme Commander's desk for final decision: how should captured liquor be distributed among officers and enlisted men? (Equally, General Eisenhower maintained, *not* on a basis of rank.)

No question was too bizarre to be ignored. He seriously considered, before rejecting, an idea that buzz-bombs be shipped up to the front and shot back into the Ruhr. He expressed willingness to see a mystery-man with a message from Marshal Pétain, for the Supreme Commander's eyes only; in this, however, Intelligence argued they could handle the situation.

While plotting the battle itself, he devoted as much time as possible to the equipment and comfort of the fighting man. He insisted that Paris be regarded as a special preserve for combat troops on leave, that they be furnished with the best accommodations, the best food, the best entertainment. He diverted scarce transportation facilities to troops' leave use. When a serious cigarette shortage developed, he ordered supply officers to give more than twice as much ration to the frontline forces as to those in the rear areas. (And he instructed me to cut him down to that rear-area ration; inasmuch as I couldn't smoke during office hours, however, I managed to give him part of my own ration, without his knowledge. A heavy smoker with no other vices and a job which demanded nerves only cigarettes could soften, he needed them.)

Sometimes, he was faced by problems unknown to military

regulations. Venereal disease is an issue known to all generals. But General Eisenhower had to answer a political question: The French and the Belgians wanted him to close all brothels. With admirable tact, he replied that it might be better if the respective governments took appropriate action; he would issue parallel orders within his own province, *i.e.*, to Allied troops under his command.

The manpower shortage he predicted long before D-Day emerged into stark reality. Replacements became a worrisome, then a pressing issue. General Eisenhower directed all rear-area commanders to use Allied civilians to the utmost, to shave down office forces to an absolute minimum. Even these and other measures were so inadequate that, by the time the Ardennes was past, more drastic steps had to be taken.

Perhaps that was the reason for his impatience with Army criminals. He was especially irate one day when, inspecting a Normandy hospital, he realized some of the men were there for self-inflicted wounds. And he was stern, as only a West Pointer and a dedicated war commander can be, with the hundreds of court-martial cases brought to his attention for final review every week.

The Eisenhower ire really began to grow inflamed at the avalanche of reports, from every type of source, on the increasing lack of discipline by Allied troops. Americans, unfortunately, were the principal offenders. Every week brought in more stories of rape, of murder, of calloused looting. One day, for example, the General noted in our office diary his reactions to that particular visit by the Judge Advocate General:

> Betts, 10:30. Reports that disciplinary conditions are becoming bad. Many cases of rape, murder, and pillage are causing complaints by French, Dutch, etc. Am assigning special inspectors to job at once. His reports substantiate those received from other sources.

The very next day a conference was held to discuss the tragic problem. Ike was particularly disturbed at the news that his cocky 101st and 82nd Airborne Division troops were on the rampage. Strong measures will be taken immediately, he emphasized to his staff. And he suggested strong medicine: a public hanging in the case of rape.

With all this, General Eisenhower had to take time for a Supreme Commander's courtesies to the usual flood of V-I-P's, some of them important, some of them semi-important, some of them downright bores.

He conferred with visiting American Red Cross officials, with Congressmen, with diplomats, with show people, with well-wishers, with key press figures, and with High Brass.

He would have a social-business lunch with Lady Mountbatten, famed for ambulance work, and the British Surgeon-General. A lunch soon after that might include as guests anyone from an Ambassador (a very sodden, mumble-mouthed Ambassador upon one occasion) to a Congressman (twenty-two of them on one memorable day!). An American admiral, passing on the rumor that Congress was to enact a bill authorizing five-star admirals and generals, might be followed by a prisoner-of-war emissary, such as Count Bernadotte, later to play an historic role in Palestine. Some might be old friends, such as Robert Murphy and Ambassador and Kathy Harriman. Others might be formal and stiff, such as the Russian Ambassador to France, in to discuss Russian prisoners liberated from the Germans and Russian slave-labor refugees set free in Reich territory. The visitor might be both personal and official, such as the London doctor who tended Ike's bad leg. Or a group of visitors might come in admiration, such as a group of French-Americans who stressed their appreciation for the Paris liberation by presenting the General with a beautiful gold watch.

The most important visitors, of course, were those directly connected with the day-by-day war: Generals Bradley, Patton, Gerow, or Devers; Field Marshal Montgomery, Admiral Ramsay, Admiral Stark . . . or the more intimate associates, Beetle,

Lee, the chiefs of staff sections, the planners, Air Chief Marshal Tedder, Tooey Spaatz, and many others.

I got a special kick out of seeing the new rank of many of our American callers. A large number had progressed quickly since I first met them in the London of 1941–42 and the North Africa of 1943. For example, there was Joseph McNarney, whom I first met in London when he was a colonel, one of the seventeen officer "observers" in civilian clothes and one of the little advance guard for some million and a half Yanks destined to come to London; he was a major general.

I also enjoyed the visits of Top Brass, men like General Marshall and his British opposite-number, Sir Alan Brooke. General Marshall spent almost a week in Europe in October, flying direct from Newfoundland to Paris and working in a visit up to the front. And Mr. Churchill was, as always, a most welcome, invigorating guest, although General Eisenhower was hard put to keep the Prime Minister from tours of the battle area.

Headliners from the show world rarely crossed into our official world at Versailles. I enjoyed meeting lovely Madeleine Carroll, for I admired her wonderful Red Cross work in France—she was one of the very few people from Movieland who knew what the war was about, what it meant first-hand. The same was true of Fred Astaire, whose sister was a mother-confessor to thousands of G-I's back in the London "Rainbow Corner" Red Cross Club; he and the General talked at great length the night he and his troupe came out to Versailles for buffet dinner. The evening was topped off when we rolled back the rugs to witness an intricate demonstration of the Astaire dancing ability.

Bing Crosby was another guest from Hollywood. I was somewhat surprised to see that he had little more hair than the General. But his natural charm—Crosby is the personification of the happy-go-lucky, friendly, buoyant American—made him even more attractive in person than on the screen, where he reigns supreme. General Ike asked about a song in an old Crosby movie but couldn't remember its name. "Does it go like this?" Bing asked, crooning as naturally, as unaffectedly, as a man in his bath.

He was directly responsible, however, for saddling me with a real headache.

"I'm going back to the States soon," he told Ike. "Isn't there anything you'd especially like, anything I could send you?"

The General mentioned hominy.

And Crosby mentioned that fact on his nation-wide radio program back in the United States.

The result was inevitable. For weeks we were deluged with hominy in every shape and size, in packages ranging from tiny parcels to mass-lot cases. I had to dispose of them, mostly to hospitals and staff messes. Thereafter, General Ike was careful about mentioning personal whims to outsiders.

I, too, learned a lesson about butting in on the General's private life. It all started when a London artist asked me to obtain permission for her to paint General Eisenhower's portrait. I declined. She then tackled Tex, Jimmy Gault, even Air Marshal Tedder and Beetle, all without success. Then, she caught me one day in Paris and pleaded her case with great logic; I weakened when she promised to take only fifteen minutes of the General's time. That would permit an over all likeness, at least, she said.

"She's so persistent I've got to admire her," I told the General. "Besides, she *is* a distinguished artist—and she'll take only fifteen minutes."

Very reluctantly and only with Tedder's added urging, he agreed.

She stayed more than two hours. I got hell from the Boss.

As far as I know, it was the General's last portrait.

The only way in which General Eisenhower could escape all these office worries and V-I-P's was to ride out into the field on his beloved "tours." This he did at least once or twice each fortnight.

A typical week during this period started with a visit to General Bradley's headquarters, where he immediately reduced a general officer for failure in combat direction of his armored division. The next day he and the 12th Army Group commander visited V

Corps, an armored division, and the 8th, 9th and 29th Infantry Divisions. In the latter's area, he took a good look at Germany; in all areas, he talked to the principal commanders and enjoyed extemporaneous chats with groups of troops on the firing line. The final stop that evening was Ninth Army headquarters at Maastricht, Holland.

The following day General Ike became a V-I-P, traveling to Brussels for a series of official welcomes by the Regent, the Prime Minister and the Senate. He delivered a speech, visited the Unknown Soldier's tomb, lunched at the palace, and attended a reception in his honor. That evening he returned to Bradley's headquarters, leaving the next day for more visits to First and Ninth Army Divisions. He got a firsthand view of the ruins of Aachen—and a firsthand view of the mud, when he slipped and fell flat on his face in the mire, to the cheers and laughter of hundreds of gleeful troops. The following morning was spent in a series of top-level conferences at 12th Army Group headquarters.

In less than five days, Ike had visited every sector of the First and Ninth Armies—covering five countries, France, Belgium, Holland, Germany, and Luxembourg.

I first saw Luxembourg in October, driving General Eisenhower up to General Bradley's headquarters in Verdun on Friday the thirteenth. General Ike left at the crack of dawn next morning on a trip to Liege, where the King of England had invited all leading American commanders to a special luncheon.

Since General Bradley was moving his headquarters to Luxembourg and since I couldn't attend His Majesty's affair, I stayed behind to join the 12th Army Group commander's aides in the last convoy. The ride was educational as well as enjoyable, for the route took us right through historic World War I country around Verdun; I shuddered at the trenches of a quarter of a century ago, now little more than ridges on the landscape. I shuddered even more at the frequent signposts to Metz, still in German hands. But we turned off that highway long before reaching the fortress city.

Luxembourg was a sort of Old World haven from the New World of Hitler's Europe. Although hemmed in by France, Belgium, and Germany, the tiny nation's capital showed little physical war damage. I found it picturesque and charming—and clean, spotlessly clean, after the mud, manure, and mire of France. Although the front was only a dozen or so miles away, I luxuriated in the comfort of a hot water bath, little more than a memory back in the supposed splendor of Versailles.

Generals Eisenhower and Bradley returned that evening. I was just as shocked as General Ike when dinner turned into a full-fledged party: everyone but General Bradley had forgotten the Supreme Commander's birthday. There was an orchestra, liberated champagne, cocktails, a four-star cake, all the trimmings. It was a gay evening, despite nearness of the wars; General Eisenhower obviously was deeply moved by Bradley's thoughtfulness and hospitality.

The next morning Ike got in another full day of inspections. Returning to our little CP at Gieux for only an hour or so, he then set out for visits with General Patton at Nancy, General Devers at Vittel, and General Patch's Seventh Army, as well as the French First Army in that same sector. He was back in Gieux that night.

Three days later I made my last trip as General Eisenhower's chauffeur.

It was gloomily memorable in every respect. We started out for General Montgomery's headquarters in rain so heavy it reminded me of a London pea-souper fog. The road was visible only a few yards ahead throughout the long drive and the foggy mist was so heavy my windshield was little more than a runny, gray sheet of water. We crawled along at a discouraging speed. As an added handicap, I had to avoid the cracks, holes, and debris left by war in the highways of France and Belgium. In some spots rain had created large lakes of water over wide stretches of the road. The trip was even worse for our motorcycle escort, who found the going so rough that we lost our way several times; riding through the storm in the open, over jagged, water-covered roads, they were soaked to the skin, cold and half-drowned.

My first visit to Brussels wasn't enhanced by the knowledge that our destination was Field Marshal Montgomery's headquarters. This was the only place in all of Western Europe where the commanding general never invited me in with General Eisenhower, for the same official and social courtesy tendered visiting Brass. Here, as always, I was that untouchable of untouchables, a *woman* in the no-woman's-land of Montgomery territory. I waited sulkily in an anteroom while General Eisenhower discussed with Monty the assault on Antwerp. My hands shook from the strain of the trip; I was chilled through and through. Shivering there in Monty's headquarters, I recalled the remarks of friends who said I had an easy, soft job driving the Supreme Commander. And, as soon as someone pointed out my quarters, I went straight off to bed, without stopping for supper.

The trip back to Versailles the next day was as bad as the journey down, a tense, foggy, soggy nightmare. But it was my last chore as a driver.

Five days later a message from Washington bore the happy news I could join the WAC's.

The electrifying cable climaxed more than a year of anxiety and hope. I had yearned to become a WAC since early days in London, becoming even more restless with my unique position as a civilian in North Africa, in England, and in France. As the only civilian member of the official family, I caused untold difficulties in the Army world where every breath and movement is dictated by strict regulations. Furthermore, as one who had gone through the Blitz, a torpedoing, the North African campaign, the pre-invasion era in England, the V-1, the Normandy campaign, the liberation of Paris, and the push up to the Rhine—I wanted to get into the war officially, not as a beyond-the-pale civilian only suffered, not welcomed, by the frowning Army. I wanted to become a formal, normal participant in the war, instead of a sideshow freak civilian.

Moreover, living and working with Americans under every conceivable sort of circumstance had injected a certain amount of American blood into my Irish outlook. I thought more like an American than a Briton, I lived like an American and talked like an American. My English inflection was dropping to a straight Yankee drawl; "cawn't" had become a hard, nasal "can't," and, I'm afraid, my once-precise vocabulary had degenerated into typical American slang . . . not to mention a full reserve of curses inherited from contact with such masters as General Patton and a score of others. I knew the American Army inside out; the British Army was a complete, foreign puzzle. Most of my friends were American, not British.

So I wanted to become a WAC.

The War Department message on October 14 was a highlight of my wartime career, bringing reality to an old, old dream. The only hitch: I could not continue to drive the General. After all my experiences driving General Eisenhower, I was greatly disappointed at this unforeseen development in becoming a WAC. But the achievement and the privilege were worth it. Besides, driving had become, by now, a mere sideline to my duties in the office; it was natural progress.

The swearing-in ceremony was simple, an anticlimax to the spectacle I'd always pictured. My old friend, "T.J." Davis, the Adjutant General, came in one morning and did the honors quickly. It was the third time I had sworn allegiance to the United States; the first took place when I started duty with the American Army, the second when I began working for General Eisenhower. I got up from the desk, raised my right arm, and repeated the officer's oath. Grinning, General Ike pinned gold bars on my shoulders, "T.J." gave me some aide's insignia, but I proudly fastened on the WAC pins.

Then I went back to work. Second Lieutenant Kay Summersby, Army of the United States.

There was little change in my official or social life. My uniform was exactly the same, except for the new insignia. My job was the same, except for the absence of an occasional driving trip; those had become more and more rare, however, and I failed to miss them after a short time. I lived with the WAC's, just as I had before.

I noticed two slight readjustments. Firstly, as a Second Lieutenant, instead of a rankless civilian, I fully realized for the first time the awesome rank of the Brass with whom I was now so well acquainted. Secondly, I had to learn—and remember—to salute.

The newness soon wore off, however, and I fell back into the routine of my job. The Boss worked long hours, which meant I was at the desk from early morning till late at night. Most of the telephone calls and the visitors cleared through my office, for one thing; for another, I had to keep up with the General's ever-increasing "fan mail." The press mention of his birthday on October 14 resulted in a landslide of letters and gifts, each of which had to be acknowledged. And the days were so busy that I often had to remain in the office at night to catch up with correspondence. The only free hours were those after the General left for his house.

One night he stopped by my desk. "I'm knocking off, Kay. Why don't you? It's late."

I explained that handling his office routine during the day left little time for attending to the "fan mail." "Only time I can get any work done on this stuff is when you've left for the night," I added.

He smiled. "And to think I'd never received even *one* fan letter when you drove me and Wayne Clark that first day in London—now look at you!"

He was right. That part of my job had increased in direct proportion to his popularity and fame. But I enjoyed it all the more, reading and answering letters from people, great and small, who knew why the war was being fought. Some had been writing since North Africa days; I felt as though I knew them personally; they were friends.

One month after General Eisenhower's birthday I finally got

out of the office on a trip. The General was headed for Third Army headquarters in Nancy; General Patton had asked him to be sure to bring me along. I was thankful for the break in routine and appreciative of the compliment, for Blood-and-Guts was one of my favorite commanders. In a moment of impulse, I took Telek along.

Our visit in Nancy was doomed from the beginning.

It all started at lunch. General Patton sat at the head of the table, General Eisenhower on his right, Shavetail Summersby on his left, an array of generals and colonels down the table—and Field Marshal Telek under the table. Willie, Patton's white bull terrier, just as tough as his master, was outside.

Suddenly, war broke out at our feet. Willie had wandered inside and found a little black Scottie in the private, holy domain at Patton's feet. He attacked with typical Patton fury. Telek fought back with all the canny courage of his Scot ancestors. The noise was straight from the jungle, loud and wild and deadly.

General Patton let loose with every curse in his celebrated vocabulary. It was classic, that tirade, but I was too frightened to hear it. I was terrified for Telek.

It took four generals, the Theater's top Brass, to separate Willie and Telek. And even then they had to throw water on the fighters.

General Patton banished Willie to an upstairs room, apologizing profusely.

"This is Willie's home," General Ike maintained. "We should lock up Telek."

Georgie Patton shook his head. "No, Sir! Telek outranks Willie, so Telek stays right here. Willie is confined to quarters, under arrest. That's Army protocol."

Then he shouted, "But my Willie was chewing bejesus out of your Gawdamned little Scottie—rank or no rank!"

That afternoon, Patton came back from an inspection trip and hurried over to the special suite fixed up for General Eisenhower in Nancy's most luxurious hotel. Walking in to propose a before-dinner cocktail, however, he found complete chaos.

The suite was filled with smoke, flames, and a screaming French fire brigade. General Ike stood in a corner smiling wanly as Patton blew in.

"Nice place you've got here, Georgie," he said amidst the pandemonium. "Only thing is, they lit the fireplace for the first time, in my honor—and it doesn't seem to have a chimney. It's a fake!"

Somewhat chastened, Patton invited the General and me to a private dinner and immediately launched a warm discussion of old memories he and General Eisenhower shared. I went on up to my room about ten o'clock, finding it so cold that I had to use the rug on the floor as an extra blanket. The discussion below, I knew, would continue far into the night. General Ike always suffered a slight morning-after head following these chats with Georgie Patton.

Sure enough, he was a very grumpy and stern four-star general when he set out on a hospital inspection the next morning.

Back in Versailles, November faded into December and the weeks dragged by until a Saturday, December 16.

That day started off auspiciously with the news that President Roosevelt had nominated Ike for a new rank—five-star General of the Army.

It also marked the long-awaited wedding of Mickey and Pearlie, in an impressive ceremony at an arctic chapel of Versailles palace. Tex did the honors in giving away the bride, who was sweet and blurry-eyed and very unmilitary in her all-white wedding gown, in contrast to her two bridesmaids, Margaret Chick and Sue Sarafin, who both wore their WAC uniforms but still managed to look quite feminine. Pearlie had everything a girl could want at her wedding, everything from an historic church to civilian-like sniffles in the rear of the distinguished audience.

General Eisenhower turned over the von Rundstedt house for a grand reception attended by as much Braid and Brass as that in a War Room conference. As both Pearlie and Mickey were old members of the official family, he had all the luxuries on hand

My office at Rheims. *Official U.S. Army Photo*

Acme Photo

At the Prince of Wales Theatre, London. Left to right: John S. Eisenhower, Miss Tony Porter, myself, General Eisenhower, General Bradley, my mother, Mrs. Vera MacCarthy Morrogh.

Passing the ruins of Hitler's Berchtesgaden retreat. Left to right: Brig.
Gen. T. J. Davis, S/Sgt. Harold Berg, driver for General Clark,
General Clark, myself, and General Eisenhower.

The General signs the famous table of signatures in Hitler's eyrie at
Berchtesgaden. General Clark awaits his turn.

. . . rivers of champagne, a beautiful French wedding cake, and a kiss for the bride from her Boss.

I didn't get much work done that day, noting only in the diary that the General had his 9:30 A.M. conference with top staff members and that General Bradley came up from Luxembourg to spend the night with General Eisenhower, to talk about replacements. Both of them attended the wedding and showed up briefly at the reception afterward.

My final diary entry for that Saturday mentioned that the First Army's attack found the going heavy.

And I added vaguely:

"The German has advanced a little."

General Eisenhower said the advance was in a sector known as the Ardennes.

CHAPTER XV

O N SUNDAY, December 17, I couldn't have been more oblivious to the war suddenly raging through the Ardennes. Pearlie and Mickey were starting their honeymoon in Paris, where Butch had given them his hotel suite. And like many others in Versailles, my brain was somewhat drowned in the champagne which had flooded the McKeogh-Hargrave nuptials. In fact, half of headquarters was soggy with the silence of plain, unadulterated, ordinary hangovers.

Dimly, I heard General Ike, Beetle, and General Bradley discussing the new German attack, which General Eisenhower deemed dangerous enough to warrant ordering an armored division toward each flank of the spearhead. I learned that General Bradley was returning to his headquarters at Luxembourg to deal with the situation. In the diary I noted, "The German is dropping paratroops in the Liége area."

Still, it didn't seem any different from any other day of this routine period. I made a diary entry that First Army continued to encounter heavy resistance to its attack.

On Monday, however, it was apparent even to me the Germans had launched a full-scale counter-offensive.

The more pessimistic staff members predicted a drive on Paris itself, plus a blitz through to the huge supply center at Liége and the key port of Antwerp. First reports said the Germans were using three entire armies made up of as many as twenty or twenty-four infantry, armored, and motorized divisions.

I found it a grim coincidence that the entire attack was directed by none other than General von Rundstedt, who apparently launched his assault even while we toasted Pearlie and Mickey in his own Occupation residence in Versailles.

General Eisenhower cursed the bad weather, which grounded all our planes and aided the enemy assault. He also worried about the 4th, 28th, and 106th Infantry Divisions and the 9th Armored Division—all spread out thinly in the crucial area; he was particularly anxious when General Bradley reported the 106th Division, newly arrived in the Theater, as badly mauled. Intelligence added to the general gloom by admitting they couldn't locate half the German armor.

Then General Ike caught a second breath. "If this is the heaviest attack they can put on," he remarked, "we're okay."

There was a tense conference at 3:30 o'clock that afternoon.

Regardless of this new danger, General Eisenhower had to continue with his regular routine. He was especially perturbed over the old problem of replacements, now growing to a head. In fact, the issue was so strained that he put out a new order for the hiring of all civilians possible, to replace soldiers, and ordered SHAEF's own personnel chief on a trip back to the War Department to beg for reinforcements.

That same day the 101st and 82nd Airborne Divisions arrived in the Ardennes, the former taking over the key road intersection at Bastogne and beginning its heroic defense of that point.

Reports received in SHAEF were garbled, contradicting, and rather terrifying. Communications were in an absolute snarl. The Germans were using American vehicles and American uniforms. Whole units had been wiped out. The destruction of equipment was terrific. German armor was smashing everything before it. Our air was helpless, weathered in. The enemy was reported variously from Paris to Antwerp. Rumor succeeded fact. The result was uncomfortably close to chaos.

Early the next morning, December 19, General Eisenhower left for Verdun in an attempt to get a tight grasp on the slippery situation and confer with all his top commanders. Patton's cocky, confident attitude was superb amidst all the apprehension, he told me later.

While there, General Ike realized General Bradley, with his communications cut into shreds and his headquarters in the awkward position at Luxembourg, would have difficulty commanding troops on both sides of the German break-through. This was when he made the controversial split of command, giving Field Marshal Montgomery direction of all forces to the north, including most of the First and Ninth Armies; General Bradley, forces on the southern side of the flank. General Patton was to be given extra divisions and make a fierce bite into that southern flank.

General Ike returned to Versailles that evening, weary from the rough trip but happier now that command problems were straightened out.

The morning of December 20 was D-Day in our own SHAEF sector of the break-through—Intelligence reported a suicide squad of at least three score Germans headed toward Versailles.

As I got the story, First Army Intelligence had captured a German officer in American uniform and given him a good first-degree grilling at Liége. He finally confessed to being one of a band of some sixty specially-trained men led by Otto Skorzeny, the scarfaced S.S. commando chief who maneuvered the daring rescue of Mussolini. The crew, composed largely of men who spoke English —some of them had been in the United States—and wore American uniforms, was equipped with proper identification papers, all sorts of captured American vehicles, even suicide-pills and capsules of acid to use as desperate weapons. Their single mission, to be accomplished with ruthless, fanatic zeal: the assassination of General Eisenhower.

To say this report upset the SHAEF staff is pure understatement.

Security officers immediately turned headquarters compound into a virtual fortress. Barbed wire appeared. Several tanks moved in. The normal guard was doubled, trebled, quadrupled. The pass system became a strict matter of life and death, instead of the old formality. The sound of a car exhaust was enough to halt work in every office, to start a flurry of telephone calls to our office, to inquire if the Boss were all right. The atmosphere was worse than that of a combat headquarters up at the front, where everyone knew how to take such a situation in stride.

The intended victim was the only officer at SHAEF unperturbed by the report. General Eisenhower had the war, the Bulge, to worry about; he couldn't be bothered by this one fantastic story.

The staff insisted he move in from the von Rundstedt house, which was comparatively isolated from the Trianon. They pointed to the lonely, wooded stretches along the road; they emphasized the Germans knew every inch of that territory, from their Occupation days. They said the General's security was impossible under such circumstances.

Finally—only after his closest associates begged, as personal friends rather than staff officers, him to leave the von Rundstedt house—he reluctantly moved into the compound.

"But only so you'll forget about this damned business and get back to the war," he growled.

With General Ike thus ensconced in Tex Lee's flat over the office, security then ordered Ruth Briggs and me to follow suit. We moved into quarters over a garage only a sort distance from the office. None of us was permitted outside the area. Security explained to Ruth and me that we knew too much about top-level affairs to risk our safety. They even asked General Eisenhower not to walk outside the office, for fear a sniper might have slipped through the toe-to-toe guard.

We were prisoners, in every sense of the word.

This new, personal tension, coupled with the flood of bad news and rumors from the Ardennes, left most of headquarters frankly apprehensive and depressed. Ike, the one solely responsible for the success or failure of our counter-attack and therefore the only one entitled to the luxury of depression, had to smother his own feelings and act as the eternal optimist, the confident buckerupper. And he carried off the role with perfect aplomb.

The same day he received this report of the Skorzeny assassins, along with other heartbreaking news from the actual front, he prepared an order of the day for every member of the Allied armies. In it the Supreme Commander called not only for an ironclad halt to the German attack, he also stressed the offensive, an all-out offensive to take this opportunity of destroying the Germans—while the enemy was out of his pillbox and his deep fortifications. "Destroy the enemy on the ground, in the air, everywhere," he urged. "Destroy him!"

The message was a masterpiece of the positive against the negative, aimed at stomping out the current traces of fear and defeatism.

Next day, on the twenty-first, weather still was as tenacious an enemy as the German. Heavy ground fog and mist blanketed most battle sectors. Air and ground chiefs alike railed bitterly at this continuing handicap to our efforts to stop the Nazi spearheads. General Eisenhower encouraged his field commanders' plans for a counter-attack the following day. I wrote in the diary:

> Another night tonight of uneasiness. E is just pinned to his office all day; at night he goes upstairs and sleeps in Tex's flat. I stay across the way from the office. Everyone's confined to the compound. What a life—

Then I made the one-minute walk to our garage "home," where I lay awake for hours envisioning death and worse at the hands of S.S. agents. Sleep was impossible—with the tramp, tramp, tramp of heavy-booted guards patrolling our tin roof.

Morning brought news that General Patton was loose, pounding toward relief of the besieged 101st Airborne men at Bastogne. It also brought news that the German attack was continuing without pause, still aided by ceiling-minus-zero weather. General Eisenhower directed 17th Airborne Division to come over from England, 11th Armored to re-assemble and prepare for action despite its late arrival from the British Isles. In addition, he ordered every available service soldier into the field, whether cook or clerk, K.P. or drill sergeant; rear echelon troops were to be employed as heavily as possible. Six French infantry battalions were ordered to join these service troops and defend the critical Meuse bridges at any cost.

Intelligence reported German forces in the north stronger than first anticipated, then worried over reports of German divisions withdrawing from the Russian front—someone from SHAEF must get in touch with Stalin for information, they emphasized.

On our personal front, Intelligence passed along a report the sabotage-assassins had made their way into Paris proper. It was said they would rendezvous at the Café de la Paix.

This warning failed to bother the General. He came out of his office cell grumbling, "Hell's fire, I'm going out for a walk. If anyone wants to shoot me, he can go right ahead. I've got to get out!"

Suddenly, the weather broke. The Air Force, after days of straining at the leash, began pounding enemy railheads, bridges, dumps, headquarters, and other vital areas. The *Luftwaffe* put up its strongest fight yet, however. And Patton reported his progress slowed by mines, demolitions, and similar obstacles. Regardless, General Eisenhower said he thought the situation looked much better. I added in the diary, "Worked very late, then back to prison."

On the twenty-fourth all our air concentrated upon Nazi airfields and grounded a good portion of enemy fighters. This and continuing fine weather permitted fighter-bombers to blast away at roads, transport, and troop concentrations without the harassment of aerial duels. The weather also afforded ground forces an opportunity to get moving once more.

No one thought much about that night being Christmas Eve, although I recalled longingly the plans of General Bradley's now-harried aides for a huge party at 12th Army Group. The big event in Versailles was the arrival of a packing case from Washington, by air: it contained hundreds of the Boss's favorite seafood, big, delicious oysters, a welcome present from the White House press secretary, Steve Early.

Reports flowing into the General's office on Christmas morning

weren't exactly optimistic. Divisional commanders screamed for
more men, although replacement depots had been scraped bare.
London advised bad weather would keep the precious 17th Airborne in Britain. Monty sent a message he hadn't enough strength
to attack. Another message carried the news that half a regiment
of the 66th Division had been torpedoed en route to France, with
very few survivors.

General Ike, apologetic because the long-awaited Christmas
Party was impossible, invited some of his intimates to dinner.

I thought him more depressed than at any time since I'd met
him. He was low, really low.

On the following day, however, headquarters sensed a new air
of confidence which started down at the lowest levels and surged
right up to the Supreme Commander's office. Ike himself agreed,
officially: the Germans were stopped.

Patton's 4th Armored Division was in firm contact with Bastogne's defenders. The Meuse was well protected by sufficient re-
serves. The enemy could go no further.

While field commanders turned to regrouping and planning
problems necessary for a return to the offensive, General Eisenhower once more took up some of his office headaches.

For one, his message to Moscow suggesting close military liaison between West and East received a quick reply. Premier Stalin
said he would see any officer the General cared to send as his representative. Ike immediately detailed a three-man team headed by
Air Marshal Tedder; they were ordered to Moscow as quickly as
weather would permit.

Also, the General had to resume his arguments against the idea
of an over all ground commander, an idea which seemed to stem
almost exclusively from the British and hint broadly at the appointment of one man: Field Marshal Montgomery. A message
from General Marshall stated the British Chiefs of Staff favored
this view. On December 27, not long after an air raid in Paris
damaged part of his train, the General traveled to Brussels for a
special conference with Monty, who insisted that even his own

Chief of Staff leave the room while he and Ike talked. On his return, General Ike hinted that Monty hammered the one-ground-commander-plan again.

Several days later the Field Marshal sent a long message saying General Eisenhower's proposed operational directive was bound to fail, in his personal opinion. Furthermore, he still believed there should be one permanent commander for all ground forces. Monty left no doubt as to who should be that commander, as far as I could see.

The General didn't say much about this situation. But he and Beetle agreed in a regular morning conference that Montgomery had changed considerably since the day in Bari, just one year before, when Monty said he wanted to "join the team."

"You must have the patience of an angel," I remarked to General Ike.

"If I can keep the team together, anything's worth it," he replied soberly.

But he sent a stiff reply to Monty's message, forwarding the much-discussed directive and saying the idea of a single ground commander was out of the question. The Field Marshal answered immediately, saying he was worried for fear his message had upset the Supreme Commander, who now could rely upon him 100 per cent to make the directive work.

Actually, the one man who smoothed out relations between Monty and SHAEF, where even British members of the Allied team often protested some of the Field Marshal's actions, was Monty's own mustached, cordial, diplomatic Chief of Staff. Freddie de Guingand, with his sense of humor and his sense of proportion, was the eternal negotiator between Monty and many sections of SHAEF, including the Supreme Commander. He deserves much credit for preserving upper-level Anglo-American peace during the war.

By December 29 the Skorzeny threat was so dissipated that not even the over-cautious security officers could keep General Ike from moving out of his office-flat prison into the comfortable Presidential House nearby. They then called off a favorite daily drama, a "double" who traveled to and from the von Rundstedt house every morning and evening in the General's car, to confound spies.

I ended my 1944 office diary with a note that a State Department envoy had just revealed the existence of an underground group inside Germany, working for peace.

That same night Hitler promised the German people victory in 1945.

The New Year, still befogged by conditions in the Ardennes, brought General Eisenhower a French problem so delicate it required Chief-of-State attention, so explosive it threatened to destroy French support of the Allies.

It all started when the General, acting upon good military advice, decided to evacuate the city of Strasbourg. Otherwise, he said, the Strasbourg-Colmar area would give the Germans an open invitation to make another Ardennes out of that sector. His idea was to pull back to a stable, straight front and permit several divisions to aid Patton in a flank attack to the north. A few mobile battalions might be left temporarily, with orders to pull out in the face of a strong enemy assault; we simply didn't have the troops to defend Strasbourg. From a purely military standpoint in the current crisis, he added, the city was not worth defending.

The French bitterly opposed this decision to turn a liberated city of some three hundred thousand people back over to the Germans. General Juin said the line must be held at all costs; the evacuation would constitute a major defeat for the French, probably start a blood-bath, and, incidentally, give the Nazis a major propaganda weapon. General de Gaulle carried the fight to topmost levels with personal appeals to President Roosevelt, Prime Minister Churchill, and Premier Stalin. And he sent General Eisenhower a courier letter which implied that unless two divisions were left in Strasbourg, de Gaulle and his forces would walk right out of the war. The Prime Minister himself came to Versailles for talks with Ike and de Gaulle. Stalin agreed with the Free French leader that Alsace must be defended to the death.

In his report to the Combined Chiefs, General Eisenhower commented:

> Originally, I had considered that the matter of Strasbourg was merely a conflict between military and political considerations and that I was completely justified in handling the question on a purely military basis. However, as I studied the French views, it became evident that the execution of the original plans for withdrawal might have such grave consequences in France that all our lines of communication and our vast rear areas might become seriously affected through interference with the tasks of the service troops and through civil unrest generally. Clearly, the prevention of such a contingency became a matter of military as well as of political necessity.

The General concluded in his report after the Vosges campaign, ". . . no militarily essential ground in the Vosges was lost and Strasbourg itself no more than threatened."

Coincidentally, the General worried over replacements. Most divisions, hard hit by the German counter-attack, were under strength. Every commander right down the line from army group to company level begged for replacements.

As a drastic step, the Supreme Commander ordered a major, final comb-out of all rear-area commands. Thousands of office personnel, officers and enlisted men alike, were shaken loose from unimportant jobs. Civilian employment climbed to new heights. One headquarters began wholesale use of Italian prisoners of war, who were checked for loyalty and then formed into regular service troops. Men who had known nothing but office work suddenly found themselves in training areas close to the front. The WAC's took on additional burdens of clerical work, to free men who could serve better by carrying guns. We even did away with our "Shellburst" CP at Gieux, to save personnel. Offices were consolidated, one to do the work of two. Service units were stripped to mere skeletons of their former rosters.

If the subject hadn't been so grim, it would have been funny.

Even so, I got a tremendous kick in seeing desk-bound officers who but recently talked incessantly of their desire to "get out into the field, with troops," now moving heaven and hell to convince Topside their paper work was essential to the war effort. They had a field day with charts, reports, and surveys intended to prove the extreme importance of their office—and, of course, themselves. Most of them got into the field, with troops.

General Marshall gave his usual co-operation, sending Lieutenant-General Ben ("Yoo Hoo") Lear over from the War Department to make the rear-area shakedown of personnel still more intensive. General Ike gave Lear complete authority and encouragement to be as ruthless as militarily possible; needless to add, the War Department general, already regarded as a very senior and grumpy man, but actually a somewhat lonely and charming officer, was not received at the various headquarters with warmth and love.

General Marshall also arranged for the 2nd Infantry Division, scheduled for another Theater, to be diverted to Europe. He promised an influx of some six hundred officers each month. Ike's personnel chief emphasized that, although SHAEF knew the War Department was engaged in world-wide war, the Allies might very well lose the European battle unless more replacements were made available; he suggested a request for several Marine divisions. General Ike discussed with the Chief of the British Imperial General Staff a plan to withdraw, secretly, some British and American troops from Italy and bring them to the Western front.

A third thorny issue in this trying phase erupted when the press announced our split command in the Ardennes. Some of the British papers again plugged for a unified ground command; American papers protested vehemently at a British general directing United States troops. General Eisenhower explained this militarily, as a temporary measure dictated by the German split of our forces.

But a new problem arose when General Bradley learned he would eventually get back only the First Army; the Ninth would stay with Monty. Ike explained, over and over, that this had been the plan from the beginning; I, personally, knew this to be the case, for he had mentioned it upon numerous occasions. Bradley, however, showed open resentment at losing the American Ninth Army to his British colleague; in fact, he was downright sore. He also indicated an unhealthy state of mind among his staff, who complained not only at losing the Ninth Army but at the flood of publicity on Field Marshal Montgomery. I found this to be true when I made a trip up to 12th Army Group; my friends, the aides, asked in semi-joking terms, "Whose side are you on, Monty's or Bradley's, or just whose?"

General Ike was most hurt at this new development, for Bradley was one of his closest friends and had been, since the beginning, the most co-operative of all field commanders. It was the first and only time he displayed real anger and disagreement. Ike's personal wound was proportionate.

But with their friendship, mutual respect, and natural forgiveness, both soon returned to their normal relationship.

Even with the battle demanding all possible attention, the General regularly had to drop all else for any one of dozens of side-issues.

He learned, with personal as well as official sorrow, of the death of Admiral Ramsay in a take-off accident at the Versailles airfield. He heard that Monty's plane had been shot up by buzzing enemy fighters, and promptly sent along his own C-47 for the Field Marshal's use. He discussed ammunition and rubber shortages with visiting members of the War Manpower Commission. He played cocktail host to the Prime Minister. He gave Mark Watson of the Baltimore *Sun* a forty-minute interview emphasizing the need for curbing home-front optimism, a need he had underlined as far back as August. He conferred with the Dutch Prime Minister on the stark plight of the starving population in Holland, especially in Amsterdam. He gave General Bradley a well publicized award for his role in stopping the German attack. He talked by telephone with Mr. Churchill, on subjects ranging from Monty to Stalin.

He sent a long reply to General Marshall's message that the Chief of Staff had his doubts about General Lee being the man to supply front line troops. He welcomed Katharine Cornell to headquarters.

He fumed at the black market, especially when Beetle reported concern over civilian thefts of vital war supplies. He blew up at the news that a well organized ring was shipping such items as champagne back to London by American planes; a truckload of wine had been found in a U.S. Army truck parked outside an English pub. The final touch came when thieves rifled his own liquor closet at the forward CP.

And, so quietly that no one quite realized what had happened, he achieved the highest rung of the tall military ladder: General of the Army.

The very tiny circle of five stars appeared on each Eisenhower shoulder almost by metamorphosis, refuting staff rumors the new design would call for a straight, staggering line of five huge stars. And it seemed to fit the General's modest demeanor. He wore collar insignia only when in combat jacket and he abandoned the overseas cap, which required rank, for the more sedate visored hat. If anything, the new five-star prominence was submerged as much as possible. Only the new red license plates on his car advertised the presence of the General of the Army.

(Patton, by way of contrast, was loaded with Brass. He wore three glistening stars on each shoulder of his snug battle jacket, three more on each collar point, and three on his overseas cap— presenting an unforgettable, impressive sight of fifteen blinding stars.)

As a West Pointer, a professional soldier, General Ike must have experienced a near-holy emotion at reaching his new pre-eminence. But, as usual, he kept his personal elation—like his personal depressions—to himself.

During this same period, Butch quietly acquired another stripe, which glowed conspicuously above the old ones on his sleeve. Several times, however, he complained that Army people had more respect for his former rank; a commander seemed far above a captain, in Army circles.

Even I picked up a little something, a British decoration, the British Empire Medal. Prime Minister Churchill was responsible for it, for he mentioned upon one occasion in North Africa that he thought I deserved some sort of formal recognition for my services. (The medal was finally awarded more than three years later, when I was once more a civilian, in a ceremony aboard the *Britannic* in New York.)

Meanwhile, the Battle of the Ardennes drew to a close.

The tension began lifting by January 14, with a new air of confidence so strong it was almost touchable. On the fifteenth, Intelligence estimated roughly, from prisoner-of-war studies, the Germans had lost approximately eighty-three thousand killed or wounded; the report proved to be most conservative. Beetle felt so relieved he suggested we move headquarters up to Rheims within a month. Other reports indicated the Germans had moved 400 to 500 fighters back to the Russian front. The Soviets were just about to capture Warsaw and the newspapers claimed their forces to be within fifteen miles of the Reich border; Premier Stalin sent a message promising to declare war on the Japs as soon as the Germans were defeated.

On January 16 the First and Third Armies linked up in firm contact at Houffalize and, as General Eisenhower put it, "turned their full strength eastward against the retreating enemy."

The Battle of the Ardennes was completely under control, just a month after it had started.

In his official report to the Combined Chiefs, Ike emphasized that the Germans had breached a forty-five-mile gap in Allied lines and penetrated more than sixty miles eastward to a point only four miles from the Meuse. He admitted, further: the attack delayed Allied offensive operations by at least six weeks.

But, with wry humor, he added:

The counter-offensive, however, was not without its effects upon the enemy . . .

During the month ending 16 January, my commanders estimated that the enemy suffered 120,000 serious casualties and lost 600 tanks and assault guns. He also lost about 1,620 planes—a severe blow—and his fuel stocks, after nearly a month of large-scale effort, were reduced to a bare minimum.

The tactical aircraft claims for the month included also over 6,000 motor transport destroyed and 7,000 damaged, together with some 550 locomotives destroyed and over 600 damaged.

By the end of our own counter-offensive the enemy had lost 220,000 men, including 110,000 prisoners of war.

More serious in the final analysis was the widespread disillusionment within the German Army and Germany itself which must have accompanied the realization that the breakthrough had failed to seize any really important objective and had achieved nothing decisive.

By January 17, things had simmered down so much that even Monty and Patton were back into routine. The Field Marshal sent a message praising the First and Ninth U.S. Armies. General Patton telephoned, worried about nothing more than promotions.

Ike asked General Spaatz and several of us over to his house that night for a home movie, insisting that Tooey bring his guitar. The two of them let off the past month's accumulated steam by booming out a medley of slightly off-key but boisterous West Point songs.

The worst part of the war seemed over.

CHAPTER XVI

WHILE the armies wound up for a new punch aimed at knocking the Germans right back to the Rhine, life at headquarters resumed a somewhat orderly pace for the first time since the break-through.

Monty requested, and received, permission for a few days' overdue rest in England. I made a note to organize some evening bridge sessions for General Eisenhower, to give *him* a bit more relaxation after the past nervous month.

Telek and Caacie contributed to the new air of routine by providing the General's household with six new pups. Although not yet three years old, Telek was a father for the third time; he regarded his latest offspring with complete nonchalance. I didn't blame him, for Caacie snarled every time her husband stopped by to play with the babies.

In the WAC house, we celebrated the girls' promotions. They all donned oak leaves and kidded me unmercifully, pointing out that, as field-grade officers they probably would have to kick me out into other quarters—how could majors live with anything as lowly as a second lieutenant? More seriously, we all rejoiced at their new rank; they needed it in the Brass-heavy atmosphere of SHAEF.

I concentrated upon the piles of letters which poured in to wish the Supreme Commander a merry Christmas and a victorious New Year, and to congratulate him upon his handling of the Bulge. And all of us pitched in to jam huge packing cases with the candy, clothing, cigarettes, foods, books, sweaters, and other gifts which had descended upon Ike over the holidays from well-wishers in all parts of the world. Then we shipped those boxes off to front-line hospitals.

The late January news was good, too. The Russians, claiming sixty thousand prisoners in Budapest, were staking everything on a gigantic attack; Hitler ordered every man, woman, and child to defend the Fatherland against the Soviet hordes, now regarded as the Reich's Number One enemy. Air Chief Marshal Tedder and his group returned from Moscow with word the Allies now had solid liaison with the Kremlin, which gloated over the picture of Germany fighting a literal two-front war. Our own Intelligence was happy to learn a long-lost Panzer division was not hiding behind our front, but in action against the Russians. Tooey Spaatz was readying a steady three-days-and-nights bombing onslaught against Berlin for morale purposes; the operation's apt code name: "Thunderclap."

General Eisenhower, although troubled by his leg, reflected the general atmosphere of optimism. He relieved only one divisional commander the rest of that month. The Theater-wide comb-out for combat replacements received an added push when Harry Hopkins, en route to the Big Three meeting scheduled at Yalta, disclosed that eighty per cent of the current draft in the United States would be sent to Europe.

Ike then left for Marseille and a visit with General Marshall, over for a meeting of the Combined Chiefs of Staff in Malta and then the Yalta conference. With the Boss away, I borrowed skis and tried out several Versailles hills, giving it up after several hours because of the frozen snow and the fear of putting myself out of the war with a broken leg.

The General returned in good spirits, chiefly because of General Marshall's promise: "As long as I'm Chief of Staff, I'll never let them saddle you with the burden of an over-all ground commander." Marshall promised to push that idea at Yalta. The Chief of Staff also advised Ike of his support for diverting troops to Europe, in opposition to Navy demands for emphasis on the Pacific war. Furthermore, he gave General Ike *carte blanche* in using younger men in top field commands; older officers, he said, could be used for training purposes in the United States. This close co-operation and mutual respect between Generals Eisenhower and Marshall was, in addition to being one of the mainstays of the European war, a beautiful thing to behold amidst all the other staff rivalries and jealousies.

With all this, it looked as though January would end as a quiet, hopeful month. Quite suddenly, however, General Ike found himself bogged down—again—in troubles with the French.

It came first in the form of captured documents showing the Germans as reinforcing their forces in the Colmar Pocket in order to create a great Nazi victory for home consumption and to have the Swastika flying in Strasbourg by January 30. Inasmuch as the Supreme Commander had yielded to arguments to hold Strasbourg for broad political as well as military reasons, even though it seemed partially inadvisable during the Bulge, he now displayed great concern over this new threat to the city.

Also, the overall timetable was behind schedule in that particular area. Attacks launched on January 20 by two French corps against the north and south sides of the Colmar Pocket had failed to make much progress.

General Ike had a long talk with de Gaulle's Chief of Staff, General Juin, through an interpreter. It was explained that the Colmar Pocket must be eliminated, that French troops must make an all-out effort as great as their British and American Allies to the north, not only for the campaign's sake but for the new glory of Free France. General Juin replied somewhat heatedly that American Intelligence greatly underestimated German strength in the sector and expected superhuman miracles of very weary, ill-equipped, decimated French soldiers. The intended "pep talk" ended with General Juin leaving in rather a huff.

Afterward, it developed that the temporary interpreter had bungled the entire conversation between Ike and Juin, leaving the latter with a distinct impression the SHAEF staff was highly critical of French forces.

Impatient with "channels" procedure, General Ike went straight-away into Paris for a chat with General de Gaulle. The Allies couldn't afford to let a few coals of misunderstanding burst into flames of resentment and possible discord. General Eisenhower emphasized he meant no criticism of the French Army; he simply wanted to impress upon all concerned the extreme necessity for the clearing of the Colmar Pocket. Toward that end, he was sending a heavy American corps to carry the load of battle between the two French corps. General de Gaulle minimized any misunder-standing and pointed out his troops had been impeded by the enemy's numerical superiority, by a shortage of key equipment, by fatigue, and by weather.

It was one of the war's most satisfactory meetings between General Eisenhower and General de Gaulle, a man-to-man talk in the style General Ike always preferred—direct, frank, factual, and cordial.

Nine days later the Franco-American force battered its way right into Colmar.

That same day, February 3, Beetle returned from the Combined Chiefs of Staff meeting with word that another man-to-man talk had staved off troubles with another Ally, the British. Sir Alan Brooke, Britain's top Army chief, mentioned doubts if General Eisenhower were "strong enough" for his job. Beetle immediately suggested the two of them speak bluntly, off the record. The Chief of the Imperial General Staff then gave as one reason for his statement the fact that Ike paid too much attention to the desires of his field commanders. Beetle retorted by stressing Ike's cordial contacts with his commanders and by pointing out the Supreme Commander could hold together an Allied team only by a com-bination of diplomacy and sternness with individual personalities such as Monty, Patton, Juin, and many others. If the British high command doubted the Supreme Commander's ability, Beetle added, they should put their cards on the table before the Com-bined Chiefs of Staff. Horrified at such a thought, Sir Alan agreed to General Ike's many abilities and conceded, flatly, the Allies had no other man who could take or hold down the Supreme Commander's job anywhere near as competently as General Eisenhower. All in all, Beetle told Ike, the chips-down talk between the two men had cleared the air and strengthened Anglo-American relations on high levels.

With General Bradley still fuming because SHAEF permitted Monty to keep the U.S. Ninth Army, General Ike left the next morning for a chat with the Twelfth Army Group Commander at Namur and another series of troop inspections. I went along, joining the General that night in a bridge bout with Bradley and one of his staff. For once, we lost. The following day he visited three army headquarters, even more corps, and a number of divisions, from Maastricht to Bastogne. Learning that Germans seemed to have advance word of our attacks, he ordered a ban on the mention of dates on any telephone.

Some of the news was bad: Communists in Belgium threatened to withdraw their support of the government, almost two score V-1's landed in Antwerp in one day, weather continued to cover battle areas with snow, sleet, and rain. However, the "Thunderclap" air bombing of Berlin was a huge success, a Secret Service report quoted the Japs as being highly critical of their German partners, Nazi fighter-plane pilots were ordered to fight only when necessary (because of a fuel shortage), and the Russians shoved several bridgeheads across the Oder.

After a delicious dinner of oysters sent over by Freddie de Guingand, we had a short night's rest and then headed back the next morning to Versailles, where General of the Army Eisenhower found Lieutenant Eisenhower awaiting him. John was on his way to an assignment at 12th Army Group: he and his father, who was overjoyed at the reunion, talked well into the early morning hours.

General Ike's leg was troublesome, from the trip and the weather, but he radiated happiness. That was the eve of his great spring offensive in Europe.

In North Africa and in England I hadn't paid much heed to

the universal idea that General Eisenhower was, as the British press once put it, only a "Chairman of the Board," an executive who directed the diplomatic, political, and paper-work part of the war, with no say in the actual field fighting. I myself, as a civilian driver meeting front-page personalities, had little interest in the actual campaigns as such or in the General's participation in those battles.

By now, however, as an officer in the Army, a member of the inner circle at SHAEF, and a sort of confidential secretary to the Supreme Commander, I had a new, intense interest in the war fronts themselves. It was both official and unofficial. And, by the nature of my duties, I fully realized for the first time just how complete was General Ike's responsibility in the combat command. He was Supreme Commander in every possible sense of the word.

I also understood why, with a force reaching the staggering total of four million men (4,600,000 by the end of March), his was the overall view. He couldn't afford the luxury of anything less. When Bradley howled because SHAEF gave Monty the Ninth U.S. Army, Ike knew the Field Marshal needed that army for half of the two-pronged spring offensive. While Patton bawled at being held in check, General Ike knew Third Army power was being hoarded for a surprise push. When the Air complained of losses over a Ruhr target, he realized that target was part of a pocket to be reduced weeks later by ground forces. His was the grand view, often incomprehensible to those with smaller views.

This time, while commanders elsewhere demanded action, the vast operation to clear everything west of the Rhine began on February 8 with a strong offensive from the Nijmegen area.

General Ike was jubilant next day, although bedded down with his bad leg. The doctor from London, over to try another diagnosis, ordered a thirty-six-hour rest. And, to everyone's surprise, the Supreme Commander followed orders. He had a telephone moved to his bedside, of course, so as to keep in touch with the new attack. First reports were somewhat discouraging, the Canadians running into floods resulting from the January thaws; men sometimes fought waist-deep in water, while armor stalled on soggy ground.

On February 10, First Army reported the last and most important Roer dam, Schwammenauel, in safe hands—clearing the way for Ninth Army's moonlight assault on February 23, as the other half of Monty's northern drive to push to the Rhine.

General Eisenhower, meanwhile, continued to encounter difficulties, both personal and official. He had a growth taken from his back, leaving him, as he phrased it, "in stitches." Monty demanded two more American divisions. An American newspaper fell for Nazi propaganda by forecasting "terror bombing" of German cities. Reports charged French soldiers with stealing U.S. vehicles in Colmar, where Allied relations were none too cordial. The Polish Government in London refused to recognize decisions taken at Yalta. The French wanted to take three whole divisions out of the line for regrouping, refitting—and a domestic parade-tour.

Ruth Briggs was the unwitting "wet blanket" one night in mid-February. She and I had been invited over to the General's house for dinner and a movie; in the course of the meal she mentioned something about a truck, a code truck, stolen from the 28th Division. General Ike, even as Supreme Commander, hadn't heard about it. He blew up.

The theft threatened to turn into a full-blown international incident. As I understood it, the codes in that truck were at least partial, if not complete, keys to the same code used not only throughout the American Army but also by parts of diplomatic staffs. The Americans were understandably worried, first starting to accuse the French Secret Service, then the British, then the Russians; finally, it was thought the Germans now had the equipment, through an ingenious theft managed in such a way as to cause suspicion among the Allies. Whole teams of Counter Intelligence Corps agents combed the area. Cables sizzled back and forth across the Atlantic. At least one high-ranking officer was put under arrest of quarters for permitting the precious truck to be left unattended all night. Eventually—almost a month later—the missing truck was found; American agents dragged a river to locate most of the priceless codes. The last I heard of it, they came to the conclusion that black marketeers stole the truck and, finding nothing of resale value, abandoned it.

The twenty-second of February was a big day at headquarters, even though the Supreme Commander was down in Normandy inspecting troops and Red Cross clubs with General Lear.

First of all, it was the start of a truly gigantic air assault to clear the way for Monty's Big Push a month later. On that one day Operation "Clarion" sent from bases in five countries the unbelievable total of almost 9,000 Allied aircraft for blasting of German railway grade crossings and signal points, canal locks, road junctions, and other key targets. Secondly, Ninth Army launched its attack toward the Rhine to link up with the Canadian thrust pushed out a fortnight before. Thirdly, it was the day of our last move in France, to Rheims, heart of the famous champagne country.

Rheims—"Ransse" to the French, "Reams" to the troops—gave SHAEF better access to forward areas, in keeping with the Eisenhower dictum. But the space and the furnishings were a comedown from the Trianon in Versailles. Instead of a grand hotel in the shadow of a royal palace, we now worked in an old red schoolhouse. Later the site was to become historic; in February, more than two months before the surrender ceremonies, it was only an old red schoolhouse, nothing more. The General's office was minute, an overgrown filing cabinet, not even as large as mine. Outside, trains and trucks provided a factory-like atmosphere compounded mostly of dirt and noise.

General Ike's residence was a large chateau owned by one of the champagne barons. The rest of the Brass moved into quarters along the main street; the heavy convoy traffic then was diverted to two streets which passed right by the windows of our WAC house, a hideous little building hardly enhanced by that convoy clatter day and night.

Rheims, however, marked the beginning of two new eras in my personal life. I became a first lieutenant—and an aide.

As the first female five-star aide in American military annals, I found little change in surface matters. My pay increased eighteen dollars per month and I put on a newly created insignia, a blue shield decorated with a circle of five white stars, topped by the aide's eagle.

But, inside, I glowed. Gone were the days of driving and civilian-status worries. Now I was on the Inside, not the Outside; I had an official Army job provided by strict regulations. Instead of confidential secretary, receptionist, odd-jobs handler, and a lowly Shavetail office clerk, I was a first lieutenant and aide to General of the Army Eisenhower, Supreme Commander, Allied Expeditionary Force. The WAC's had won another victory; they now had a five-star aide. (I kidded Sally Bagby, Tooey's aide, when her Boss got his fourth star the next month; would a major aide to a four-star General outrank a first lieutenant aide to a five-star General of the Army? The question opened an entire new field of high-level protocol.)

The General arrived two days after our move, happy at SHAEF being pried from Versailles and purring over the military air of our new headquarters. He and Beetle immediately started talking about plans to hold SHAEF personnel for the American occupation staff.

After an impatient three days in his new office, he was off again —to see, firsthand, last phases of operations to clear the Rhine's long west bank. I went along, thankful for the opportunity to leave Rheims and to see the gang at General Bradley's headquarters, which General Ike used as a base for his travels. During the three-day tour he managed to see just about every major commander in the field, hitting, among other units, the British Second Army, Canadian Third Army, and the American First,

Third, and Ninth Armies. He even visited the new Fifteenth Army, formed to handle operations in the hold-out Brest peninsula and plan occupation duties in Germany. After seeing a number of German cities, he remarked, "I know you'll be glad, Kay, when I tell you this: they're all in ruins, just like Aachen. Maybe they'll make up for places like Coventry, London, Rotterdam and St. Lô!"

March battle news came in like a lion. The day of our arrival back in Rheims, Monty's Canadian and American Armies linked up in the Geldern sector. Three days later, Cologne fell to the First Army. That same night, March 7, General Bradley telephoned the Supreme Commander with electrifying news: a small armored spearhead had found a bridge still intact over the Rhine, the Ludendorff railway bridge at Remagen.

This was a superb example of General Eisenhower's active, literal, field command of the war, a typical answer to uninformed critics who accused him of being a red-tape general completely out of touch with the actual fighting. Bradley already had begun exploitation of the bridge, but he called to get Ike's concurrence. The Germans had presented them with one of the choice plums of war; should they junk present plans and risk throwing everything into the bridgehead? General Ike acted with a born soldier's lightning-fast decision: grab it, pour in everything we have, get not less than five divisions across as soon as possible.

(Results justified the risk. Within two days the bridgehead was three miles deep. The Germans, belatedly horrified at finding a bridge still over the Rhine, battered bridge and troops with bombs, long-range artillery, rockets, everything in their arsenal. But anti-aircraft gunners teamed with a Ninth Air Force sky-umbrella to inflict heavy damage on most of the German air force; engineers continued to strengthen and repair the battered structure as thousands of men and vehicles poured onto the east bank. The center span collapsed on March 17, but, again, engineers kept up the flow of traffic with supplementary floating bridges and other equipment. By March 24, only seventeen days after Bradley's telephone call and despite fanatic German harassment, the Remagen bridgehead was a huge bite out of Germany—twenty-five miles long, ten miles deep. And it bulged with three entire corps ready to lash out into the Reich itself.)

Due to a bad bout of flu, contracted from the rainy ride to and from General Bradley's headquarters, I missed most of this early-March excitement. I also missed, for the first time, a shipment of V-I-P's: the Prime Minister, the Chief of the Imperial General Staff, Madeleine Carroll, and others. I found General Ike worrying over the wording of a message to His Holiness, the Pope, who had sent him a specially blessed rosary.

Next day, the General bedded down with a cold. I took advantage of his absence to collect some office equipment in Paris, where I also got to see my only USO show of the war. It was good, that show, featuring Noel Coward, Marlene Dietrich, and Maurice Chevalier. All received a big hand, except Chevalier, then tarnished by collaboration rumors. He received polite applause, none from me.

The following week offered little more around headquarters than the usual variety of routine. Agents reported finding more coding equipment from 28th Division's stolen truck. General Eisenhower backed up his soldiers and insisted upon the B-Bag "gripe column" in *Stars and Stripes*. He presented the Presidential Citation to 101st Airborne Division just outside of Rheims, visited the Third and Seventh Armies. Beetle reported approximately 130 German prisoners suffocated to death in a troop movement by train; General Marshall demanded a full report, fixing responsibility.

One day there was a report of Himmler sending a representative to contact the Allies *re* a Western surrender. Another day, General Alexander disclosed receipt of peace feelers from General Karl Wolff, chief S.S. officer in northern Italy, suggesting a parley in Switzerland. (Alexander's reply: unconditional surrender only, no terms.)

General Ike, meantime, fell into such a state of nerves that

Beetle insisted he take a brief rest-cure. An American had written
to offer use of his villa in Cannes. Even so, it took Beetle four
whole days to convince the General he must get some relaxation
or face a nervous breakdown. Ike agreed only with the reserva-
tion that General Bradley come along. And, per usual, he filled
up the plane with extra passengers: Tex, Ruth, Ethel, Nana,
and me.

We took off on March 19 for five days on the Riviera, which
I hadn't seen since 1939. It was as peaceful, wasteful, luxurious,
and lovely as ever, even in the middle of a war. I wrote in the
diary:

> The trip took us just under three hours. The weather per-
> fect at Cannes . . . blue sky . . . so wonderful to get away
> from the marshalling yards at Rheims, plus the dirt. The
> villa where E is staying, "Sous le Vent," is a most delightful
> place. Never have I seen such wonderful bathrooms. We
> were told that the house cost over three million to build and
> furnish. Ruth, Nana, Ethel, and myself staving at a very
> nice villa about 1½ miles away.

General Eisenhower, incognito and unable to walk around, retired into the peace of his villa. General Bradley and aide arrived
the next morning to keep him company. The rest of us took off
for Monte Carlo. In order to at least pretend the civilian status
required by Monaco, the men shed caps and insignia and rolled
up their sleeves; we girls followed suit, wearing slacks. But our
holiday mood evaporated in the Monte Carlo of 1945; it was
rather pitiful, in spite of the divine setting, with only a few
broken-down old ladies fiddling at the tables. Ruth was the only
one in our party who carried away any roulette money.

All in all, the stolen holiday, brief as it was, made time and the
war stand still. We all left the Riviera feeling rested, refreshed.
Generals Ike and Bradley had to get back for the Big Push.

This was Monty's show, all the way—and a typical Montgomery performance, with all the ingredients of incredible prepara-

tion, wheel-to-wheel barrage, mass assault, and victory. Inasmuch as it led to a steady succession of advances and resultant war news which wiped the operation from public attention, Operation "Plunder" is worthy of more than passing notice. For one, it was the main "power crossing" of the Rhine. Secondly, General Eisenhower regarded it as the epitome of Allied warfare.

"Plunder" started back in England with meticulous exercises on rivers and banks similar to those expected in that Rhine sector. It also started with the construction of special craft, some of them forty-five feet long; with intensive Navy-Army studies of amphibious landings.

Then, on February 21, the Air Forces began a month-long bombardment carefully tailored to the ground assault set for late March. With the crossing aimed at encirclement of the vital Ruhr, initial bombing efforts concentrated upon eighteen key bridges and viaducts serving every main railway route out of the Ruhr. Before the month was out, ten of the eighteen bridges were destroyed, two seriously damaged, and another two damaged. Heavy and medium bombers smashed old records: on March 11, for example, more than one thousand Bomber Command planes rained about five thousand tons on the Essen rail center; the following night, even that new record was smashed, with still more planes and still more bombs. The RAF began using its 22,000-pound monsters. Almost the entire weight of the Eighth Air Force was concentrated upon airfields for jet planes, a growing worry to the high command. In one memorable operation, Italy-based bombers pounded Berlin to draw fighters from the Ruhr; Eighth Air Force fighters protected the bombers. The armadas also hit hard at airfields, gun and mortar sites, barracks, defense works, camps; all were strafed relentlessly, as well as bombed. During the four days beginning March 21, aircraft from Italy, western Europe, and Britain hurled more than forty thousand sorties against Germany.

At eight o'clock the night of the twenty-third, Monty loosed his famous Desert Rat barrage against the east bank. When British commandos entered Wesel an hour later, they found the sector so perfectly bombed and shelled that only thirty-six casualties were reported in the taking of the communications center. The British Second Army crossed over on the left; the American Ninth Army, on the right.

At one o'clock in the morning of March 24, the airborne attack began, the two divisions making contact by afternoon.

This two-hour landing represented an historic degree of planning, timing, and fighting—a peak of joint effort by two Allies. As General Eisenhower described it in his report to the Combined Chiefs: "An Allied operation in the fullest sense."

Unadorned facts and statistics stagger the imagination: the 6th Airborne Division came from England; the RAF and the U.S. Troop Carrier Command together furnished 669 planes and 429 gliders. The 17th Airborne came from France in 903 planes and 897 gliders of Troop Carrier Command. Not one of these planes or gliders was molested by enemy aircraft . . . and little wonder. Fighter escort on the approach was provided by 213 planes from Fighter Command, plus 676 more from Ninth Air Force. Over the target area, 900 British aircraft supplied the cover while 1,253 fighters of Eighth Air Force put up a screen east of the Rhine. The sole aerial losses came from heavy ack-ack, which accounted for only four per cent of this colossal sky armada.

That same night of "Plunder," the all-out crossing in the north, General Patton sneaked his 5th Division across the Rhine south of Mains, taking 19,000 prisoners in twenty-four hours, building up a bridgehead nine miles long and six miles deep within another twenty-four hours. The next day, Third Army put over two more bridgeheads; the next, Seventh Army got across near Worms and, the next, linked up with the Third, which had two more lodgements. On April 1, French II Corps established a bridgehead at Philippsburg.

Thus, as it was outlined at SHAEF, the great Rhine was breached all along its length—according to plan.

Sir Alan Brooke admitted General Eisenhower's championship

of this plan had been right. He had no doubt of it, for he, Ike, and Mr. Churchill were standing on the east bank of the Rhine not long after Monty sent his forces across.

As for operations to the south, General Eisenhower covered them thoroughly and finally in his report:

> No defeat the Germans suffered in the war, except possibly Tunisia, was more devastating in the completeness of the destruction inflicted upon his forces than that which he suffered in the Saar Basin.

Then, after this tribute to the Seventh Army forces in that mass attack by some fifteen divisions, he emphasized the great tactical direction of warfare in that area between two army groups:

> I unhesitatingly class General Bradley's tactical operations during February and March, which witnessed the complete destruction of the German forces west of the Rhine, as the equal in brilliance of any the American forces have ever conducted.

After all these campaigns up to the Rhine and the crossings themselves, I lost interest in the grand strategy. From then on, like everyone else, I became lost in the confusing but exciting avalanche of individual victories and new advances and mass surrenders which made up the month of April.

March went out with an announcement that an average of ten thousand prisoners came into Allied hands every day during the month, apart from heavy losses in dead and wounded. (I found the last day of March more noteworthy on the personal front because General Ike was already in the office, stern-faced and silently chastising, when we all showed up that morning.)

While trying to keep up with the marauding armies, the Supreme Commander had his hands full in the final phase.

General Marshall advised that Mr. Churchill and the Combined Chiefs of Staff disagreed with the Eisenhower operational plans. Among other things, there was pressure to give priority to a drive into northern Germany, instead of an offensive from Kassel toward Leipzig and the Russians. This school emphasized the political-psychological effects of early entry into Berlin, the necessity of bringing the U-boat war to an end, opening up supply lines through North German ports, acquiring use of Swedish shipping, relieving the Dutch, occupying Denmark and Norway, and using the great plain country. General Ike contended the main function of his forces was to crush the German armies, not to occupy empty ruined cities. He stressed the tactical benefits of a Kassel thrust, showed the northern plains to be in poor condition for mobile warfare, and argued that Berlin no longer was a military objective of major importance. General Bradley was to rush toward Leipzig, meet the Russians on the Elbe, or, if the Soviet advance failed to come as fast as expected, to seize a bridgehead on the Elbe and be prepared for further advances to the East. The general idea, Ike declared, was to meet the Russians and split Germany in half. The northernmost assault would come next in priority, then the chase into the Nazis' so-called National Redoubt in the Alps.

A message from Moscow quoted Stalin as in complete agreement with the Eisenhower directive; he promised detailed plans for co-ordinating the expected link-up. That same day, however, a message from Mr. Churchill hinted resentment at alleged belittling of British troops. General Ike was quite upset—until he learned poor decoding was responsible for what he regarded as a nasty crack by the Prime Minister. The next day, Ike was told he would be military governor of the U.S. occupation zone; the next, General Arnold, over on a visit, whispered a rumor that General Eisenhower was to become Chief of Staff in Washington.

On April 4, there was a brief flurry of fear over a last-ditch secret weapon. Some said it might be gas; others, rockets. Kesselring was reported as telling Hitler he refused to use this new weapon: it could only bring a horrible bloodbath to both sides.

That first fortnight of April was a field-day of Allied reports:

Official U.S. Army Photo

Big Brass in Germany. Seated: Lt. Gen. Wm. H. Simpson, Gen. George S. Patton, Gen. Carl A. Spaatz, General Eisenhower, Gen. Omar N. Bradley, Gen. Courtney H. Hodges, Lt. Gen. Leonard T. Gerow. Standing: Brig. Gen. Ralph P. Sterling, Lt. Gen. Hoyt S. Vandenberg, Lt. Gen. W. B. Smith, Major Gen. Ralph P. Weyland,

With Telek, in Berlin.

Kassel cleared . . . Weimar and Erfurt cleared . . . Ninth and First Armies encircle Ruhr pocket, largest double envelopment in history, trapping twenty-one divisions . . . Prisoners become a problem . . . Ruhr pocket split in two . . . Karlsruhe, Schweinfurt, Rheine fall . . . Fourth Armored at outskirts of Chemnitz . . . Jena cleared . . .

General Eisenhower visited Frankfurt, found it badly damaged, but made initial preparations for the great headquarters to be established there. He talked with Bernard Baruch in Rheims, chortled over the news of von Papen's capture, visited General Bradley at Wiesbaden and then toured a long list of corps and divisions, ending up at General Patton's headquarters.

That night—April 12, just as the 2nd Armored gained a beachhead on the east bank of the Elbe—we heard the tragic news of President Roosevelt's death.

I was in Paris, where people walked hurriedly along the streets in unaccustomed solemnity. Many, men and women alike, walked up to Americans with tears in their eyes. Some simply shook hands with silent understatement. Others tried to express what they felt. Even the G-I's were hushed, unusually quiet and dignified. It was as though everyone, regardless of nationality, had lost a personal but mutual friend. I doubt if any world figure's death caused as much universal, sincere grief. As for myself, I just couldn't believe it. America without Franklin D. Roosevelt— it seemed impossible. General Eisenhower, returning the next day to Rheims, said softly it was a shame the President didn't live long enough to see final victory, now it was so very close.

It was close, too. Within a few days the Ruhr pocket collapsed, with eighty thousand prisoners taken in the first twenty-four hours; the total finally reached 325,000. The Second British Army reached the Elbe. The Canadians found resistance collapsing in North Holland; they reached the sea on April 15. Arnhem fell, followed by such cities as Baden-Baden, Leipzig, Magdeburg, Nurenberg.

While General Eisenhower saw his first Nazi concentration

camp, insisting upon a firsthand view of the atrocities (although Patton himself admitted to downright nausea at the horrors), I flew east in a B-25 with Tooey Spaatz and others for my first visit to Germany. We landed near Marburg. Sally Bagby and I, quartered in our first German house, got our first touch of the new fever covering Germany: looting. Ashamed but excited, we went through every drawer, cupboard, and shelf in the building—but too many had been there before us. Not as much as a Nazi flag was left. We glared even more fiercely at the few Germans on the streets next morning before our takeoff.

On the seventeenth, the Military Assistant, the Naval Aide, and I accompanied General Eisenhower on a flying trip to London, where he was dining with the Prime Minister. We were to leave the next morning, but Mr. Churchill insisted that Ike stay over for a Cabinet meeting. The Prime Minister, incidentally, had remarked to General Ike at dinner the night before that the Russians already were becoming difficult, refusing to let our correspondents into Vienna. After the Cabinet meeting, the General invited Mother and me out to Telegraph Cottage for a quick lunch prior to our departure for Rheims.

The rest of April was one grand, happy mess at headquarters. Everyone agreed it was only a matter of days before war's end. Meanwhile, Allied armies streamed over the crumbling Reich, taking more than one million prisoners in the first three weeks of the month. Supply lines stretched farther than in the 1944 dash across France: 15,000 cargo planes supplemented by stripped heavy bombers became literal "flying boxcars," flying over 20,000 sorties during the month to bring almost 60,000 tons of freight to the racing spearheads. (One item: 10,255,609 gallons of petrol.) Every afternoon they returned to bases loaded with evacuated casualties and Allied prisoners liberated by the advances.

General Eisenhower and all of us at SHAEF staggered with work. Members of Parliament arrived from London to see the horror camps. My "fan mail" job, increased by a flood of congratulatory letters, suffered in the rush of problems descending upon the Boss. We had calls from the Prime Minister, who was upset over the food situation in Holland and the coming Russian link-up, among other things. He had sheafs of messages from General Marshall, on subjects ranging from a request for Generals Hodges and Bradley in the Pacific to agreement with the idea that a party of Congressmen and leading editors tour the concentration camps for eyewitness evidence of Nazism. He kept close touch on advances into the National Redoubt area, where some advisers still feared a desperate to-the-death stand by the Nazis.

On April 25, the Prime Minister telephoned to transmit a Swiss message claiming Hitler to be the victim of a complete nervous breakdown. Himmler reportedly would propose surrender to the Western Allies. (Two days later, BBC announced the Himmler approach and quoted Ike as saying "not interested," unless the Germans promised unconditional surrender, to *all* the Allies.) Next was a message from General Alexander *re* the forthcoming surrender of German forces in Italy; it looked real this time, he said.

The day of April 25 was more notable for another event: patrols of the U.S. 69th Division met elements of the Russian 58th Guards Division in the Torgau area, on the Elbe.

The Eastern front and the Western front had melted into one. The Russians and the Allies had joined forces; Hitler's wildest nightmare of a two-front war was bitter fact. Germany was split in two.

(Later, a Second Lieutenant, William D. Robertson of Los Angeles, from that link-up patrol came in to present General Eisenhower with the sheet-and-stick flag used to identify themselves in their meeting with the Russians. Ike promoted the lieutenant and his soldiers one grade, on the spot. The soldiers were Sergeant James J. McDonnell of Peabody, Massachusetts, Corporal Frank B. Huff of Washington, Virginia, and Corporal Paul Staub of New York.)

Some of the headquarters staff protested bitterly, but unoffi-

cially, because what they described as "political influences" kept
the Allies from entering Berlin just about the same time as the
Russians. Berlin had been the objective of everyone in the western
armies, starting 'way back in North Africa. And there was widespread resentment that the push couldn't continue straight into
Hitler's capital. But the decision was out of our hands.

Throughout all this period, the plight of the Dutch became
more and more pressing.

Western Holland was isolated, cut off by the advances of our
troops, facing wholesale starvation. At the same time, German
defenses there were so strong the Allies would have to halt their
final push into Germany in order to mount an attack strong
enough to batter into western Holland. On the other hand, if
such an attack were launched, the enemy would open dykes and
flood the entire country—ending its fertility for many years to
come, showering further miseries upon its people.

The German commander, General Blaskowitz, was warned
that holding onto Holland would not, in any way, affect our
military power or slow down the coming German collapse. He was
further warned that opening of the dykes would constitute an
immortal crime, an indelible blot upon his own military honor
and that of the German Army.

The General was unimpressed. But Seyss-Inquart, Nazi Commissioner for Holland, came up with a possible solution: a truce.

On April 27, General Eisenhower sent two staff officers to
Holland. They found General Blaskowitz unwilling to consider
surrender as long as any form of resistance continued inside
Germany. But, possibly because of nightmares about future war-
crimes trials, he agreed to the Commissioner's plan.

The Seyss-Inquart proposal was simple: inasmuch as the
Germans refused to surrender and the Allies hesitated to make
an all-out attack, why not keep the present battle-line exactly
as at present? If so, the Germans would co-operate in the introduction of relief supplies. They also would promise to cease any

further repressive actions against the Dutch and to abandon any plans for flooding of the country.

The Combined Chiefs gave General Ike a free hand in negotiations. With the Dutch people and their nation's soil held as hostages, he had little choice. Besides, it was only a matter of days or hours before a complete German surrender—at 3:00 A.M. on April 28, for example, two correspondents checked with him on a rumor in the United States that the war was over.

On April 29, the Supreme Commander sent Beetle, along with other Allied staff officers and a Russian representative, to meet General Blaskowitz. Both sides agreed to the truce, the Germans re-emphasizing their promises, the Allies postponing any further advance. Free dropping of food by mercy planes already had begun; now relief poured into devastated Holland. The Canadians stood fast, grimly, on their so-called Grebbe Line —just waiting for the word of Germany's collapse.

That same day General Alexander messaged General Eisenhower the Germans in North Italy would surrender effective at noon, May 2.

I wrote in my diary:

At midnight the German radio announced Adolf Hitler has died at his post.

CHAPTER XVII

EXACTLY eight days after hearing that midnight announcement of Hitler's death, I was:

(1) The first British woman to enter defeated Berlin.

(2) One of the only three western women permitted to witness Nazi Germany's formal surrender, and

(3) One of the few survivors from a great sea of vodka which
flooded the Russianized surrender hall in Berlin.

However, in the week leading up to this climax, neither I nor
anyone else at Supreme Headquarters had time for conjectures
about the future. The war might end at any minute of any hour;
perhaps with the next telephone call to our office. We were pro-
portionately busy.

Despite the surrender suspense, General Eisenhower had to
wade through the usual collection of problems, V-I-P's, and political worries. Major visitors included the Under Secretary of War,
the American Ambassador to France, the Harvey Gibsons, a
group of Mexican generals. Generals Tooey Spaatz and Ira Eaker
came in to talk about going home soon. General Marshall ordered
First Army's General Hodges to return "with all possible speed,"
for eventual duty in the Pacific. General de Lattre de Tassigny
declined, successfully, to evacuate his French First Army from
Stuttgart. The Prime Minister called several times, much disturbed over Russian landings in Denmark. Staff and War Department officials brought in studies on redeployment of European forces to the Pacific, plus demobilization plans.

Like everyone else around the world, I spent every free moment planning V-E Day celebrations. The girls and I set up a

big reception, to be held at our WAC house. We named May 6 as the date; that seemed safe enough. And I suggested another kind of party to General Eisenhower.

The latter started from a casual conversation in the officers' mess. I heard one of the lieutenants across from me remark, "Seems sort of funny that I'll finish out the war without seeing the Supreme Commander."

I looked up. "Don't you work here at SHAEF?"

"Ever since London," he replied. "I was down in Algiers with AFHQ, too."

"And you mean to tell me you've never seen General Eisenhower?"

He looked at my aide insignia, then said sarcastically, "Well, we can't all be aides, you know."

Back in the office, I told the General of my talk in the mess. "There must be dozens of officers right here in headquarters who've never seen you, let alone met you," I added. "How about having some sort of 'open house,' or a cocktail party, before SHAEF breaks up?"

He saw the reasoning behind my idea and, foregoing his normal reaction to social events, decided to stage such a party. Colonels and general officers would be excluded, as he had met most of them. Guests would range from lieutenant colonel down to warrant officer, the men who'd never had an opportunity to meet their Commanding General, or vice versa.

"That's a very good idea, Kay," he said. "We'll certainly do it—right after the official surrender."

Throughout all these first days of May, of course, all attention focused on the coming surrender. The smaller capitulations, by units ranging in size from squads right up to whole army groups, only whetted headquarters' appetite.

On May 2, General Eisenhower went into Paris with Butch to record V-E Day speeches for radio and the newsreels. That same day, the Germans in the Alps asked to whom they should surrender. (Comprising two armies, they laid down their arms on May 5.) On the evening of May 2, we heard BBC broadcast the surrender of the Germans in North Italy.

Returning to Rheims on May 3, the General learned Field Marshal Montgomery had received a new peace-feeler. The negotiating party was headed by Admiral Hans Georg von Friedeburg, the U-boat chief who became head of the German Navy when Admiral Doenitz took over from Hitler. He wanted to surrender three armies which had been fighting the Russians; it was another move to avoid surrendering to the Soviet, and to force a split between the Allies. Monty refused at once. Individual soldiers who gave themselves up would be treated as regular prisoners of war, he added. Admiral Friedeburg then asked Field Marshal Wilhelm Keitel for further instructions.

On May 4, Monty met the Germans at Lübeck. Meanwhile, at SHAEF, General Eisenhower learned that Admiral Doenitz apparently intended to make an over all surrender. A representative was to arrive in Rheims the next day; U-boats had been recalled to port. In order to make the surrender all-inclusive and truly Allied, the General immediately messaged Moscow to inquire if Major General Ivan Suslaparov would be acceptable as the Soviet representative. The Kremlin reply agreed to the choice. General Eisenhower also insisted, over Montgomery's objections, that representatives of the sea and air forces participate in the northern surrender, if any.

All afternoon we waited tensely for Monty's call. Air Chief Marshal Tedder joined the General in his tiny office; Butch, up from Paris, joined me in my office. We waited and waited. Finally, General Ike declared he was going home and could be reached there. Afraid of missing the big surrender, I succeeded in urging him to wait just another five minutes.

The phone rang exactly five minutes later, about 7:00 P.M. I answered it. It was Monty.

Butch and I eavesdropped shamelessly through the open door. The ceremony had gone through, but it was not the all-fronts surrender. General Eisenhower and Monty treated it as a tactical, sectional surrender—covering all German forces, land, sea, and air, in northwest Germany as well as Holland, Schleswig-Holstein, and Denmark. (The papers were signed that night and the surrender became effective at eight o'clock the next morning.)

Although dead-tired, the General sat down and dictated a special message to the Prime Minister praising the courage and determination of the British people throughout the long war years. Then he and Butch went off for dinner.

There was another message from Monty that evening, saying the Germans were flying to Rheims the following day, due in about noon, to discuss the general surrender of all German forces.

I went home late, looking forward to the important day ahead. More personally, I rejoiced in the news report that London was abolishing air-raid warnings; to me and to all Londoners, that was the official end of the war.

There wasn't much work being done in our red schoolhouse when I arrived the next morning. Most of us sat around talking about the surrender ceremony, which was to take place in the War Room; that square, pale-blue office looked exactly like a movie set in Hollywood or Elstree. All the super-secret charts and maps now were only a dull background for the clutter of cameras, cables, wires, and banks of klieg lights. Butch was outranked out of his office, which had been taken over by the Russian representatives, General Suslaparov and his bald-headed interpreter, a Soviet colonel also bearing the first name of "Ivan."

Just before noon, we learned the German party's plane had run into foul weather and landed at Brussels. They would lunch in the Belgian capital and come on to Rheims by auto, due to arrive about five o'clock.

The main visitors to our office that afternoon were Beetle, Air Chief Marshal Tedder, and Major General Kenneth Strong, SHAEF's Intelligence chief and an able German linguist as the result of service in Berlin as British Military Attaché. Beetle and General Strong, the same two who had accomplished the cloak-and-dagger negotiations in Lisbon with the Italians, were to be the principals in this surrender drama. General Eisenhower said he didn't want to see the Germans until after they had signed all the capitulation papers.

The Nazis arrived shortly after 5:00 P.M., met by two British officers from SHAEF, and escorted to a washroom.

Then they were taken to Beetle's office, where the Brass moved on down to the War Room. Ruth Briggs stood an incongruous guard while her Boss started to work on the Germans.

In our office, the suspense stretched into five, then into ten minutes. Fifteen minutes . . . twenty minutes.

Finally, Beetle came in.

The surrender, he said, would be postponed until at least the following day.

Neither Admiral von Friedeburg nor the German War Office Colonel with him was authorized to make a surrender. Furthermore, they had failed to bring a code for communication with Admiral Doenitz. Beetle, as Prussian as the best of the German General Staff when he wants to be, told them to get authority, or an officer with authority, without further delay. He then explained just how the Germans were to surrender their forces, unconditionally, without terms, to all the Allies, on all fronts. Admiral von Friedeburg was permitted to send a report of this discussion to Admiral Doenitz. It would travel by Allied code to a British Army outpost, be decoded, and then sent on by messenger to Flensburg.

No reply could be expected, Beetle added, until tomorrow.

The let-down was horrible. All staff sections closed their offices; everyone left in a gray mood. Press and Brass filed despondently from the War Room, the room still rigged for a spectacular show postponed at least twenty-four hours. I went on home to make the most of an opportunity for a good night's sleep, completely unaware it would have to last me for the next three hectic days.

The following day, May 6, gave every promise of becoming V-E Day. But the morning dragged by, the minutes loaded with lead. The telephone rang incessantly, but without importance. Eventually, however, we learned Doenitz was sending General Gustav Jodl, German Chief of Staff, to Rheims with the necessary authority for a surrender. Freddie de Guingand was escorting Jodl and his aide.

They arrived in late afternoon.

Jodl and his aide joined Admiral von Friedeburg and the German War Office Colonel; they conferred alone for quite a while, then, about 6:00 P.M., entered Beetle's office for the conference.

Once again, our office was lonely, tight with impatient tension. And it remained that way for the better part of an hour and a half . . . before Beetle came in to announce a further delay. Jodl had a code but it would take another three hours for him to communicate with Doenitz on the final decision. Meanwhile, General Suslaparov had been acquainted with the details; General François Sevez had arrived as the French representative of General de Gaulle.

The final hitch came when the Germans, playing for time to withdraw units from the Russian front, asked for an adjournment of forty-eight hours before signing the final surrender; this time was necessary, they contended, to permit communication with their outlying forces. General Eisenhower replied firmly: unless the Germans agreed to his terms immediately, he would break off all negotiations and seal his lines so no more Germans could get through. Furthermore, he warned this ultimatum would expire forty-eight hours from midnight.

By this time it was about nine o'clock. Our party was well under way at the WAC house—so we all adjourned to the reception. Actually, the party wasn't very abandoned or gay, for no one was able to ignore the event about to take place in the schoolhouse. The Rheims champagne disappeared surprisingly slowly, although one of the Russian officers, attempting to drink American rye as though it were vodka, got so drunk that he and his colleagues had to leave. General Eisenhower stayed only a few minutes, his thoughts far away from casual cocktail chatter.

"Keep in touch with the office," he told me. "Let me know what's happening."

Just after midnight, a call from the General Staff secretary indicated the big show was about to take place.

I called General Eisenhower's house, but someone had telephoned before me; he was just leaving. (His British Military Assistant, Jimmy Gault, slept through the entire proceeding; he never forgave Butch for not awakening him.)

Ruth and I hurried up to headquarters, where brilliant klieg lights blazed in the War Room. I went on to our office, somewhat disappointed at missing the ceremony. The General was pacing up and down his room, into my office, back into his room, just as he did when dictating. The atmosphere was electric with his impatience; at the same time, I thought it rather lonely and pathetic in the Supreme Commander's office. The silence was heavy with the contrast to the bustle in the War Room.

It was nearing 3:00 A.M. when Beetle stomped in, half-grinning, half-grim.

The surrender had been signed—officially, at 2:41 A.M., Monday, May 7.

There was no time for elation, for celebration. The Germans were on their way up to our office. I felt a shiver of excitement; these would be my first German Brass, other than prisoners of war and dead Germans. I shoved Telek under the desk, commanding him not to bark, to present a proud Scottish dignity to the enemy.

At the sound of heavy boots nearing our door, I rose from my desk in the same respectful attention I showed to any high-ranking officers. They marched straight by without as much as a glance, exact prototypes of filmland Nazis, sour-faced, glum, erect, and despicable. The whole thing seemed unreal.

In the inner office, they came to a parade-ground halt, clicked their heels, and saluted smartly, with no hint of the Nazi salute. General Eisenhower stood stock-still, more military than I had ever seen him. Any human curiosity at this first meeting with his enemy—it was the first and only time he was to see the German chiefs—was completely submerged in an icy West Point formality. I bent over my diary to take his words down.

His voice was brittle. "Do you understand the terms of the document of surrender you have just signed?"

I heard a "*Ja, ja,*" following General Strong's interpretation.

General Eisenhower concluded this historic meeting with two more coldly undramatic sentences: "You will get details of instructions at a later date. And you will be expected to carry them out faithfully."

Jodl nodded. General Eisenhower stared silently, in dismissal. The Germans half-bowed, saluted, did an about-face and marched back past my desk and out of the office. Telek, thank goodness, only growled.

Afterward, General Ike's face stretched into the broadest grin of his career. As the photographers milled around, he said, "Come on, let's all have a picture!" Everyone gathered near the Boss as he held two of the signature pens in a V-sign. He said Ruth and I should appear in the picture, as we had been "in this thing" since the beginning. Ruth, however, was down in Beetle's office and the group couldn't wait.

Within a few minutes, the office was empty once more. Ruth came in to chat with me; Air Chief Marshal Tedder stayed behind to talk with the General.

Almost as though it was expected of him—and without the slightest sign of exuberance—General Eisenhower remarked that the occasion called for a bottle of champagne. We repaired to his house.

The next two hours or so bore more resemblance to a group sitting around discussing a just-ended bridge game than to people who had just seen the end of a war. There was no gaiety, no joking, no laughing. The Supreme Commander spent most of the time listing those to whom true credit belonged for successful conclusion of the war; there was no gloating, no personal pride, absolutely no buoyancy. Everyone simply seemed weary, indescribably weary.

We broke it up as dawn came through the chateau windows. Ruth and I went straight to bed, without undressing.

I stumbled into the office about 10:00 A.M., groggy from only two or three hours' sleep but expecting to enjoy a light day of celebrations devoid of any sign of work.

Instead, I found V-E Day to be the worst day I ever put in at the Supreme Commander's office.

One glance at the messages awaiting the General indicated there would be no partying that day. Everything was snafu. One message stated the Germans in Czechoslovakia refused to surrender to the Russians opposite their lines; instead, the Nazis were flooding our front. A second message noted that, even while Jodl signed the formal papers at Rheims, the German radio announced the Nazis had made a separate peace with the Western Allies, not with the Russians. The latter not only complained bitterly at this report, but advised SHAEF they no longer felt General Suslaparov had been an acceptable Soviet representative at the Rheims ceremony.

The anti-climax was complete with a new demand from the Russians: a formal surrender must be signed in Berlin.

General Eisenhower messaged Moscow he would be delighted to go to Berlin for a formal surrender ceremony. Then, the Prime Minister began calling; Beetle was in and out a dozen times; other staff members added to the pressure—General Eisenhower shouldn't participate in the Berlin surrender. His advisers' principal objection was one of military protocol: Marshal Zhukov was only an Army Group commander, far below the rank of a General of the Army. Western pride and "face" were at stake. This and other reasons brought the Supreme Commander to agreement; he sent another message to Moscow, noting that his Deputy, Air Chief Marshal Tedder, would represent Britain and America at the Berlin sessions.

Throughout the day the German radio drove a deeper wedge between East and West; it announced the Nazis had surrendered to the Western Allies. No mention was made of Russia.

Around 3:00 P.M., the final blow fell. Beetle roared into the office like a madman: Ed Kennedy, of Associated Press, had smuggled into America a story on the Rheims surrender. The "scoop" already hummed over AP wires in the United States, leaving a pack of angry correspondents in France, a group of very upset gentlemen in the Kremlin, 10 Downing Street, and the White House—and a very irate Supreme Commander in Rheims. Aside from his understandable anger, General Eisenhower was hurt. He had taken the press into his confidence throughout the campaigns from Africa to Germany, often against conscientious military advice, and he was proud his confidence always had been justified. Now, at the one time when it mattered most, the AP man had shown a complete disregard for that confidence.

The rest of May 7 was all like that. Even the Prime Minister added to the general chaos in our office, by telephoning a total of eight times from London. I didn't get to open a single "fan letter," although they covered my desk demanding attention. We all went home late that night, agreeing it was the most harrowing day SHAEF ever experienced. That was my V-E Day. Fatigue made sleep elusive.

I was up early the next morning, first in the office. Among the overnight messages was one asking Air Chief Marshal Tedder to meet a Russian escort at the airport in Stendal, some sixty miles from Berlin.

General Eisenhower came in with a Happy V-E Day present for his official family: an invitation to join the Berlin surrender party.

To us, it was the final, grand gesture for the little official family, significantly typical. The General confided unofficially, he would like to go along. But, inasmuch as it was impossible, he wanted us to enjoy this last major event of the war. All his aides were invited, his Military Assistant, his Naval Aide, his

Texas Aide, and his WAC Aide, plus Nana Rae, his chief ste-
nographer. Tooey Spaatz, scheduled to witness the signing, agreed
to permit his aide, Sally Bagby, to join us.

We three girls probably were more excited than any of the
others. We would be the first three western women to enter Berlin; I probably would be the first British woman. We would have
ringside seats at the greatest show of the war.

Actually, however, the entire party seemed somewhat excited.
General de Tassigny, the French representative, failed to show
up for our departure and had to leave in a later plane. One of
General Spaatz' staff crowded into the C-47 hauling the German
group. Air Chief Marshal Tedder had his own ship, the same
one in which we had visited Luxor. The rest of us—Tooey, Jimmy,
Tex, Sally, Nana, and I piled into General Eisenhower's C-47,
settling down happily in the blue-and-burgundy cabin. At the
last moment, General Suslaparov and his aide joined us.

Arriving at Stendal, we found no sign of the Russian escort.
Forty-five impatient minutes later, Air Chief Marshal Tedder decided to proceed without the Soviets. When an American pilot
mentioned that a U.S. plane had been shot down the previous
day, Tedder replied testily, "All right, we'll wait fifteen minutes
longer. No more. Then we'll take off, Russians or no Russians."
The rest of us began scanning the sky nervously. Just as the
fifteen-minute ultimatum expired, the Soviet fighters appeared
overhead. We jumped back into the C-47 and took off.

A broad dark cloud was the first hint of Berlin. Coming in at
about 2,000 feet, stories of the city's bomb damage seemed exag-
gerated; we could see thousands of buildings still standing. But,
lowering gradually toward Templehof airport, we saw the truth
behind this optical illusion: the structures were little more than
rubbled walls, completely gutted. Berlin was a ghostly skeleton.
Smoke still rose from her bones.

Even Templehof showed smouldering ruins as we landed, pulling onto a debris-littered runway not far from a smoking airport
building. General Suslaparov jumped out immediately, then

turned, as Marshal Zhukov's representative, to welcome Air Chief Marshal Tedder to Berlin. (I believe it was the friendly General's last official act; he has never been heard of since that noon of May 8.) A band played the various national anthems; everyone stood at super-stiff attention. There was an inspection of the guard of honor. The Air Chief Marshal made a brief speech.

Several dozen cars were drawn up a short distance away. Their appearance—glistening limousines side by side with battered, windowless, tiny vehicles—pointed up the Soviet's pitiful poverty of transportation. On the biggest day of their war they could only offer this junkyard collection of automobiles to carry the Western Allies to the big surrender. The Brass moved sedately to their assigned cars. The rest of us waited, then joined in a free-for-all rush.

Stepping into the car was just like stepping into an ill-kept stable. The Russian driver had all the odors of any man who never bathed in his life, plus those of a soldier just through fighting, plus those of countless bottles of vodka. Luckily, the car had no window glass.

And as our long convoy started off, at breakneck speed, I saw our driver was about as familiar with automobiles as with soap. He jammed on the gas, put one hand on the horn, released the brake—and we were off. I watched the back of his thick neck, to keep from looking at the car only a few feet ahead; we were traveling about forty miles per hour through the streets.

Then, I turned to concentrate on the view. The damage was appalling. Whole blocks were little more than fields of stones and bricks. Buildings still standing were burned out, mere shells. There were no German civilians, no automobiles, no windows. Some houses still smoked, from the recent fighting. Most, however, were grim monuments to U.S. bomber raids by day, RAF bombers by night.

Any initial pity I felt was erased by memories of London's Blitz, of Coventry, Plymouth, Dover. Berlin, awful in its utter devastation, was only multiplied retribution for Rotterdam, War-

saw, the enforced destruction of towns such as St. Lô. Any remaining traces of pity disappeared at the sight of long lines of
dead-faced humans now classified primly as Displaced Persons,
trudging through the ruins of Berlin, dragging rag-shod feet,
sometimes riding wagons piled high with pitiful belongings, heading dolefully for France, Belgium, Holland, Italy, Czechoslovakia,
Yugoslavia, all of Europe.

At each intersection, where the Germans had erected street barricades, I saw my first Russian WAC's. No British, American, or
French girl would have been caught dead in their uniforms:
knee-length boots, shapeless skirt, a three-quarter length tunic
tightly belted at the waist and bulging out in a dozen queer
places. A rifle slung over the shoulder keynoted a sober, soldierly
appearance. They wore no make-up, made no attempt at a feminine appearance.

They made a frantic effort to salute each speeding car, finally,
however, breaking into smiles. Altogether, I thought them quite
efficient and military, although rather frightening in their obvious toughness.

In the suburb of Karlshorst, which was comparatively undamaged and therefore chosen as the surrender scene, we all disem-
barked before a row of houses for the Brass.

A tall Russian general walked up to us three women and, wonder of wonders, introduced himself to us in English. It was General Andrie F. Vasiliev, who later headed the Russian delegation
to the United Nations.

"Where did you learn to speak English?" we asked.

"In Algiers . . . and now, may I show you to your quarters?"

"Quarters?" Nana asked. "But we'll only be here an hour or
two."

The General looked confused. "But, my dear ladies, you may
be here a week!"

Meekly, we followed him down the street to a small two-story
house, where he left us. Inside, we found a bathroom incapable
of use—and, upstairs, a score of shouting Russian soldiers.

We ran back to the house occupied by the Brass, with our nylons, and our uniforms creating something of a sensation among soldiers along the way. There were no wolf-calls, but a wolf-look is no different; there were few salutes. It seemed queer not to see G-I's or Tommies; Berlin was a completely Russian city.

We found all our party gathered in Air Marshal Tedder's house, the only clean building in that area. The rest of the day and the evening was spent in waiting.

First, we waited hungrily for food. It appeared about 2:30, black and pink caviar accompanied by wine and liquor; perhaps this was a luxurious V-I-P touch, but most of us would have exchanged a carton of cigarettes for a ham sandwich and a cup of coffee or tea. The faucet water was sheer poison, untouchable.

About 3:00 P.M., we listened to the German radio: announcements of V-E Day by President Truman, Prime Minister Churchill, and General de Gaulle. There in Berlin, the Russians made it plain there was no V-E Day till after their own ceremony; the speeches from Washington, London, and Paris fell flat, as far as we were concerned.

Air Chief Marshal Tedder left to pay his respects to Field Marshal Zhukov; Jimmy Gault and Tex Lee went along to present a lovely SHAEF flag to the Russians on behalf of General Eisenhower.

Meanwhile we sat . . . and sat . . . and sat. An hour passed. Two hours. We tired of our favorite pastime, comparing notes on the Russians, agreeing on two major points: (1) the Soviets have about as much regard for time as a South Seas native, and (2) it was a good thing our delegation hadn't been headed by General Eisenhower, for he would have returned to Rheims in a huff at this insulting delay.

Six hours after our arrival in Berlin, we learned we might have to spend the night there. The surrender ceremony was delayed by the arguments of Anglo-American, French, and Russian interpreters over the meanings of the smallest phrases incorporated

in the surrender document. No one knew just when the big show
would go on.

Desperately, we tried to get back to Templehof for hand luggage. Larry Hansen, the pilot, said his crew might dig up a few
extra toothbrushes for us women. After an hour and a half of
negotiation, the trip was permitted.

Then the Russians allowed us to enter the surrender building
only a block away, a former engineering college for the German
Army. The staff worried about getting a message through to
Rheims, where headquarters expected us back hours before; the
Russians were erecting special equipment for the communication.
Personally, I was more worried about food. Joined by other hungry
voices, I found our cries resulted only in bottles of a very light
beer; no food.

The power failed just as darkness fell. A helpful Russian supplied candles. Nana typed out some of the surrender documents
while High Brass held candles over the typewriter. The hours
crept by in this flickering, impatient atmosphere.

About 10:30 we were summoned to the surrender hall, all our
irritation and restlessness fading into sheer excitement at the
ceremony about to take place.

The huge room was banked with klieg lights, blinding as we
stepped in from the dim hallway. Everything seemed to be set
up for the sole convenience of the Russian press, who numbered
close to 100 and swarmed around in shouting bedlam. Movie
cameras were ready in almost every conceivable spot. Microphones
sprouted from the floor, hung from the ceiling; they and the
klieg lights created a veritable spiderweb of wires and cables.
A long table at one end of the room commanded all attention; obviously, this was for the highest High Brass. From it stretched
three other long tables, for press and lower Brass. Set apart, under
the balcony, was a short table apparently reserved for the surrendering Germans.

Sally, Nana, and I took our places at the center table, flanked
by the other two tables, with a good view of the table at the head

and that intended for the Germans. The noise was deafening. Virtually everyone at our table was a Russian general, most of them extremely young, bull-necked, short, and burly. We all smiled at each other helplessly, each placed in solitary confinement by the barriers of language.

There was a momentary silence as Marshal Zhukov, a short, stubby officer with a stern expression, entered the room. Everyone stood up. I noticed Zhukov was smaller than General Spaatz, who was on his left, even shorter than the Air Marshal, who was on his right; but he had neither Tedder's mischievous eyes nor Spaatz's schoolmaster grin. As we sat back down, he called the conference to order.

I was surprised at the way a civilian, later identified as Andrei Vyshinsky, hovered over the entire proceedings, deferred to even by Zhukov. Even in this moment of Soviet military victory, the Kremlin was stepping in to take charge. Vyshinsky found no detail too small for his attention, whether it be a whispered conference with Zhukov or the location of a propaganda movie camera.

With final details arranged to everyone's satisfaction, the signal was given for the enemy's entrance.

As a door opened just behind the empty table, a silence smothered the babble. Every pair of eyes in the room focused on a tall German officer in smart blue-gray Field Marshal's uniform, his chest covered with decorations and medals, his head poised high. He looked a little like Boris Karloff, this man; and his haughty manner was that of the born actor, the born Prussian. It was Field Marshal Wilhelm Keitel.

He stepped stiffly to the table, jerked up his silver-headed baton in a curt salute, and sat down.

The noise rose again. No one seemed to notice as the other two German principals took their places beside Keitel. While the latter stared straight ahead, his head rigid, his chin lifted to a near-ridiculous, pompous level, Colonel General P. F. Stumpf took the seat on Keitel's right, his *Luftwaffe* uniform failing to cre-

ate quite the same ponderous sense of dignity as that of his supe-
rior. On Keitel's left was Admiral von Friedeburg; the former
U-boat chief also lacked Prussian arrogance, relaxing slightly at
the table; his eyes had deep, dark circles, those of an ailing man.

Seated only two yards away, I had ample opportunity to study
the German Brass. Keitel was, by far, the dominant figure; his
disdainful dignity radiated hate. Behind him, however, among
the aides, was a youthful colonel whose handsome, brutal face
advertised a pure-Nazi arrogance even more fearful than that of
Keitel. I couldn't take my eyes off this officer's horrible expression; if the Germans ever make war again, I thought, he will be
among the top generals, relentless in his revenge. (Afterward, I
learned this colonel was educated at Oxford, spoke perfect English, was a fanatic Nazi, and one of the Third Reich's most brilliant young officers. I wonder where he is now?)

Although I had a close-up view of both the head table and
that of the Germans, the aggressive, mob-like behavior of the
Russian newspapermen permitted me only occasional glimpses
of the actual signing.

Keitel, I noticed, carefully pulled off one gray glove before
taking the pen. He looked up contemptuously at the boisterous
newsmen, then scribbled his signature across the surrender papers, moving hastily, as though anxious to dispense with a dirty
job. Some of the reporters and photographers climbed on tables
to get a better view; two had a brief fist-fight; all yelled and pushed.
Friedeburg and Stumpf signed hurriedly while Keitel glared
without seeing, the incarnation of the traditional icy Prussian.

Zhukov and Tedder signed as representatives of the Allies, followed by Generals Spaatz and de Tassigny, as witnesses.

The Air Chief Marshal arose, almost naked without his familiar
pipe, and asked in an emotionless, high voice, "Do you understand the terms you have just signed?" I was startled; the Air
Chief Marshal had asked almost the exact question which General Eisenhower put to Jodl and von Friedeburg back in Rheims;
Tedder was, as always, the perfect Deputy Supreme Commander.

As the Germans nodded, Zhukov gave them the order of dismissal. The Nazis arose as at a parade-ground command. Keitel again jerked his baton in brief salute. They left the room with an exit equally as dramatic as their entrance. (The next time I saw Keitel he was in the dock at Nuernberg, his military bearing crumpled, his fine uniform only a memory, his decorations gone, his sandy hair thin and rumpled, his expression that of a beaten, broken old man. Von Friedeburg committed suicide.)

Now, even for the Russians, V-E Day was official.

My watch hands neared the midnight mark as we all scrambled out of the hot surrender hall. Some of the Russians were singing, waving bottles. The cameramen were taking down their equipment. The English, French, and Americans sort of clung together, shaking hands vigorously, clapping each other on the back. Bottles appeared and the mingling between East and West became more noticeable.

Amidst all the noise, we learned of a grand banquet to be held within the hour. Sally, Nana, and I hastened to repair our make-up, some sixteen hours old, sharing a pool of precious tissues, lipstick, powder, and rouge. Nana, ever the canny Scot, even provided me with a spare pair of hose to replace my laddered stockings.

We went in to our old seats about 1:30 in the morning.

The surrender hall was even more impressive as a banquet hall. All the press and movie equipment—*and* the press—had been removed. In the balcony was an orchestra. Behind every other chair was a waitress, Soviet WAC's wearing gaily colored blouses.

Taking my seat, I blanched at the liquid artillery before each place: bottles of champagne, red wine, white wine, and—the Soviet secret weapon—vodka.

The Russian general across from me smiled encouragingly, then made peace overtures with a crazy combination of textbook French and pidgin English.

Great arc lights suddenly snapped on, flooding the room with a brilliant glare. I noticed a movie camera in one corner. Not all the equipment had been removed, as I thought upon entering; part of this scene was to be preserved for Russian posterity.

The first of the coming barrage of toasts was proposed, naturally, by Zhukov, to, naturally, Premier Stalin. We waited awkwardly for the English interpretation by a Russian officer, then the Soviets all performed a bottoms-up, followed by their Western Allies. I used champagne. Later, I degenerated to water; even champagne, at that pace, could be disastrous.

For almost four hours, the entire assemblage spent its time hearing toasts proposed and interpreted, then bottoms-upped. The head table seemed to be in a perpetual uproar, as Zhukov, Tedder, Spaatz, and De Tassigny each jumped up to out-do the others in flowery toasts from their respective four nations. Piles of *hors d'oeuvres* appeared periodically, consumed methodically by the Russians. There were other dishes, too; no one noticed them. After each toast, the Soviet women refilled every glass. I reached an understanding with my waitress; she winked as I refilled with water.

I wasn't the only one. Glancing around, I soon learned most of the Russians were playing possum. Only a few were all-out in the vodka game. The rest slyly substituted wine, smiling broadly at the growing intoxication of their Allies from the West. The General across from me was one of the conservatives.

Suddenly, however, he leaned over the table, "Why you not drink vodka?" he asked sternly. "You cheat. Wine!"

I looked him straight in the eye. "You cheat, too. That's *vin, pas de vodka.*"

His frown melted into a smile, then into a long, long laugh. For once, the British and the Russians understood each other. From then on we each toasted the other before lifting our glasses of wine or water.

By five o'clock in the morning, even the expert interpreter couldn't understand the toasts. The majority of the banquet guests were drunk, good old-fashioned drunk. Among the few survivors still afloat were Zhukov, who didn't drink, his High

Brass companions at the table, a few wise Russian generals, and we three women. One of the Western Allies crumpled onto the table after a last-effort toast. Several Russians literally went under the table. Another in our party disappeared. The tables' strict seating arrangement was abandoned as everyone became neighborly, breaking up into groups. Songs bubbled up in four languages, Russian predominating, closely followed by the American. The orchestra, which had struck chords for each and every toast, began to sour as vodka penetrated to the balcony.

As the party broke up just before dawn, Sally, Nana, and I agreed there had been between twenty-four and twenty-nine individual toasts, each requiring five to ten minutes for translation, plus the musical chord, and the final, deadly bottoms-up. We all agreed we had been in on the V-E party to end all V-E parties. I felt I could never face another glass of water or wine in my life.

As a final gesture, our more sober Russian hosts arranged a quick tour of the city.

Somewhat fearfully, I got into a car with another member of the SHAEF staff. He seemed out, out cold. The Russian driver and his companion grinned understandingly and we took off.

In the new daylight, Berlin was dead, a corpse. We saw Brandenburg Gate, the capital's triumphal arch, still standing but little more than a battered memento of old German victories. The Russians were building their own triumphal arch a short distance away. The Reichschancellery was a pile of ruins: I was amazed at the tiny balcony where Hitler screamed his speeches; it was small, very tiny, not at all the impressive scene I recalled from prewar newsreels. The site of Hitler's suicide and cremation was closely guarded by Russian soldiers. The Tiergarten, Berlin's own Hyde Park, was a ghastly battleground littered with burnt-out German tanks, helmets, leafless trees, and other debris from the recent fierce fighting.

At the Adlon Hotel, I got out to fulfill a 1939 wager I would be there for the war's end. I couldn't buy the required drink, however, for the Adlon had become nothing more than a shapeless acre of rubble. A Russian rushed up, shouting "No, no! Mines! Mines!"

Hurrying back to our car, I found my companion awake, glassy-eyed. I sat tensely as we drove toward the gutted Reichstag.

Suddenly, my SHAEF friend leaned forward, locked his arm around the driver's neck and tried to choke him to death. The car zigzagged. I screamed helplessly. The other Russian pulled out a huge revolver. Somehow, despite his instinct to shoot and my instinct to break into hysterics, we managed to pull the driver free.

As the car pulled up before the wreck which once had been Hitler's Reichstag, I begged someone else in the party to take care of our homicidal; he was vodka-mad, out of his mind. I crowded into another car, no longer interested in playing the tourist. I wanted to get "home," to the orderly routine of SHAEF.

Our C-47 took off from Templehof just before seven o'clock that morning.

Speeding toward Rheims, it carried the souvenirs of that great Russian V-E party—a sodden mass of dead-tired people whose eyes blurred with lack of sleep for twenty-four hours, whose heads throbbed louder than the engines, whose nostrils ached with the overpowering, sickening cloud of vodka fumes.

The war, at long last, was over . . . and the surrender thoroughly celebrated.

CHAPTER XVIII

A T THIS time, General Eisenhower had no idea of the spectacular acclaim awaiting him in London, Paris, New York, Amsterdam, Prague, Brussels, Washington, Luxembourg, Belfast, Warsaw, Moscow . . . half the world.

He was more concerned with his own personal celebration of V-E Day.

Just how the Supreme Commander would celebrate had been an old question around headquarters, a subject for endless debate. More sedate staff members bet on a dinner dance in Cannes or an official party in Washington. Younger, more imaginative officers, over-awed by the privileges of a five-star general, suggested a bachelor affair at Patton's headquarters, a Russian-style banquet in Rheims, or a soiree in Paris.

The General himself had no such grandiose, wild dreams.

To celebrate the victory, he simply wanted to see—for the first time in three years—a good, light show.

A sudden invitation to appear before the British Cabinet provided the perfect opportunity. Arrangements were made for the long-awaited theater party, with tickets to *Strike a New Note*. General Bradley was invited along as a special guest, as well as Jimmy Gault and I. Happily, the General's son John was in Rheims, for a few days' leave from the First Infantry Division, and able to join his father in this social excursion.

The festive air began on the flight over to England. General Eisenhower and I won 100 francs in a bridge game with General Bradley and Jimmy.

The latter ran into difficulties with customs officials at Northholt airfield. They questioned his frank declaration of eighteen bottles of champagne. But when he explained, "It's for General Eisenhower's V-E party," the authorities smiled and turned their backs.

We all had lunch at Telegraph Cottage and a champagne buffet that night in General Bradley's suite at the Dorchester Hotel. General Eisenhower had thoughtfully invited my mother and Tony Porter, a WREN friend; Mrs. Gault, and Sir Louis and Lady Gregg.

All of us remarked that our host, resplendent in a tailored summer uniform, looked boyishly happy.

When he appeared in the box at the Prince of Wales Theater, the entire audience rose to its feet and almost shouted the roof off with un-English abandon. They cheered, whistled, stomped, and applauded until, bowing to cries of "Speech!," he leaned on the rail and signaled for quiet.

The General spoke briefly, emphasizing his delight at being back in England. "It's nice," he grinned, "to be back in a country where I can *almost* speak the language!"

We had a drink in the manager's office during the interval, and the General went behind stage after the show to meet all the company.

Somehow, the word got around that "Ike" was in the Prince of Wales. We found most of London packed outside on the sidewalks, spilling over the street. There were no attempts at autographs, there were no flags or floodlights. This was a spontaneous demonstration by thousands of Londoners who merely wanted to see General Eisenhower, perhaps touch him.

The driver didn't dare put our gear into gear. Police had to clear a small path and then push us into the open.

Our next stop was Ciro's. The General said he might be criticized for stealing a little personal fun, but he didn't care; this was his first night out, and he had waited a long time for it. He clung tightly to that mood throughout the evening, dancing impartially with all us women, completely free from any thought of the war just over or the peace just beginning. He glowed when the orchestra played *For He's a Jolly Good Fellow.*

That night was the one time in his entire war career when I ever saw General Eisenhower completely relaxed, thoroughly enjoying himself, without a care or a wrinkle of worry. The other people, bless their English hearts, sensed his feelings and gave him a maximum of privacy. Most of the time he was just another customer, although happier than most.

He and John exchanged meaningful looks when the band played an Eisenhower request: *One Dozen Roses.* It was a heartfelt tribute to Mrs. Eisenhower, expressing a wish she could have been there, too.

General Eisenhower's quiet little V-E celebration ended about 2:30 in the morning.

He was up in time to attend the Cabinet meeting and to lunch with Mr. and Mrs. Churchill. We returned to the Continent immediately afterward.

Appropriately, Supreme Headquarters moved on into Germany before the so-called "victory month" of May was over. And most of us found the city of Frankfurt very German and very devastated, just as we had expected.

But the new headquarters building, former home of the I. G. Farben empire, stood untouched, a sort of oasis in the desert of bomb damage. After command posts in a Normandy apple orchard, in Amilcar, in Southwick, and Caserta, even after Norfolk House and Widewing and Algiers and Versailles, this structure was a complete shock.

Walking into the impressive lobby, General Eisenhower remarked, "Is this an *Army* headquarters?"

The marble lobby was banked with flowers, adding to the somewhat voluptuous appearance created by a lofty ceiling and huge twin staircases. The 82nd Airborne guards, smartly uniformed in polished boots, skin-tight jackets, and dashing white scarves, were as rigid and formal as palace guards.

The whole lobby made me think of a futuristic home, a ballroom, Napoleon's tomb, a millionaire's arboretum, and a reception hall . . . all rolled into one.

The rest of that gigantic building was the same, the most ornate and spacious quarters SHAEF ever occupied throughout the war. General Eisenhower's office was large enough for an auditorium, more befitting a Mussolini or a Hitler. He immediately ordered the removal of the heavier furniture, including a fantastic desk. The room was so long (the approach made junior officers' knees quake, visibly) he had a rug put down in the center, to make it a bit more livable. My office was smaller but nonetheless grand, catching an overflow of the daily flowers posted in the Supreme Commander's office. The final touch to this new postwar SHAEF was a compact snack bar which offered Americans a delicious, if incongruous, link with home: ice cream.

On June 5, General Eisenhower flew to Berlin. Although almost a month had passed since the end of the war, it was his first glimpse of the enemy's capital.

I had no regrets at not making the trip, after hearing about it afterward. It sounded exactly like the surrender scene. This time the signing was staged for the quadripartite agreements—otherwise, the details were nostalgic. General de Tassigny was late again. The ceremony was delayed for hours by haggling over words and phrases. The western group waited and waited and waited in a cottage in Karlshorst. The actual signing took place in the same engineering school where I'd seen Keitel sign the surrender. Zhukov was advised by Vyshinsky at every step of the way. There was a huge vodka banquet as the climax.

General Eisenhower was most impressed by Marshal Zhukov. The two of them seemed to share a mutual liking which was all the more rare in the new, strained atmosphere between East and West. Both were direct, friendly, and stubborn. Zhukov insisted his guest stay for the banquet; the General indicated he had to be back in Frankfurt by nightfall. Each was politely adamant. General Eisenhower achieved partial compromise by remaining for thirty minutes of toasting festivities.

The Field Marshal had beamed broadly at receiving an American decoration making him a Chief Commander of the Legion of Merit. He said he wanted to present both General Eisenhower and Field Marshal Montgomery with a special Soviet decoration within the very near future.

Five days later, on June 10, he came to Frankfurt to keep his word. His party was ushered into my office, then into the General's. I noticed their group included a tall, well-uniformed, attractive Russian girl whose blouse was covered with medals. (She was never introduced to anyone at SHAEF and, as far as I am concerned, remains a "mystery woman" to this day.)

When the Russians present a decoration, they do it up royally, almost in Tsarist fashion. To General Eisenhower and then to Monty, Marshal Zhukov gave the almost-legendary Order of Victory. It is a gorgeous, breath-taking medal, a jagged platinum base literally covered with brilliant diamonds and rubies. Estimates as to its value ranged anywhere from $20,000 to $100,000. I put General Eisenhower's into the safe at once, worried over the responsibility.

The SHAEF luncheon for our Soviet visitors had a diplomatic dessert, an air show of some 1,600 or 1,700 Allied fighters and bombers. It was a pure show of strength, if ever I saw one.

The day following this Russian ceremony, we left for London, which waited to give the Supreme Allied Commander her most hallowed gift: the Freedom of the City.

General Eisenhower, after his long association with the British and his frank love for London, regarded this as his most important honor to date. For the first time in his career, he actually prepared a speech. He rewrote over and over, for more than three weeks. He spent every free moment on it, trying to compress into a formal address all the emotions he felt about the Allied armies and the great courage of the British people themselves. From hearing all his rehearsals in the office, in addition to timing the length again and again, I knew it almost as well as he. And I knew it for a great address.

On the morning of the twelfth, we all drove down to the Guild-hall early in order to protect our seats. General Eisenhower rode in an open carriage, accompanied by Air Chief Marshal Tedder. While we waited his arrival, the very air in that ancient, battered building seemed tense with history. It became taut as we heard the shouts outside swell into a roaring tidal wave of cheers.

When the General started his speech, I felt a moment of panic. The microphone was too far away; his address could be heard only by those in front. Then, someone fixed the mike.

His deliberate, friendly voice immediately demanded complete attention from the distinguished audience. It was vibrant with an emotion so obviously sincere and forcibly controlled that all of us later confessed to tears in our eyes.

The speech was such that London newspapers, hardly given to overstatement, compared "Ike" with professional orators from Lincoln to Churchill. But, there in the Guildhall, General Eisenhower rose above the formalized speech.

It was as though he spoke without thought, as though he spoke to one person instead of an audience. It was more of a private soliloquy, an outpouring of the heart. I knew every word of his address, yet I, too, was caught in the feeling which surged through the old building.

Unfortunately, part of Britain's victory celebration had to be "utility," or "austerity." The great Sword of Honor was as yet unfinished; the Duke of Wellington's was presented in temporary substitute.

The new citizen of London then proceeded to Mansion House, where so many thousands gathered outside that Mr. Churchill joined him for a joint appearance on the balcony. Each made a short speech, punctuated by the greatest ovation I ever expect to hear again in my entire life.

General Ike also mingled with royalty. He called upon Queen Mary, who had demanded she meet this famous man already well known to the rest of the ruling family. And he had tea at Buck-

ingham Palace with the King and Queen, and Princess Eliza-
beth.

His Majesty presented the Supreme Commander with the al-
most-sacred Order of Merit.

Although this decoration may not be as bejeweled as the Russian Order of Victory, it is one of the most precious in the British Empire's vaults. For example, Marshal Foch received it after
World War I—and General Eisenhower was the first American in
history ever so honored.

When he went to dinner that night at 10 Downing Street, most
of the guests, including Cabinet ministers, admitted they never
had seen the Order of Merit. The General sent back to his hotel
for the medal. Their unabashed awe provided the final scene to
his day's drama.

General Eisenhower had only one day back in Frankfurt before
flying to Paris for another civic reception.

But that one day was filled with protocol difficulties. The
French, apparently angry over events in Syria, advised the General no British officers could join him for the ceremonies. He replied that any honors for him as Supreme Allied Commander
would be shared by his British as well as American colleagues.

The General won this diplomatic battle. When he received the
Compagnon de la Liberation at the Arc de Triomphe next day,
his party included not only Beetle Smith, his Chief of Staff, but
two top British members of SHAEF—Air Chief Marshal Tedder,
his Deputy, and General Frederick Morgan, his planning genius
and Assistant Chief of Staff. Thus, the British were represented,
in keeping with the SHAEF tradition.

The remainder of the formalities at the Arc were formal and
brief. Beetle received the Grand Cross of the Legion of Honor.
General Eisenhower placed a wreath on the Unknown Soldier's
Tomb, saluted during "Taps," and reviewed French troops.

Then there was a triumphal tour of the city, along boulevards
absolutely jammed with cheering Frenchmen. It was almost the

same route we had taken just after the liberation of Paris—starting straight down the Champs Elysées—and there were even more crowds, if anything. Yet I couldn't help feeling the reception lacked the emotional spontaneity of the Liberation, or that of the Londoners around Mansion House.

That evening, General de Gaulle achieved a diplomatic triumph.

He succeeded in barring the British from his lavish state dinner by inviting General of the Army Eisenhower, rather than Supreme Allied Commander Eisenhower. In this way the honor guest could come only as an American, without the privilege of bringing his British associates at SHAEF . . . and it left that guest with no alternative. As some wily French official had figured, any other move by the distinguished guest would have constituted an insult. Except for that one peevish touch, however, the dinner was a great social success, in the French tradition. As an added honor, the General of the Army received the Napoleonic sword meant for the people of the United States.

The climax to this week of historic acclaim came two days later when General Eisenhower left for home, for a real hero's homecoming.

Typically, he filled up other seats on the plane, President Truman's own "Sacred Cow," with G-I's due for discharge in the States. To help with a speech to be given before Congress, he took Sue Sarafin along. Butch, Tex, and Mickey completed the roster. I was left behind to take care of the office, where General Bradley would come in from time to time to handle urgent matters.

But with all the world well aware of General Eisenhower's American tour, there was little business in the Supreme Commander's office in Frankfurt. Following the General's advice, I went off to Cannes for my first official leave of the war, my first real holiday free of responsibilities and V-I-P's.

Reading the *Stars and Stripes* in Cannes and, nine short days later, in the Frankfurt office, I realized America was smashing every sort of record in her all-out welcome for General Eisenhower.

He spoke before a joint session of Congress. He dined at the White House. He was paraded and applauded through the streets of Washington, Kansas City, and New York. The crowd figures staggered my imagination; in New York, for example, they numbered one or two million more than the four million he had under his command during the war. I felt a special kinship when he returned home to Abilene; through handling the General's correspondence, I felt as though I knew every one of the some five or six thousand inhabitants of that Kansas town.

I noted that he received a grand welcome from West Point, as its most illustrious alumnus, and that he and his family enjoyed a brief vacation at White Sulphur Springs. I was happy, too, when he made a solemn pilgrimage to Hyde Park.

Surely, no soldier in history ever received the voluntary, spontaneous, tumultuous, and varied acclaim which was General Ike's due after World War II. Even when he returned to Germany in July, the unprecedented shower of special honors continued to heap upon him, to fill his treasure chest with rare gifts, to spread a growing rainbow of decorations across his chest.

During the summer of 1945 he was the feted hero in virtually all the major cities of Europe. The gigantic reception in London, then that in Paris, were followed by similarly spectacular ceremonies in Luxembourg . . . Belfast . . . Brussels . . . Amsterdam . . . Warsaw . . . Prague . . . even Moscow.

The Moscow festivities, formal and instigated by a personal invitation from Joseph Stalin, took the General to Russia just in time for the V-J Day celebration there. Ambassador Harriman later told me he came home from late evenings at the Kremlin to find Marshal Zhukov visiting General Eisenhower at Spasso House.

A sudden V-J party had sprung up, he said, with Zhukov happily echoing the last word of General Ike's "Here's How!" toasts. The Ambassador said that sight of a high Russian hero with his arm around General Ike's shoulders, shouting "How!" over and over, was one of the most incredible sights he had ever seen in the Soviet Union. Such conviviality with a foreigner, he added, not only was a rare occasion in suspicious Russia; it was a warm tribute to General Eisenhower's popularity in the Kremlin.

In addition to the official receptions, General Eisenhower collected university degrees (Oxford, Queens, and Louvain), swords (London, Paris, Brussels), even lace (in Nottingham). One of his most cherished gifts was a special ash tray brought to Frankfurt by an American major stationed in Liége; it contained coils of the first cable laid under Ludendorff Bridge at Remagen. That ash tray never left the General's desk.

One of the loveliest personal presents General Ike received in this period was one from General de Gaulle, a jeweled platinum-and-gold cigarette case. It bore a glittering replica of General Eisenhower's five-star rank—in sapphires. The clip also was made of sapphires. Inside, the French general had signed his name and the date; the engraved script was in his own handwriting. It was in exquisite taste, the most beautiful cigarette case I've ever seen.

Despite all these high obligations of state, General Eisenhower had to concentrate as fully upon his job as he had during the war.

From the very first day after the surrender his chief task was, firstly, the redeployment of troops and equipment to the Pacific, and, secondly, the demobilization. Scarcity of transportation made both these problems even more difficult than the fantastically involved procedure of logistics. Europe was filled with men who had fought the war and who, under the War Department's demobilization scheme, had more than enough "points" for discharge. From our office went a Theater-wide directive to give top priority to these veterans, particularly in transportation. At the same time, there was the involved planning necessary for shifting to the Pacific men and materiel readily available. Naturally, the resultant staff work equaled—often surpassed—anything seen during the war.

Even the "fan mail" began to reflect home-front pressure. Virtually every one of the General's correspondents wrote to draw attention to a particular son, sweetheart, brother, husband, or friend now believed long-overdue for return to the United States. As always, none blamed General Ike himself; each letter was written only to emphasize an injustice of some sort, "which I'm sure you'll correct as soon as you hear about it."

These letters became so numerous that I got a full-time assistant, Frances Smith, a pretty and highly efficient WAC from New York City. The volume of our mail was such that I had to draw up somewhat of a stock answer upon which to base individual replies over the General's signature.

There were letters from Germany, as well as those from the United States; much of the Army was impatient with demobilization, with redeployment and with occupation life.

I still have one which was addressed to me from anonymous members of the 156th Field Artillery Battalion in a camp at Backnang, Germany. Dated July 25, 1945, the first part of that letter typifies the G-I adoration of General Ike and the general reaction to his policy of answering all mail:

... It all started when a Corporal Berard from this battalion applied for an emergency furlough following the death of his mother shortly after V-E Day. The request was refused on the grounds that his presence was not necessary at home. In a moment of anger, frustration, or what you will, he sat down and wrote a letter to General Eisenhower, then Supreme Commander of all Allied Forces and the "biggest" man this war has produced in the eyes of the Enlisted Men.

At the time the General was on a well-earned leave to God's country taking with him the best wishes of every last one of his boys. Telling you that is like carrying steel to Pittsburgh, but it has been our experience in the Army that *good* officers are like your mother; you can never do or say enough for them. The other kind falls in that classification known as those whom you can never say enough *about* ...

Before too long a period had elapsed our Corporal friend

had received a letter stating that his letter had been received and would receive immediate attention. The letter was unique in our military experience in that it was informal and yet efficient, sincere but not ambiguous, helpful but not boastful of future deeds. And signed at the bottom was the name of the writer: 1st Lt. Kay Summersby, WAC.

The letter was passed around faster than a choice bit of gossip at a sewing circle and in each case the reaction was practically SOP. "Imagine General Eisenhower or any of his staff taking the time to answer a personal letter," was the usual theme and it echoed louder with each repetition.

We wanted to write you a fan letter to thank you for answering one of our buddies and while it may not be the first fan letter you've received since you've been in the ETO the boys feel it is as sincere as any you have received or will receive, as long as you are in the ETO or the Army itself for that matter.

We couldn't and wouldn't be sincere if we didn't also tell you how envious, yes that's the correct word, we are of you in having General Ike for a boss. It's like sterling on silver or Tiffany on a diamond—tops . . .

The writer of this letter then went on to list, in general, some of the widespread beefs of soldiers in Germany:

During this period of war any physical inconveniences were taken in stride for a sensible person could easily see that there were no alternatives for the mud and mire . . . This didn't alter the fact that the end of the war was the goal . . . (and) with victory we could picture a let-down in the physical and mental side of soldiering.

How wrong the ETO veteran was! Before the ink was dry on the surrender papers, veterans of three and four years' service were doing close-order drill, taking hikes, laying out full field inspections, pitching tents by the numbers, and all the other things usually associated with basic training. Not knowing the overall picture, perhaps such training was necessary but a word to that effect would have been appreciated instead of making us march and hike simply for lack of something to do.

The next noticeable factor was the immediate discarding of the spirit of camaraderie between officers and men. Long faces were again the vogue and the provincial version of "spit and polish" typified by the would-be West Pointers again held the stage. The friendly greeting and smile was replaced by a terse, "Make the salute snappy, Soldier!" or, perhaps, "Stand at attention when you address an officer, Sergeant." Camaraderie was definitely not a part of the makeup of these knights in shining brass . . .

Next, "The Boys from the 516th F.A. Battalion" listed specific incidents which they said would "make a fair-minded Statue of Justice do handsprings":

(1) We, a F.A. Battalion of approximately 525 people, live in one large factory in Backnang while some 28 officers have four houses in which to loll. Still . . . we must use the side entrance which is, shall we say, the servants' entrance. The front door is reserved for officers and German civilians on official business. Perhaps it is my faulty memory but I can't recall an officer denying us a particular door during combat . . .

(2) When Bronze Stars were being considered for the Battalion, each officer was considered for one and that was the end. With the exception of the personnel of one battery . . . not another Enlisted Man was so recognized. This means that heroes ran close to 100% among the officers and approximately .008% among the EM . . .

(3) One or two Enlisted Men created a disturbance in a G-I beer parlor and it resulted in a "dressing down" for the Battalion C.O. by the Brigade C.G. The next day two more men got involved in a similar manner. Fearing another lecture, the entire Battalion was restricted to the building for an indefinite period. At present the restriction has been in effect for three days and as yet there has been no word of its eventual end. This, despite the fact that there is no hot

water in the building with which to bathe during weather
that has reached 80 degrees on a tar-topped roof . . .

Finally, this letter ended on a familiar note of apology, sincerity,
and best wishes for General Ike:

We are still envious of the boss you have for were it possible for him to be everyone's boss, in fact as well as theory,
we know that we who are not professional soldiers, and never
will be, would never need worry over the perverted inter-
pretations and queer quirks which orders issued from higher
headquarters often take on when relayed to us . . .
We fully realize that you and "The Boss" have problems
beside which ours are as nothing.
We regret our inability to sign this letter not only with
our names but with our hearts. We are all sufficiently Army-
wise to know what happens to people who even remotely
hint that a Lieutenant, Captain, Major, or Colonel is not
a potential five-star General . . .
Please take care of yourself and Ike too, for we would all
suffer in our future dilemmas should anything happen to
either of you. With best wishes for a new T/O that will make
you a Captain . . .

General Eisenhower was very interested in this letter, ordering
me to trace down the unit's location and then arrange for him
to make a personal investigation of the charges. Unfortunately,
by the time we hunted down the unit, first in Backnang, then in
several other spots, the Battalion had left Europe. (I'd still like
to meet the writer of that powerful little volume.)

As an example of a more subtle, touching letter—similar to
hundreds the General received during the war—I'd like to quote
one which a woman enclosed with her own letter to General
Eisenhower. It is a copy of that which she received from a soldier
Somewhere In Europe:

Dearest Lee—
You've followed me a long way without asking questions.
You've been swell about almost anything I could name and
you've stood by me through long silences, a good deal of mov-

ing on my part, and intervals when you would have been perfectly justified in doubting my sincerity.

And now I'm asking you to accept another fact with the same beautiful sympathetic shoulder you've lent me so many times in the past.

They busted me down to Private the other day, Lee—completely and, I'm afraid, irrevocably. All I'm asking of you is to take my side without hearing the details.

The reason they give on the official order is "inefficiency." But there's more to it than that. You'd have to be in the Army a long time, Lee, to know how human nature works on a man in uniform; how your job can be affected by greed, envy, and plain covetousness on someone else's part. Yes, a long time—before you learn how you can be stepped down because your ideas, theories and methods of handling men don't jibe with the fellow who is a couple of rungs higher on the Army ladder.

Yes sir, I got them all one at a time, PFC, Cpl., Sgt., was even recommended for Officer Candidate School last August—and now they took all that away at one sweep of the ax.

I'm hurt, so deep down, it feels like what Hell must be after death.

When you can look about you and see people who don't amount to a damn really, but are successful Army men, men who represent everything intolerable in civilian life, and you yourself who you give credit to for playing the game straight gets lowered beneath them—well, it hurts.

I guess this is all mixed up but perhaps it will give you a small idea what I've been going through the last three days. I've bounced back after many a setback in the past, but this has just about thrown me.

Look, I can't talk shop any more and I'm anxious to get some mail from you. Don't worry about me, Honey, I'm just plain mad now.

The Germans will be hearing from me now, if I ever run into any.

Privately yours,
Mike

The woman who sent this letter wrote one of her own along with it, typifying, again, the public attitude that General Ike would be a sympathetic listener—and, if humanly possible, do something about the particular problem. Some pertinent excerpts:

... I cannot even be sure that you will ever receive this letter but neither can I overlook the remote chance that you may.

This morning I received a letter from a dear friend of mine who is a trooper in a cavalry reconnaissance squadron somewhere in Germany. He was a Sergeant. This letter told me that he had been broken to the rank of Private.

There is something wrong here, General Eisenhower. Maybe other people have written to you protesting things of this kind and perhaps you feel that you cannot interfere. But there has been injustice done here. This is the boy's record ...

Now his stripes have been taken from him for "inefficiency." It doesn't make sense. I've never tried to understand why the Army does the things it does. I've always accepted the inexplicable things because I felt that its leaders understood far better than I what was necessary. But this I cannot accept without a protest. I beg of you to do something about it.

Michael's whole heart is in the Army. He's loved its traditions and worked with his whole heart to be a part of it. And now it has betrayed him. There is no other word for it ...

Can I plead any better for him than that letter does? I don't think so. That boy didn't deserve this. No one will ever make me believe that. Did you notice that it's going to be the Germans who will "hear" from him—and not the ones responsible for his humiliation?

I wonder if you or I or many other people could keep ourselves so well in hand when we were suffering the tortures of a Hell after death.

I said the Army had betrayed Michael. I am betraying him, too, by writing to you and still more by sending you his letter. But I'm so far away, he's been hurt so badly, and I know he doesn't deserve it. Please, General Eisenhower, I beg of you—do something for him. His name is . . .

Need I add that General Ike took a personal interest in this case, in the pursuit of justice?

Also, at the beginning of the summer General Eisenhower had to supervise the disintegration of SHAEF, the million and one troubles which arose as Supreme Headquarters dissolved. There were questions of files, supplies, equipment, which belonged to the Americans and which to the British. There were decorations and citations to be presented. There was the chore of combing the American side for personnel to fill the Occupation Offices. The fact that SHAEF was the first such truly Allied headquarters didn't help matters much in the way of precedent.

Personally, I believe General Ike hated to see the gradual death of SHAEF. He was, after all, the man who had made it work, in spite of the seemingly insurmountable difficulties caused by differences in nationality, service procedure, and a thousand other obstacles to actual Allied direction of a war. I think the late war is still too fresh to permit historians to realize just what an achievement SHAEF was in its command of an Allied war.

(As a human-interest example of that historic unity, I like to remember the Independence Day celebration staged in Frankfurt while the Supreme Commander was in America. The genial hosts at that party—held just 169 years after the new United States won its war against the hated British—were SHAEF's British officers. And it was one of the best parties I ever attended.)

In his final report to the Combined Chiefs of Staff, dated July 13 of that summer, General Eisenhower inscribed a sort of epitaph for SHAEF:

Within my own headquarters the American and British personnel worked harmoniously together, obliterating all distinction of national outlook in their zealous service to a single organization . . .

With SHAEF changed into headquarters for the American zone of Germany, the General had his hands full. In the beginning, the late Allies couldn't even agree upon a date for their first Allied Control Council meeting in Berlin. Although an early opponent of zonal rule for Germany, General Ike, as head of the American sector, found himself very much involved in the inter-zonal squabbles.

The actual chores of an Occupation commander—prisoners of war, health, education, Displaced Persons, administration, industry, war criminals, public utilities, Army routine, all the horrible headaches of any conqueror—need no elaboration.

Suffice it to say that even a five-star general has his boss. The President of the United States, for instance, sent General Eisenhower a letter which demanded investigation of D.P. complaints that Americans held them in camps under conditions as bad as those imposed by the Nazis. (The General immediately set out for Bavaria on a personal inspection tour of the camps in Third Army's area.)

President Truman, incidentally, headed our long list of summer visitors. He came down from Potsdam for the specific purpose of seeing General Ike—and to inspect the 84th Infantry and 3rd Armored divisions.

As soon as he and Secretary of State James Byrnes arrived in our office, General Eisenhower called each of us in for personal introductions. I thought the President, although lacking his predecessor's celebrated charm and personality, extremely friendly, natural, and pleasant. After the somewhat wearing poise and determined regality of many V-I-P's, his average-man cordiality was distinctly refreshing.

As the summer wore on, headquarters life as we had known it during the war disappeared entirely.

Air Chief Marshal Tedder, Generals Morgan and Strong, all the British colleagues of former days left with the demise of SHAEF. "High-point" Americans dropped out of sight every day, headed home. General Bradley departed for Washington, reluctantly following Presidential orders to take over the obsolete, red-taped Veterans Administration. Even our own office seemed empty, without Butch and Mickey, both of whom had declined to return to Europe with General Eisenhower in July.

To provide the General with a little social life, without the obligations of formal society, we occasionally had him and a few intimates over to our WAC house for dinner and an evening of bridge. Several times a week, he and I went horseback riding, following doctor's orders that the General get more exercise. He also managed to attend a West Point reunion in Cannes and go on a fishing trip in Bavaria with Beetle.

While John was visiting his father in Frankfurt one week, we persuaded the General to get a few days' rest in the villa leased to him on the Riviera. General Gerow, Jimmy Gault, and I joined the excursion; "Sous le Vent" was so crowded I had to stay in the Hotel du Cap in nearby Antibes. The weather was lovely. General Eisenhower had a real little holiday, sunbathing on the beach and motorboating in the Mediterranean.

But his one night out, at the Hotel Provençal, was almost ruined when an American Red Cross girl recognized him. We all feared the whole place would descend upon the General. I tried to convince the girl she was mistaken, in the dim light; failing that, I offered to get the Eisenhower autograph for her if she would promise not to reveal his presence. Luckily, she kept her word. And General Eisenhower remained the entire evening, without cringing in the usual glare of publicity.

Early in September, we made a trip to Austria to see General Clark for the first time since Caserta. He and General Ike hiked off to a mountain hunting lodge for some long-awaited fishing.

On that same trip, we visited Berchtesgaden. I thought the occasion especially noteworthy when, atop the mountain, General Eisenhower spotted a big sign, "Eagle's Nest—Officers Only." His neck and cheeks flamed, but, unlike Patton, he made no scene.

Instead, he turned quietly to the conducting officer and said grimly, "Remove that sign, *now!*"

A group of sight-seeing G-I's cheered so loudly their voices must have echoed into Italy.

Traveling with Brass, I could hardly stoop to cut out a piece of Hitler's carpet for a souvenir. I did, however, add my name below that of Generals Eisenhower and Clark, on the colossal, circular oak table which bore the carved names of hundreds of G-I's. And as we left an officer gave me a tiny piece of the mantelpiece.

That same month I visited Denmark. General Eisenhower's C-54, the only one in the Theater, was to be in a huge aerial display over Copenhagen; the pilot asked me, "Why don't you ask the Boss if you can come along?"

It was the first time in all my service with the General I ever asked him, directly, to make a trip. He not only gave me permission to go; he suggested that I take one of the other girls along.

I asked Frances Smith. To overcome rank troubles, she took off her stripes and insignia and we both checked in at the Palace Hotel in Copenhagen, where the Danes regarded us as something straight from Mars. The United States Minister invited us to a cocktail party that evening; I met a few people I had known back in 1937. The air crew had promised to show us around, but they didn't show up until time to leave. Neither Frances nor I asked any question; we had been in the Army too long.

Not all such trips were as pleasant as this or the one when Ambassador and Kathy Harriman arrived in Germany with a few extra days on hand before a conference in London, General Eisenhower directed me to take them to "Sous le Vent." He himself was off on a trip to Rome and Venice, but promised to join us shortly.

The holiday started off nicely, as both the Ambassador and his daughter are charming persons. For the first time since I had known him, Mr. Harriman threw off his rather cold, diplomatic demeanor and became a warm, cordial tourist. His attractive, highly intelligent daughter was, of course, her usual friendly, invigorating self. We had a wonderful time.

I began to worry at the absence of any word from General Eisenhower. The day of his expected arrival, there was no sign of a message from either Frankfurt or General Clark's headquarters.

Late that afternoon, the two of them rolled up to the villa in a car—boiling mad.

I got the worst bawling out of my war-time career . . . for not having transportation at the airfield. General Clark's aide suffered a tongue-lashing equally vehement. Yet neither of us, being in the Army, could explain there had been no message informing us of the Generals' arrival. And they weren't interested in any explanations. So the other aide and I just stood and took it.

Dinner was quite frosty that evening. Both Generals went off to bed early. An officer from the Marseille headquarters joined Clark's aide and me in an old-fashioned gripe session. When General Eisenhower came down later, apparently unable to sleep, I knew he wanted to join us for bridge or mere conversation. But we all simply stood stiffly, answering his questions with respectful monosyllables—until he trudged back up to bed, to nurse burning ears.

General Ike had more transportation troubles when he left us and arrived in Paris. The officer with him called Army headquarters for a car, but the transportation office failed to answer the telephone. He tried several other offices, without success— it was lunchtime in Paris. Finally, a sleepy colonel answered.

"Give me that 'phone," General Eisenhower demanded. "And don't tell him who's calling."

The colonel heard a voice boom in his ear, "This is General Eisenhower!"

Bemused, the colonel sighed, "Yes, God? This is Saint Peter!"

I doubt if that colonel ever joked on the telephone again.

Handling the General's correspondence brought me face-to-face with the Eisenhower temper on another occasion.

Letters were pouring in so heavily that I had them divided into three folders, "Official," "Personal," and "Fan Mail." The Official papers went to his office immediately, the Personal mail received second priority, and the Fan Mail, last.

One day the girls, shaking with apprehension, brought in the latter folder. Buried among the fan letters they had found an urgent communication from the RAF's Sir Charles Portal. I took it in to the General with some other documents, hoping he would miss the date.

But he yelled as soon as he saw it, immediately aware the paper had been mislaid three whole days. Once again, I stood dumbly while he lectured me volubly on the difference between official mail and fan mail.

In late September, General Eisenhower erupted into the granddaddy of all tempers: General Patton had made his worst and final mistake.

Everyone who could read a newspaper knew the Third Army commander had sounded off on the Germans—in a favorable way which only Patton could devise. The reaction was instantaneous and very high-level, coming not only from the War Department but from the State Department and the Foreign Office.

On the twenty-seventh, a very meek Blood-and-Guts reported in to the Commanding General's office. During the course of a long and acid conversation, he learned he might be relieved of his beloved Third Army. General Eisenhower said he hadn't made up his mind; he would sleep on it.

On the twenty-eighth, General Eisenhower came in looking as though he hadn't slept a wink. I knew at once he had decided to take action against his old friend. He had aged ten years in reaching the decision, which was inevitable in the light of Patton's past mistakes and the universal furor over this one.

When General Patton came in, followed by Beetle, the office door closed. But I heard one of the stormiest sessions ever staged in our headquarters. It was the first time I ever heard General Eisenhower really raise his voice.

General Patton was relieved from command of the Third Army, shifted to the Fifteenth "paper Army."

General Eisenhower's next worry was the prospect of returning to Washington to become Chief of Staff. Several months before—at the same time General Bradley learned of his Veterans Administration assignment—General Marshall had advised Ike of his forthcoming retirement. It was quite definite that General Eisenhower would succeed Marshall . . . only a question of time.

October brought the Harrimans to Frankfurt for another visit, en route to Moscow. They invited me to come along and asked General Eisenhower for his permission. Although he had refused to take me on his August trip to the Russian capital, he gave his consent this time.

While he and Tex left for official receptions in Amsterdam and Prague, the Harrimans and I took off for Russia.

Our first stop was Vienna, where even the bomb damage failed to hide the glamorous capital's former beauty. We stayed there two days, taking a quick side-trip to Budapest. Assistant War Secretary John McCloy's bucket-seat C-47 provided the transportation; actor Paul Lukas, in Europe to visit relatives, was our guide. Budapest was little more than a wasteland of debris, still smothered in the stench of the dead.

The flight to Moscow took about six and one-half hours, much of it over desolate country more bleak than anything I had ever seen in all my travels. We arrived at dusk, when the darkness and a light snowfall made Moscow seem even more drab and dilapidated. I was especially impressed with the absence of wholesale bomb damage, in contrast to such cities as Berlin, Frankfurt, London, Plymouth, and Le Havre.

I had three days in Moscow and made the most of them: I rode the subways, which seemed far more clean and modern than those of New York . . . I stared in empty shop windows . . . I stared at the drab people, who, in turn, stared at me and my uniform as though I were a fugitive from a museum . . . I noted how women serve as anything from police to bus drivers in Russia . . .

I learned that caviar was about sixty-five dollars a kilo; eggs, almost a dollar apiece. . . . I heard the radio announce General Eisenhower's reception in Prague, where he received a lovely oil painting of the city . . . I went to a Red Army concert, where more than 100 tall, good-looking soldiers presented the most beautiful choral music I ever expect to hear in any country. They ended with two strange songs, *Tipperary* and *There's a Tavern in the Town,* sung in Russian . . .

Ambassador Harriman arranged for me to visit the Kremlin. Inside that walled city, I found most everything as I expected. Long, black limousines sped through the gates, curtains drawn. There was a Soviet soldier at my elbow every time I went up to a glass case in the museum. The Russian Parliament and Lenin's tomb were exact counterparts of familiar pictures.

I was back in Frankfurt by October 14, just in time for General Eisenhower's birthday party at our WAC house. We all gave him silly little gifts, such as cigarettes and handkerchiefs. They were only something for him to open, token presents.

A fortnight later, on the last day of October, he gave me the nicest present of the war . . . or the peace: an empty seat on his plane, headed for Washington on official business.

I took out my first papers toward becoming an American citizen.

Arriving back in Germany after the short trip, I found the General packing. He was taking over from General Marshall, who had postponed his retirement in order to carry out a Presidential assignment in China.

"I'm going to Washington tomorrow," General Ike said as I entered the office. "But I'll be back."

He didn't come back.

CHAPTER XIX

G ENERAL EISENHOWER's return to Germany was forbidden
by the doctors in Washington. After nursing the new
Chief of Staff through a hospital siege of near-pneu-
monia, they refused to let him fly anywhere.

Perhaps it was just as well. His mission in Europe was finished,
already fading into history. A quick trip back would have been
nothing more than anticlimax, just as the rest of my own Army
life was anticlimax:

A month or so after the General's departure, I was transferred
to Berlin—along with Telek, now my very own little Scottie.
My new boss was General Lucius D. Clay, then Deputy Military Governor (and slated to become the generalissimo of
America's most inflammable slice of the postwar world). My job:
handling the stream of V-I-P's flowing into Hitler's late capital.

Somehow, I felt little enthusiasm for this new life, although it
involved meeting Cabinet Ministers, Congressmen, movie stars,
even an ex-President of the United States, Herbert Hoover. My
new rank of Captain didn't help much in the way of personal
morale; I had seen far too much rank to have any respect for it.

Actually, in Berlin I missed the daily excitement, the daily
sense of urgency which the war had given to my some three years
in the top Allied headquarters, working for the Supreme Allied
Commander. In the explosive Berlin of today, things might be
different. But in the Berlin of late 1946, I was just another person
who had been overseas too long, much too long.

I returned to the United States that November, assigned to
public relations duties at an Army post in California. There, I

became just another civilian who had been in the Army too long. A Captain, a Lieutenant, a Sergeant, and I worked hard to make our office seem busy. But the Sergeant could have done the job, alone.

I was happy to see my discharge papers in July of 1947 . . .

Now, the cycle is complete. I'm a civilian once more, soon to become an American civilian.

After the somewhat fabulous wartime career Fate gave me, however, the "readjustment" to this new life is rather challenging. I might even describe it, with massive understatement, as difficult.

Meanwhile, the war has become only a memory, a permanent memory, I hope. Like thousands of other veterans—I'm more concerned over the fragile peace. And a job.

CHAPTER XX

B Y WAY of epilogue, I'd like to answer—for once and for all—
those questions which both friends and strangers have
asked me since I first met General Eisenhower in 1942:
Who is his ghost-writer?
Dwight D. Eisenhower. The thoughts and words in every
speech he ever made came straight from his own head. Blessed
with logical mind, amazing vocabulary, and phenomenal memory,
he is a born speaker; more important, an extemporaneous speaker.

Of all the thousands of talks and addresses he delivered while
stationed in Europe, I know of only two the General prepared in
advance: one for the Guildhall ceremony in London; the other,
for his appearance before a joint session of Congress.

Few men have faced such varied listeners . . . British Cabinet
Ministers . . . staff officers . . . paratroopers about to take off for
Normandy . . . crowds gathered at civic receptions . . . wounded
men in hospitals. Yet, time and time again, his talks were so well
formed no one could believe they were off-the-cuff. I once asked
him how he did it.

"It's simple," he said. "Know you have something to say, something you *want* to say. Then, there's no need to search around
for words—they'll come."

Is he conceited?

Not even his worst enemy could stick that label on General
Eisenhower. Overbearing, arrogant, vain, egotistic, opinionated—
none of these synonyms of "conceit" could possibly be associated
with his name.

Could an overbearing general be known to his troops as "General Ike" and "Ike"? Could an arrogant general give up the pleasure of "lording" it over the Nazis at the Rheims and Berlin surrenders? Could a vain and egotistic general bawl out an aide for giving the press personal items of priceless publicity value? Could an opinionated general ever run a headquarters such as SHAEF?

On the other hand, General Ike is self-confident.

It takes immeasurable self-confidence to run an Allied army, to make decisions almost beyond the limit of human responsibility, to argue endlessly with a Churchill, to take major steps in the face of advisers' opposition. In fact, he had to be supremely self-confident to remain more than one day as Supreme Allied Commander.

Yet his Number One charm is his unaffected, unsophisticated normality. "I'm just a farmer boy from Kansas," he remarks frequently. And he believes it.

In this way he can present a completely composed appearance and manner before royalty, presidents, generals, admirals, Congressmen, soldiers, and workers alike. He never pretends to be anything other than himself—which permits the luxury of never being nervous, ashamed, or uneasy.

Some sort of false front, conscious or unconscious, is the main reason for embarrassment. And I can say, truthfully, I never saw General Ike embarrassed.

Was he just a "paper general"?

This belief that General Eisenhower was "chairman of the board," a sort of executive-diplomat without interest in the actual fighting, is the most persistent of public misconceptions of his role in World War II.

General Eisenhower directed and commanded the European war.

It was a far cry from paper work when he—and he alone—made the decision to delay, then to launch the invasion of Normandy . . . When he advised General Bradley to go ahead and build up the Remagen bridgehead . . . When he took charge of the Ardennes battle, splitting the forces under Bradley and

Monty . . . When he finally agreed to the defense of Strasbourg . . .

He was not a combat commander in the sense of a divisional commander. But he deployed divisions, armies, and army groups in the same way a division C.G. deployed companies, regiments, and battalions. He made immediate military decisions, momentous as well as emergency military decisions.

"Ike" was a general in the most exacting essence of the word; not a mere staff officer, not a "chairman of the board." With all his paper work, his executive worries, and his diplomatic troubles, he was the Supreme Commander of the armies in Europe.

How did he get different nationalities to work together?

General Eisenhower wasn't, of course, wholly responsible for Allied unity. This was a people's war; nations and nationalities drew together as never before to battle the common enemy.

But his command of Supreme Headquarters (and its resultant effect on armies in the field) surely is a military achievement unparalleled in history. It still remains for some historian to emphasize the seemingly insurmountable difficulties. For instance: national differences in military terminology, official documents, equipment, strategy, training, uniforms, and over-all outlook.

In my opinion, General Ike's own example was the primary reason for SHAEF becoming a working, victorious headquarters despite these problems. His only weapon was absolute, utter honesty. He judged every case on its merits, without a hint of bias. He submerged all nationalistic prejudices. He demanded unswerving concentration upon one goal: winning of the war. All else was secondary, even unimportant.

Roosevelt, Churchill, Stalin, de Gaulle—all knew General Eisenhower would tell them the truth, without diplomatic or nationalistic shadings. The same went for each member of the SHAEF staff, regardless of uniform or rank.

Secondly, the General pounded home this "our team" win-the-war theme at every opportunity. He repeated it, endlessly, at staff meetings, in formal speeches, in talks with men in the field, in directives, in press conferences, even in informal conversation. It was his religion, contagious as fever. He also warned and threatened against nationalistic arguments—and cracked down ruthlessly on those who engaged in petty quarrels.

As a result, the personnel of SHAEF were as neutral, efficient, and non-flag-waving as any headquarters in recorded time. They even defended SHAEF actions against their own governments. They became Allies.

How did he react to criticism?

The General never sulked against criticisms.

Partially, I guess, he took it all as part of his job. Also, he took the view he was doing the best job possible and would continue to do so until relieved or commanded to do otherwise. His self-confidence—and the continual pressure of fighting the war—allowed him to avoid such pitfalls as anger, arrogance, and alibis.

Did he ever worry about losing the war?

Never, as far as I know. He may have experienced personal depression over temporary defeats and disasters—Kasserine, the Bulge, air losses, casualty figures, and the like—but they remained purely personal.

With his position and his personality, he was the perfect picture of confident optimism. He never uttered a defeatist word; he prohibited defeatism among his staff. Even his friends never heard a truly pessimistic word from General Ike.

Of all the generals, admirals, field marshals, and air marshals I met during the war, only General Patton exuded more consistent, confident optimism than General Eisenhower.

Was he a bug on discipline?

First, last, and foremost, General Eisenhower is a soldier. He also is a West Pointer.

These facts—plus his almost fanatic devotion to the single duty of victory—led him into many actions during World War II which some regarded as harsh.

It is important, however, to understand his brand of discipline. He was coldly incisive if a subordinate failed to live up to his job.

But, as long as that subordinate performed his duty, he received *carte blanche* from the General, who was generous in the way of promotion and decoration, who backed both clerk and field commander in crises, and who was cordial in personal relationships.

Also, the Eisenhower discipline was that of an American, not the stiff, uncompromising, upper-class formality of the European military man.

General Ike gave full, equal attention and courtesy to privates, second lieutenants, generals, and chiefs of state. He was a good listener, a sincere listener, a respectful listener. And, after hours, he relaxed completely. The atmosphere in his quarters was that of a business executive, not a five-star General.

When he approached a group of troops for one of his break-ranks chats, the soldiers invariably yelled "Ike!" or "Ike's here!" Soldiers don't give an over-strict disciplinarian that sort of welcome.

Did his own staff like him?

His immediate staff, official family, frankly worshipped "The Boss." Most of our admiration stemmed from his natural thoughtfulness.

When Mickey was ill, General Eisenhower ordered food sent down from his mess; he stopped by the hospital every other day. He did the same for Sue Sarafin, when she had a bad auto accident in Algiers; for Beetle, when he was in hospital in England; in fact, for all of us, at one time or another.

The point: no secretary or aide had to remind him of these little courtesies. They sprang from his innate kindness, on impulse, even while directing a huge war.

Examples of this unceasing thoughtfulness could be quoted hour after hour. I've already mentioned many of them in this book, as far as my personal experiences are concerned. Anyone else in the official family could do likewise, for he treated us impartially, like a real family.

This same feeling permeated the entire headquarters staff. He was liked and respected for himself, not merely as the Commanding General. Loyalty and friendship come to him without effort. Despite all the bitter incidents and arguments bound to occur during a long war, I really doubt if any man who served on the General's staff harbors any active dislike for him today.

What did he do for relaxation?

As I've outlined more fully in the preceding pages, General Ike's pleasures are simple.

His chief, consuming hobby is bridge; he has little patience with poor or half-hearted players. Secondly, he favors the relaxation of Western pulp magazines; he finds them soothing and entertaining; they require a minimum of mental work.

He is a moderate drinker, an immoderate smoker. His interest in history is unusually avid. He enjoys golfing and horseback riding. He likes movies, Wild West versions if possible. He dreams of fishing with all the intensity some men reserve for hunting, stamp-collecting, women, photography, or gardening.

He can cook, but, being neither *gourmet* nor *gourmand*, he can take his food or leave it.

This simplicity of pleasures marked his entire personal life during the war. Unlike some High Brass who wallowed in luxury and king-like grandeur, General Eisenhower preferred to have his headquarters in the field. Abhorring social pomp, he felt more kinship with an easy chair than a ballroom floor or a formal dinner table.

Neither his personal appearance nor that of his entourage had any of the showmanship and glamor so dear to personalities such as Patton, Montgomery, and MacArthur.

All in all, his personal tastes—except, perhaps, that for history—are those of an average man.

What do you think is the one secret of his success?

No single characteristic lifts a man from the crowd.

Yet General Eisenhower does have one outstanding distinction: his unconquerable honesty. It is, I believe, the one trait which makes everyone respect him, regardless of the circumstances or one's own opinion. It is, further, the one trait which permitted him to talk with identical candor to heads of many countries, to rise above the quicksands of nationalism, to weather the storms of criticism, and to retain the loyalty of his staff.

Honesty seems to be an increasingly rare characteristic of the world's leaders. Possibly that is the reason for the universal respect for General Eisenhower. I find it unique that a man of his prominence has never once, as far as I know, been accused of dishonesty or a lack of integrity.

There are dozens of other keys to his success. To name a few:

At SHAEF he had that rare gift for selecting a brilliant staff and then, unlike numerous leaders who mistrust others' ability, delegating complete authority. Any executive knows this quality is a cornerstone of success; among the military, it is so unusual as to amount to something near genius.

General Eisenhower is a natural leader . . . He has the knack of putting the other person at ease . . . He is a wonderful listener . . . His personality is unaffected . . . He inspires both loyalty and respect . . . He is enough of a disciplinarian to command efficiency . . . His mind is almost frightening in its lucid logic . . . He is a marvelous extemporaneous speaker . . . He is self-confident without being conceited, modest without being timid, natural without being awkward. He is thoughtful and warm in his individual contacts.

His military, executive, and diplomatic abilities require no explanation.

And he has that million-dollar grin.

Is he perfect? Doesn't he have ANY faults?

The answer is obvious. Naturally, being a man instead of a machine, General Eisenhower would be the first to roar at any idea he is near-holy.

He has a temper which should be accompanied by red hair and an Irish or Italian ancestry. His anger is offset, however, by its extremely perishable quality. No matter how violent or lengthy the argument, General Ike never holds a grudge; the incident is forgotten once it is over.

Any other debit entries in the Eisenhower ledger depend upon the accountant. What one person dislikes, another admires; what one envies, another loathes.

Some officers, for instance, hated his strong ideas on discipline; others found them in the best military tradition. Some thought him too charitable with Patton; others believed him too harsh. Many believed him too stubborn.

So it goes. Whether certain of the General's characteristics are perfect or imperfect depends entirely upon the point of view and the individual preferences of the viewer.

The wide-eyed, gushing type of verbal portrait painted of General Eisenhower does him no service. I think it insulting and ridiculous to paint any man or woman as perfect.

Why didn't he accept a nomination for President in the summer of 1948?

Let me say, quickly, at the outset, I have no inside information on this touchy subject, I have not seen the General since long before the conventions, I know absolutely nothing of his own ideas on the topic, and I know very little of American politics.

But I can say this: in his casual conversations during World War II, General Eisenhower made it quite clear he regarded himself as a soldier, with no political ambitions whatsoever—not even political inclinations or interest. He was painfully definite in his opinion of politics in general.

The acrobatics to draw him into the campaign were, to me, ridiculous and foolhardy from the start. I can only assume the politicians believed no man, not even one of the General's integrity and announced views, could resist the lure of the Presidency.

Nonetheless, his disinclination to accept either the Republican or the Democratic offers came as no surprise to me or anyone else who heard the statements he made during the war. For us, the fact that he said he had no political ambitions or desires ended the whole debate.

Still, as a will-be American citizen, I cannot squash the conviction General Eisenhower has more stature and popularity for the position of President than any other figure on the scene. I further believe, personally, America needs him as President in the world of today.

However, I'm not even a voter yet . . . which immediately precludes any additional discussion on this question.

Is he liberal or conservative?

Here again, people believe I am evading or downright lying when I say, flatly, "I don't know."

During the war period when I drove the General and worked in his office, I never once heard him discuss such questions as racial discrimination, capital *vs.* labor, international politics, or any of the other usual signposts to political conviction. He was too busy directing the war—with more problems and responsibilities than any one man should shoulder—to put a conversational toe into such dangerous waters.

For most persons, it is sufficient that he is honest and possessed of unquestioned integrity.

How did all his fame and popularity affect him?

When I first met General Eisenhower in London, to drive him just one foggy block, he was unknown except to the War Department. To the public, he was a faceless, anonymous general.

Three and a half years later, he left Europe after achieving a classic military victory. He had carved a niche for himself in history. He had become the world's most famous and honored general.

When he left Frankfurt the awesome events of those three years had aged him.

But, otherwise, the General Eisenhower of 1945 was exactly the same man I had met in 1942—unchanged.

Could there be a greater tribute?

INDEX

INDEX

Milton Keynes UK
Ingram Content Group UK Ltd.
UKHW041442081124
2704UKWH00037B/158